EMMANUEL LEVINAS AND THE POLITICS OF NON-VIOLENCE

Emmanuel Levinas and the Politics of Non-Violence

VICTORIA TAHMASEBI-BIRGANI

UNIVERSITY OF TORONTO PRESS
Toronto Buffalo London

Toronto Buffalo London

www.utppublishing.com

ISBN 978-1-4426-4284-3

Library and Archives Canada Cataloguing in Publication

Tahmasebi-Birgani, Victoria, 1961–, author
Emmanuel Levinas and the politics of non-violence / Victoria Tahmasebi-Birgani.

Includes bibliographical references and index.
ISBN 978-1-4426-4284-3 (bound)

1. Levinas, Emmanuel – Criticism and interpretation. 2. Nonviolence – Political aspects. 3. Nonviolence – Moral and ethical aspects. 4. Nonviolence – Philosophy. I. Title.

B2430.L484T34 2014 179.7 C2013-903794-2

University of Toronto Press acknowledges the financial assistance to its publishing program of the Canada Council for the Arts and the Ontario Arts Council.

University of Toronto Press acknowledges the financial support of the Government of Canada through the Canada Book Fund for its publishing activities.

For my beloved son, Siavash

"انسان دشواری وظیفه است"

(احمد شاملو)

Contents

Acknowledgments

With gratitude to Asher Horowitz, for many years of intellectual guidance, encouragement, and support. I continue to be inspired by his passion for rigorous thinking, by his critical approach to the projects of modern political philosophy, and by his exceptional intellectual integrity which ceaselessly resists disappearing into the comfort of the given.

I would like to extend a special thanks to Shannon Bell for all her unflinching help and support. My engagement with Emmanuel Levinas began in her graduate course in which she introduced Levinas to her graduate students. I would like to extend a special thanks to Alice Pitt. Over many years, her probing questions helped push my intellectual journey in new and interesting directions.

I would also like to extend my deepest gratitude to Gad Horowitz whose continuous presence and support has greatly shaped my journey in life. His course in "spirit of democratic citizenship," among others, has greatly influenced my subsequent academic work and research.

I am grateful to Daniel Quinlan, my editor at the University of Toronto Press, who saw this book through its many iterations, and to Matthew Kudelka for copy editing the manuscript.

To my mother: I love you. Your amorous presence in my life continuously renders possible the manifestation of a love that does not expect much in return. And to my father, who believed in me and pushed me to break the traditional gender boundaries in a culture which, like any other culture, was mired with sexism and misogyny. And finally, to my dear son, Siavash: the spirit of this course is for your young, kind, and generous heart *Azizam*.

I would like to dedicate this work to the memory of thousands of political activists who lost their lives during and after the Iranian revolution of 1979, especially to my three close friends, Mohammad, Bijan, and Ghassem, three beautiful souls whose only crime was to dream about a better world.

List of Abbreviations

Works by Emmanuel Levinas

BPW	*Basic Philosophical Writings.* Edited by Adriaan T. Peperzak, Simon Critchley, and Robert Bernasconi. Bloomington: Indiana UP, 1996.
BV	*Beyond the Verse: Talmudic Readings and Lectures.* Translated by Gary D. Mole. Bloomington: Indiana UP, 1994.
CPP	*Collected Philosophical Papers.* Translated by Alphonso Lingis. Pittsburgh: Duquesne UP, 1998
DF	*Difficult Freedom: Essays on Judaism.* Translated by Sean Hand. London: Athlone Press, 1990.
EN	*Entre Nous: Thinking-of-the-Other.* Translated by Michael B. Smith and Barbara Harshav. New York: Columbia UP, 1998.
HO	*Humanism of the Other.* Translated by Nidra Poller. Urbana: University of Illinois Press, 2003.
IRB	*Is It Righteous to Be?: Interviews with Emmanuel Levinas.* Edited by Jill Robbins. Stanford: Stanford UP, 2001.
LR	*The Levinas Reader.* Edited by Sean Hand. Oxford: Blackwell Publishers, 1989.
NTR	*Nine Talmudic Readings.* Translated by Annette Aronowicz. Bloomington: Indiana UP, 1990.
OB	*Otherwise Than Being or Beyond Essence.* Translated by Alphonso Lingis. Pittsburgh: Duquesne UP, 1998.
PM	"The Paradox of Morality: An Interview with Emmanuel Levinas," in *The Provocation of Levinas: Rethinking the Other.* Edited by Robert Bernasconi and David Wood. London: Routledge, 1988.

RPH "Reflections on the Philosophy of Hitlerism," in *Critical Inquiry* 17 (Autumn 1990). Translated by Sean Hand.

TI *Totality and Infinity: An Essay on Exteriority*. Translated by Alphonso Lingis. Pittsburgh: Duquesne UP, 1961.

TO *Time and the Other*. Translated by Richard A. Cohen. Pittsburgh: Duquesne UP, 1987.

Works by Mahatma Gandhi

ASMET *An Autobiography or The Story of My Experiments with Truth*. Ahmedabad: Navajivan Publishing House, 1927–9. Volumes I and II.

CWMG *The Collected Works of Mahatma Gandhi*. New Delhi: Publications Division, Ministry of Information and Broadcasting, Government of India, 1988. Volumes 19–33.

MPWG *The Moral and Political Writings of Mahatma Gandhi*. Edited by Raghavan Iyer. Oxford: Oxford UP, 1986–7. Volumes I, II, and III.

NVPW *Non-Violence in Peace and War*. Ahmedabad: Navajivan Publishing House, 1948. Volumes I and II.

SWMG *Selected Writings of Mahatma Gandhi*. Boston: Beacon Publication, 1951.

EMMANUEL LEVINAS AND THE POLITICS OF NON-VIOLENCE

Introduction

The injustice and alienation introduced by the arbitrary workings of political powers in every human enterprise will disappear; but the social injustice, the power the rich hold over the poor, will disappear at the same time as political violence.

Levinas, DF 60[1]

Politics as it stands, separate from ethical and moral considerations, has exhausted itself in the twentieth century and now into the twenty-first. Atrocities committed in the name of Truth, Justice, Equality, Liberation, Freedom, or God – we have exploited and exhausted them all in an effort to justify a means to an end in an incessant flow of political struggles both local and global. For Emmanuel Levinas, the question of the political is primarily a question of one's relationship with the absolute alterity of the other human being. As such, the question of politics is irreducibly bound with the question of ethics. If there is no other, why should there be the question of politics at all? If this other is always reducible to the same universe as that of the subject, why bother with questions of justice, liberation, and democracy in polity? On some fundamental level, Western moral philosophy has been on a quest to answer to Cain's sincere question about his brother's fate – is he, in fact, his brother's keeper? Or as Levinas puts it, "Does the subject arrive at the human condition prior to assuming responsibility for the other man?" (RPH 63). This question is both political and ethical and reveals the limits of ontology – if ontology is taken as the persistence of the same in its own being, that is, as the founding moment of the political and as providing a satisfactory answer to the nature of one's relationship with the other. That is to say, this question immediately links the responsibility of the political to the ethical, divorcing the political from the concerns of a being for its own maintenance, and displacing the origin of politics from ontology to the ethical realm. My central claim is that Levinas' ethics is already an ethicopolitical undertaking and that his proposed ethical relation could inspire a new radical praxis, one that, in its unfolding, transfigures both ethics and politics.

This book takes as its primary observation that nearly every revolution or social movement in modern human history has turned against itself. The human aspiration for freedom and justice has almost always been turned into its opposite and has itself inaugurated a new dynamic of oppression and domination. It is in this context that the political implications of ethics – of one's responsibility for the other – have become some of the most pressing issues for the world community. The urgent need to engage with these issues stems from the following well-documented observation: existing national and international political organizations have failed to eliminate the threat of global – and local – wars and, indeed, have contributed to an increase in violence, atrocity, and wars of all kinds. The old divisions of class, race, gender, poverty, illiteracy, and religion have not only become sharper but also have acquired new characteristics and intensity. And, what is most important, the new world order has increasingly divided the world into North and South, into the privileged and the unprivileged. The upsurge of religious fundamentalism in the South (which has emerged as the dominant form of struggle against neocolonialism), in tandem with the triumphant return of neoliberalism on the back of globalization in the North, has divided the world into two seemingly polar opposites. In this new world order, the old divisions between the dominator and the dominated, the oppressor and the oppressed, are no longer based on direct and visible exploitation of one by the other. A new form of invisible exploitation and injustice has emerged: a small minority live wasteful, luxurious lives, broadly indifferent to the destitution and poverty of millions of others. It is in this context that definitions of ethics as being content with not causing harm, as being and letting be, exhaust itself and most clearly demonstrates its political and ethical bankruptcy.

Within this new dynamic, the question of responsibility, of non-indifference to the other whose exploitation and destitution may not directly be of my doing, becomes pertinent: I am responsible even for the harm that I have not done. For Levinas, the current responses to global human suffering – to genocide, exploitation, domination, tyranny, and political-economic violence – are ineffective and insufficient. These responses take a multitude of forms: private or public charity that eventually exacts its own costs; a blind and violent reaction that is unaware of its own injustice; the investment of hope in a state's impersonal and bureaucratic machinery; or, even worse, pervasive indifference to the others' suffering. For Levinas, all of these attempts at disalienation are already alienated; his ethics, one may argue, amounts to a radical objection to both the violence that is launched in the name of liberation and the anaesthetization of the political in the name of reason.

Let me then say from the outset that this project stems from a rather clichéd insight: struggles against oppression cannot be automatically justified; it cannot be assumed that they are "just" on the basis of their opposition to oppression. The negation of political evil is not necessarily the assertion of "good" – something that has been made plain in many of the conflicts – and in the responses to these conflicts – we have encountered in the past century. To problematize the relationship between the ideas of "good" and "evil" is immediately to delink the hitherto unproblematic relationship between justice and liberation; it means pausing over the ethics of political struggle and asking questions such as these: What is it that makes a political struggle against injustice a just praxis? Do we need to justify our political struggle, or is the injustice of the system one rebels against itself the justification of that rebellion? Are the criteria for justifying one's rebellion independent of the forces against which one fights? What is the relationship between justice and liberation? In short, through what sets of issues can the ethics of political struggle be thought of and understood? Central to these sets of concerns are the ways in which the subject of the political struggle or radical-political subjectivity[2] is imagined in relation to ethical relations. Building on Levinas' ethics of one's irreducible responsibility for the other, I maintain that the consequence of separating ethical subjectivity from radical-political subjectivity is the reduction of politics to replacing one totality with another – to fighting against one dictator but not necessarily against the dictatorship. To bring these two terms into an alternative relationship, therefore, is to revisit both ethics and politics and to examine other possibilities of formulating ethicopolitical subjectivity.

Ethical Subject and Political Praxis: A Theoretical Background

Much has been written about the relation of Levinas' ethics to politics, and further exploration is under way.[3] Following Levinas' insight into ethics as first philosophy, I contend that there is an urgent need to articulate ethics (non-indifference to the other) as first politics. For Levinas, the horrendous reality of the past century points to something fundamentally disturbing about the ways in which the political is defined, especially within the dominant Western philosophical tradition. On the one hand, the Western polity and the justice of its social and political arrangement (i.e., the state) are measured by the ways in which the members of that community treat one another and by the level of rights and freedoms they obtain. A community's legitimacy is based on how it defines the insider and the outsider, the self and the other. Needless to say, the inside can sometimes be extended to the minority – and the outside to the majority – of that same community. So, ethics – that is, justice – is articulated in terms of one's responsibility to the same: I am responsible for those with whom I share blood, ideology, values, a nation-state, race, gender, sexual orientation, and so on.

Of course, the Western polity has developed a multitude of ways to conceptualize responsibility for the other who is deemed an outsider. It has even devised a multitude of strategies for addressing various degrees of outsideness: partial outsider, complete outsider, complete but understandable outsider, complete and not understandable (yet controllable) outsider, the outsider on the fringe, the assimilable outsider, the non-assimilable outsider, and the irreducible outsider who can be neither comprehended nor assimilated nor controlled. So there are nuances in the ways in which the modern Western polity produces and then treats the outsider – nuances that correspond to the degree to which the outsideness is perceived, which I do not intend to elaborate here. Suffice it to say that ideas such as liberal pluralism, respect for differences, and tolerance are examples of the kinds of responses that political theory has generated in its relation to the exteriority. Yet a common thread binds all these responses together – benevolence, which is the central philosophical underpinning of Western liberal states, and which is expressed most clearly in those states' social policies.

The problem of how to meet one's responsibility for the other through benevolence has been an important one in political philosophy. I argue, following Levinas, that the core of the problem is that in Western philosophy the coming into existence of the subject is signified through the fall and separation of the particular from the One – from the universal. As such, being-subject appears on the scene as the result of a fall and is forever defined as a deficiency, a sin, and/or a perversion. Logically, then, if this being-subject is to achieve unity, closure, and salvation, it must be reassimilated into the One. Hence, responsibility for this fallen, perverted particular emerges as benevolence – defined as a general desire for the good of others – and as the disposition to act so as to further that good, which, although benevolence contains a sort of invitation, is nonetheless, at its core, a violence. In short, benevolence, enacted within the dichotomy of particular–universal, begins with knowledge of the possible and anticipates a fixed outcome. Levinas offers a radical critique of the subject as a particular instance of a universal whose pathos is to be reassimilated into that same universal, by either explicit or implicit forms of violence, such as benevolence. First the subject is produced as a deficient other; then it is saved from its own flaws by being incorporated into a totality; in this way, the good conscience of the redeemer is again reaffirmed. Therefore for Levinas, benevolence ultimately stems from the worry for the other generated by the same – in contrast to the fear for the unique and irreducible alterity of others – and as such, benevolence reinforces the law of the same.

Rousseau, Marx, and Nietzsche all tried to interfere with this construction: Rousseau's "amour-de-soi" and "pitie" linked the love of existing as the foundation through which one suffered with the other. Nietzsche, as Adorno rightly pointed out, saw in benevolence the total degradation of human dignity,[4] to the extent that he rejected the idea of friendship and instead tried to think about the ethical relationship through one's relation to the enemy. Marx provided the concept of work as the basis of social relations between humans, in order to intervene with the idea of the One into which every fallen particular must reassimilate.

I contend that Emmanuel Levinas is the only thinker to break decisively with this construction. In Levinas' ethical relation, the other is absolutely irreducible and incomprehensible; this irreducibility of the other in proximity and the asymmetrical relationship between the self and the other create the curvature of social space in which the responsibility for the other is brought to bear.[5] For Levinas, the other is inassimilable and irreducible to the same; the otherness of the other is precisely the core of its singularity and of its humanity,[6] over and above the rights she[7] shares with the rest of humanity. The absolute alterity of the other is not the result of a fall but is in fact the nucleus of her humanity. Levinas' ethics demands that one be infinitely and irreplaceably responsible not merely for the other, but for her irreducible alterity. Therefore, in Levinas the questions of the social and the political do not emerge in terms of the bond, the similarities, or the differences between the self and the other. These conceived or real differences ultimately serve to reassimilate the other back into the same, or to compare, evaluate, and hierarchize. Furthermore, Levinas does not posit the question of one's responsibility for the other in a reciprocal framework: the responsibility suggested by Levinas bears no relation to the response one may or may not receive; my responsibility is perceived as separate from and independent of the other's response.

Building on Levinas' conception of the alterity of the other as irreducible, I will be developing two dual critical moments as the core constitution of the ethicopolitical subject: radical passivity and rebellion, and freedom and responsibility. These two moments, as the two crucial modalities in which ethical and radical subjectivities meet to forge the ethicopolitical subject, are the theoretical basis of this book.

The first moment is what I deem the moment of radical passivity and of the rebellion against injustice that emanates from this radical passivity. I will be arguing that the collective mobilization of subjects against injustice presupposes a primordial sensibility at the heart of the human, one that marks it as radically vulnerable to the call of the other. Unless it senses injustice – that is, without a simultaneous inwardness and openness that allows the other's plea for justice to leave its inscription – the subject can neither feel nor hear nor respond to the other's call. Rebellion against injustice, therefore, assumes this modality of sensibility, radical vulnerability, and receptivity.

The second moment involves the tension between responsibility and freedom. In Levinas' ethics, the relationship between freedom and responsibility undergoes a radical transformation: freedom is not the first – and does not need to be perceived as the first – to claim its own dignity.[8] In Levinas' ethical relation, beings do not relate to one another through their freedoms; also, the relationship with the other is not through relatedness – be it similarity or difference – but rather through the non-relation of proximity. So freedom, as a theme, becomes relevant only after the initial an-archic sensibility and openness, and only after my responsibility for the other has already marked the subject with its claims. Therefore the realization that I am the only person responsible for the other – even in being responsible for the responsibility of the other – foregrounds the question of freedom. Freedom and the rights of human beings are inseparable from one's responsibility for-the-other. In other words, responsibility for-the-other is the condition of the possibility of freedom. Freedom is neither the first nor the second; rather, it is a pre-originary beginning that emerges out of the ability of the one to respond to the call of the other. That is to say, freedom is the realization of one's irreducible responsibility for the other, made possible through substituting praxis.

I want to relate these two moments to the questions raised at the beginning of this introduction, namely, the inquiry into the grounds for social and political struggle against oppression and injustice. Levinas' ethics helps us think about the justness of political struggle not in terms of the evil of the forces against which one fights, nor in terms of the level of rights and freedoms one struggles to gain. These issues have to be addressed in light of one's responsibility to the absolute alterity of the other. The question is whether freedom emerges primarily as part of a multiplicity of consciousness in search of its own rights and freedom and whether social movements are about the alienated self or about the excluded other. Building on Levinas' ethical relation, this book will argue that what justifies a struggle is whether the subject, in the struggle, suffers with, and for, the other. If, as Levinas would have it, the struggle against oppression is the most profound adventure of subjectivity, it is simultaneously the very turning back of the subject to itself. This profound inward journey is signified by passivity more passive than passivity, marked by the traces of a rupture brought about by the other's suffering. Levinas judges the majority of twentieth-century revolutions as devoid of this profound journey, and as such he describes them as projects wherein "*the disalienation itself is alienated*" (CPP 143).[9] Therefore, the polemic posed in this book is the predicament of the excluded other, not of the alienated self.

Levinas' ethics helps us pose new questions in relation to the politics of struggle: How must a political struggle legitimize itself? How does a political struggle articulate its inside and outside, its friends and enemies? And more important, what are the foundational narratives that ignite the imagination of a liberatory movement? Does such a movement solely concern the rights and freedoms of those who are already deemed members? Alternatively, is the idea of rights and freedoms informed by responsibility for the other's justice? And if so, how is this responsibility articulated in relation to oneself, to the other, and to a third? In short, how can we bring back the question of responsibility to freedom, justice to liberation, peace to violence, and ethics to politics? To think about these questions in relation to the two moments outlined above is to think about a political order not just in terms of the rights and freedoms it grants – and limits – but to also place this human endeavour in relation to a larger concern or a larger order. It is, as Levinas insists, to theorize an ethicopolitical order that, instead of being based on limiting the freedom (and hence the violence) of autonomous individuals, instead rests upon the responsibility of one-for-the-other and, equally important, upon the limitations that arise from this responsibility (BPW 168–9). At another level, part of addressing the nature of this responsibility entails questioning political and philosophical discourses through which notions of enemy and friend are constructed, inclusions and exclusions are formed, alliances are reached, punishments are devised, and violence is legitimized. Therefore this book is, in part, an attempt to envision an ethicopolitical arrangement that goes beyond class society and its state, and beyond violence as the basis of the state's legitimacy.

In chapter 1, "Levinas' Ethicopolitics: Beyond the Western Liberal Tradition," I address the problematic relation between ethics and politics in the thought of Levinas. First, I discuss some general criticisms directed at Levinas, who judges his ethics to be contradictory and irrelevant to, or as an abandonment of, the political. Much of the literature on Levinas, when it discusses the relationship between his ethics and his politics, ends up elaborating the extent to which the ethical is necessarily interrupted and, as such, abandoned by the political necessity and the requirements of justice, equality, symmetry, comparison, and reciprocity.

In contrast, I will establish an alternative reading of Levinas' ethics and politics, one that is based in the logic of "betrayal"[10] rather than on a mutual exclusion, or abandonment. I will be arguing that the logic of betrayal, because it allows for degrees instead of dichotomizing itself into two poles, enables Levinas' ethics not only to be concretized in the political, but also to function as the measure of legitimacy of the political itself.

Indeed, we find in Levinas an intricate, complex, and sometimes obscure relation between ethics and politics; certainly, they are not one and the same in his thought, and Levinas himself insists on the separation between the two. My approach to Levinas' ethicopolitics does not intend to erase the critical distance between the two; rather, it addresses the political implications of Levinas' ethics for a specific sociopolitical context, that is, for liberatory political praxis, and for an alternative mode of thinking about political subjectivity. I undertake this task via notions of radical passivity, substitution, and justice – all central concepts for Levinas – where he comes closest to addressing the relationship between ethics and politics.

Second, since most of Levinas' readers focus on his notion of the "third" as the inevitable moment in which ethics is abandoned for the sake of justice and politics, I challenge this reading by developing Levinas' notion of the third as the simultaneous, but uneasy, embodiment of two different orders of justice – what I, after Levinas, call formal and ethical justice. I discuss these two simultaneous orders of justice as they pertain to the political, illustrating that Levinas' ethicopolitics simultaneously contains formal justice and transcends it, and as such, far exceeds the universal, formal equality of liberal ethics and politics.

Finally, this chapter expands on Levinas' radical critique of the liberal concept of the individual, on his rejection of the liberal notion of peace, and on his explicit criticisms of the liberal economic arrangement, to argue for the incommensurability of Levinasian ethicopolitics to liberal politics.

The task in chapter 2, "Radical Passivity, the Face, and the Social Demand for Justice," is to argue that Levinas' notion of subjectivity, or what I term post-individual individuation, is irreconcilable with the prevailing definition of the subject provided by modern liberal discourse. Insofar as Levinas views the core constitution of the subject in terms of its exposure to the other in radical passivity, and not in terms of personal freedom and self-sufficiency of reason, it provides a new horizon for the work of liberation. This approach is not meant to replace the agency of the self with "radical passivity"; rather, it builds on radical passivity as one aspect of the self in order to create space for a radical non-violent political praxis.

To extend this point, I believe that this distinction is fundamental on many levels: radical passivity as a mode of agency, and not the agency of the self, is posited against a notion of agency founded on a colonial conception of the self. At one level, I contend that radical passivity is fundamentally distinct from normal passivity (the passive–active dichotomy) in which the agency is denied or paralysed. Instead, radical passivity opens the subject to an alternative mode of agency, a praxis that is accomplished by means of responsibility for the alterity of the other's face – her justice. At another level, I aim to provide a deeper appreciation of Levinas' subject as an agent of social change who cannot be exhausted in and by totality or by the dominatory practices of power. Most important, I hope to demonstrate that Levinas' conception of the subject, of the other, and of their relation departs from a sense of sociality that frames itself in terms of a fair, equal, and reciprocal commerce among individuals. In its place, Levinas' ethical relation poses fear for the other's suffering and death as the commencement of the social and the political. My central thesis in this chapter is that the political, rather than being issued from consciousness of one's rights and freedoms, originates in the radical exposure of the sensible to the destitution of the other and to her demand for justice.

I begin chapter 3, "Substituting Praxis and Political Liberation," by arguing that while being for-the-other is originally signified in the radical passivity of one-for-the-other's suffering, responsibility is concretized by means of what Levinas terms "substitution." Building on this notion, this chapter develops substitution as the structure of ethicoliberatory praxis. To establish a link between Levinas' substitution and the work of liberation, I first elaborate on substitution as an ethicopolitical undertaking or praxis rather than merely an ethical sensibility. I call this praxis "substituting praxis" to differentiate it from a praxis that is grounded in the virility of an autonomous agent. Substituting praxis, I argue, embodies one's response to the other's demand for a justice in which the singularity of the other and all the other others, the third, is both defended and respected. Second, I challenge the standard reading of Levinas, which reduces Levinas' being for the other's justice to works of private or public charity. I contend that substituting praxis involves more than a demand of a "good conscience"; it also embodies the exigency to rebel against injustice committed against the other. I coin this moment "ethicoliberatory praxis." Developing from Levinas' proximity, the third section of this chapter is an elaboration of the contours of this praxis on the spirit of youth and sincerity, on freedom as responsibility, and on his approach to (non-)violence in relation to the third. In this section I distinguish liberatory praxis from an intentional act in which the other is ultimately treated as an object "for" the same. In the fourth and final section of this chapter, I discuss Levinas' approach to (non-)violence, especially as it pertains to liberatory movements. Every rebellion against injustice raises the question of violence in relation to a third. In every work of injustice there is a persecutor; the other as persecutor confronts me with two seemingly contradictory demands – that is, to rebel against injustice while also being responsible for the face of the other, even that of the persecutor. I maintain that substituting praxis satisfies both these claims simultaneously, for it insists that the work of liberation be both revolutionary and peacefully patient.

The final chapter, "Levinas and Gandhi: Liberatory Praxis as Fear for the Other," attempts to demonstrate how Levinas' ethicopolitics is substantiated in a historical movement – here, Gandhi's non-violent decolonization struggle. I suggest that Gandhian non-violent revolutionary praxis embodies the two distinct dimensions of Levinas' ethicopolitics: radical passivity, and rebellion. I hold that Gandhi's political orientation, his *Ahimsa* and *Satyagraha,*[11] addresses the central concern that Levinas raises throughout his ethical-philosophical inquiry – that is, to recall a more an-archic modality of peace and justice that is based in something more fundamental than the individuals' rights and the power of their freedom – two central pillars of the modern Western conception of liberation. In the first and second sections of this chapter, I argue that Gandhi and Levinas both adhere to an eschatological-ethical peace, one that simultaneously serves as a radical critique and as a transcendence of the rational peace of "bourgeois man." For both, a permanent peace cannot arise out of rational peace signed under the shadow of war. Rational peace assumes nothing beyond a totality within which individuals conduct commerce; under it, political systems function in fear of the violent spectre of the other(s). It follows that a permanent and ethical peace requires an eschatological vision that resists disappearing into the totality of either war or rational peace.

Levinas offers the event of speech as a possible structure of sociality within which ethical peace can be imagined. Hence, in the third section of this chapter, I discuss Levinas' approach to the event of speech as the moment of eschatological peace, and explore its implication for the other as the "persecutor." Yet despite offering a few examples, Levinas is not clear on how his vision of eschatological-ethical peace must be approached in the concrete-historical dimension. Gandhi helps Levinas by providing examples in which the eschatological structure of peace becomes a concrete reality and redefines revolutionary praxis as nonviolent struggle for the justice of the other. I link Levinas' insight into the structure of speech to the Gandhian motto "love the enemy" and to his attempt to change the enemy's heart rather than overpower her. I demonstrate how the example of Gandhian praxis and Levinasian ethics allows us to approach the political opponent as an interlocutor rather than as an opposing force, thus offering liberatory praxis an opportunity to mark its radical distance from violence. Levinas' approach to the event of speech, I suggest, offers an alternative structure to liberation and makes possible a substituting praxis in which fear *of* the other is replaced by fear *for* the other. In this way, political struggle is fundamentally redefined for the better.

1
Levinas' Ethicopolitics: Beyond the Western Liberal Tradition

> The moral consciousness can sustain the mocking gaze of the political man only if the certitude of peace dominates the evidence of war.
>
> Levinas, TI 22

(i) Levinas and the Political: General Discussion

Although Levinas' ethics and philosophy have been influential in Europe and in North and South America for decades, the political implications of his work have been largely neglected. Levinas' reception in the English-speaking world has been primarily through religious philosophers, phenomenologists, and deconstructionists.[1] Only recently has the relation of Levinas' ethics to politics gained attention.[2] Yet most of these works remain within the general tenets of Western liberal thought and its conception of politics, justice, and the state;[3] only a few works, such as Howard Caygill's *Levinas and the Political,* explore the intersection of Levinas' thought with radical traditions in political philosophy.[4] Although, due to the growing importance of Levinas' work, analytical and pragmatist philosophers such as Hilary W. Putnam, Richard J. Bernstein, and Richard Rorty have begun to address and engage Levinas' thought,[5] there still exists no substantial work on the relation between Levinas and the left, notably in critical theory and Marxian political philosophy.[6] In this context, there is an important gap in literatures on Levinas' ethical relation and its implications for both radical thought and liberatory praxis.

One of the most prevalent, but false, arguments against Levinas' ethics is that he leaves the political to the realm of ontology, and the question of ethics to transcendence, so that the gulf between them is unbridgeable. One reason for this misreading is the apparent "impossibility" of Levinas' ethics – each of us is infinitely and irreplaceably responsible for the other, to the point of being responsible for the other's responsibility and his faults, so much so as to give our life for the other. To translate this "impossibility" into political language, as Levinas explains it in "Philosophy, Justice, and Love,"[7] I am responsible even for the one who persecutes me (EN 106). The question of the political is first the question of the other's rights and freedoms – it is about my infinite responsibility for rights and freedoms, which are not "mine." To unconditionally accept Levinas' ethics as the basis of one's political praxis is to be infinitely guilty of one's "un-ethicality."

This seemingly impossible demand of Levinas' ethics has prompted many social and political theorists to dismiss Levinas' ethical relation and to question its relevance to the political. Alain Badiou, in *Ethics: An Essay on the Understanding of Evil,*[8] argues that Levinas' ethics is victim-centred and that it valorizes otherness, difference, and victimization. Therefore Levinas' ethics, in its obsession with human beings' potential for victimization, is a form of nihilism.[9] I will not engage with Badiou's criticism in its entirety, but I believe that Badiou's reading of Levinas' notion of the victim is problematic, and therefore his argument that Levinas equates humanity with the identity of the victim needs to be re-examined.

Most people are the victims of some unjust economic, social, and/or cultural relation. One of the radical demands of Levinas' ethics, contrary to Badiou's claim, is that both the oppressor and the oppressed be responsible for the other. In other words, the victim, precisely *because* of her victimization, is responsible for the treatment of her persecutor in her struggle for liberation. If victimization means being deprived of one's voice, agency, and moral autonomy – that is, in addition to being cut off from the hope of a humane and dignified life – then Levinas, by holding the victim ethically responsible for her actions, gives voice and agency back to the victim.

In reading politics into Levinas' ethics, the other challenge we face is the potentially conservative implications of his ethics. Levinas' radical heteronomy can be read either as a renunciation of the autonomy of the human individual, or as advocacy for a traditional collectivity. His notion of one-way responsibility of me for the other, or his curvature of social space, if misread and applied to a concrete social and political situation, can be twisted into a reaffirmation of existing social and political inequalities and the stereotypical roles assigned to different classes, genders, and races. For example, Gayatri C. Spivak, in "French Feminism Revisited," voices her scepticism of whether Levinas' ethics can have any positive effect on collective struggle against forms of social inequality such as gender oppression.[10]

The consequence of misreading Levinas' ethics as "impossible" is that his ethics is dismissed as either impractical or irrelevant to political praxis and political struggle; this in turn reduces the applicability of his ethics to events such as the performative speech or communicative dialogue. Thereby foreclosed is an in-depth exploration of his ethics in relation to political praxis and liberatory political struggle. Furthermore, this seeming impracticality has led many Levinas'commentators on Levinas to reduce his ethics to yet another support for Western liberalism, and his ethicopolitics to a mere deepening of this project. Indeed, Levinas' reading of liberalism is a complex one: he does not seem to negate liberal ethics, nor does he offer a wholesale critique of liberalism. Yet I believe that he is careful to maintain a critical distance from liberalism. I see this critical distance as the most productive point of entry into the discussion around ethics and politics in Levinas' thought. By discussing the fundamental distance between Levinas and Western liberalism as it relates to subjectivity, peace, and economic justice, this chapter offers an alternative reading of Levinas, one whose central claim is that his ethicopolitics is a radical critique of the modern liberal project and can offer a great deal to liberatory political struggles whose goals extend beyond liberal capitalism. Consequently, my central thesis in this chapter is that Levinas' ethicopolitics is not reducible to Western liberal democracy, which defines the political as the postponement or suspension of war – as an oscillation between violence and rational peace.

Misreadings of Levinas' thought have this is common: they completely ignore his attack on totality and universal history. In his early work *Totality and Infinity: An Essay on Exteriority* (1961),[11] Levinas radically critiques Western philosophy's efforts to build a totality in which the individual is but an instance. In terms of the individual, he challenges those approaches that prioritize *categorization* and *comprehension* over *singularity* and *uniqueness*. His insistence that the other cannot be reduced to any category stems from this deep insight: that this sort of reduction is precisely what subjects whole categories of others to political violence and genocide. Levinas simultaneously criticizes and displaces both the liberal, modern conception of the individual and the grand Hegelian philosophies of history in which the individual's ultimate meaning is revealed only in the last instant. He demonstrates how the modern notion of an individual is still a particular moment of a totality–unity, from which the individual is assumed to be engendered and to which he/she will finally return.

This double move allows Levinas to transcend the idea of totality: instead of regressing to a traditional conception of subjectivity, thereby assimilating the subject into a collectivity or a universal world history, and instead of adhering to a modern notion of an autonomous individuality, Levinas posits a notion of individuation that is post-autonomous and post-individualist and that resists recuperation by totality and universal history. This individuation involves neither a particular moment of a totality nor an autonomous self-sufficient individual who waits for final judgment in the distant future, when history fulfils itself. In fact, Levinas rejects Hegelian world history as the ultimate court of judgment. As Robert Bernasconi suggests in "Different Styles of Eschatology: Derrida's Take on Levinas' Political Messianism," Levinas' conception of eschatology reintroduces judgment into every instant of history.[12] Levinas' ethical exigency demands that the subject *interrupt* and *disturb* history in every instant and be *judged* in every instant. Bernasconi is right when he argues that the meaning of Levinas' "beyond history" is not a "waiting for a Godot who will never come," but rather an incessant demand on the subject to question history's workings at every turn.[13] Bernasconi contends that this moment in Levinas' thought is signified through "eschatology," an event that poses the possibility of interrupting history here and now. He cites Levinas in *Totality and Infinity*: "It [eschatology] is reflected within the totality and history, within experience. The eschatological as the 'beyond' of history, draws beings out of the jurisdiction of history and the future; it arouses them in and calls them forth to their full responsibility."[14] Indeed, as Bernasconi concludes, Levinas' eschatology is not about anticipating the future, but about interrupting the present.

However, Bernasconi does not further develop his insight into Levinas' ethical interruption, nor does he explore its significance for the political. In fact, all literatures on Levinas have underemphasized and underdeveloped the ways in which the subject interrupts totalities and the implications of this for the possibility of a radical political praxis. In this context, the following questions must be addressed: What are the constitutive events, as Levinas envisions them, that prompt the subject to interrupt history? What are the ethical exigencies on which the

Levinasian subject disturbs the totalizing account of history? What are the political implications of such interruptions? These questions will be addressed in chapter 2. Suffice it to say here that Levinas recognizes the ground for interrupting totalized history on two trajectories: the subject's radical sensibility to the suffering and death of the other; and the effect of the subject's non-violent rebellion against injustice committed against the other. The subject comes to *be* through her radical exposedness to the other who is proximate; and her sociality – her relation to the other – is signified through her call for justice for the others. The subject interrupts history in every instant not to demand her own rights and freedom, but more important, to rebel against injustice committed against the other (to whom the subject is not necessarily related by family, nationality, politics, geography, or ethnicity). For Levinas, ethicopolitical subjectivity is instantaneous with the radical interruption of totalized history. The individual comes to be signified as a subject precisely in her struggle against the oppression of the irreducible other, to the point of giving her life for the other. This call for justice does not originate in an understanding of humanity in its universality or particularity; rather, it stems from a concrete, immediate, and face-to-face encounter with the other whose suffering calls me, and no other, to respond and to act. This call makes every subject singular in her response-ability to the call of the other and to her demand for justice. This reading opens Levinas' ethics to a radical political endeavour that is different from any political project thus far, be it liberal, Marxist, or conservative.

Still, Levinas' metaphors and hyperbolic language, especially in his early works, have been strongly contested. His use of "paternity" as the event of fecundity, and as the instant in which "the ego becomes other to itself" (TO 90–2),[15] is questionable when translated directly into the political. Also, his descriptions of the irreducible other as the poor / the widow / the orphan / the stranger, with their traditional connotations, raise the question of whether he is forever inserting categories of real people into these abstractions, making the existence of these categories a necessity itself – or as Badiou claims, signifying the other as always a victim.

I provide a more progressive reading. Indeed, I believe that these categories play a fundamental role in establishing a radical connection between ethics and politics in Levinas. His emphasis on these categories of the poor, the widow, the orphan, and the stranger reveal his attempt to open his ethics to those economic, social, and cultural categories in which the destitution of the other originates. In this way he also seeks to address these important questions: Am I my brother's keeper? What is in it for me? If for Levinas the beggar signifies economic poverty, the widow, existing oppressive gender relations, the orphan, social powerlessness and vulnerability, and the stranger, those kept at the margins of the economic, the social, the political, the cultural, the legal, and the state, then these are the oppressive structures against which Levinas' ethicopolitics is oriented.[16] The other is not reducible to her victimhood or her oppression; that said, it is the other's victimization that bothers me and for which I am unconditionally responsible. Relations of oppression reveal their vileness through the face of the corporeal other who suffers. My responsibility for the other takes a concrete form in my struggle against all forms of oppression that subjugate the other.

In choosing these categories, Levinas raises an important question about one's responsibility for the other. One meaning of this formula, as I read it, is that the struggle against the other's oppression cannot be delegated to another person or institution. In the modern liberal state, responsibility for the other has become largely an administrative matter, relegated to the state, which through its charity is supposed to distribute means of subsistence among the most disfranchised individuals. The state plays a crucial role in promoting justice and equality; meanwhile, the individual is left to carry out sporadic acts of charity and benevolence, which reaffirm and sustain the self more than they help the other. Levinas returns the urgency of the struggle against inequality and injustice to the political, placing it firmly on each and every individual's shoulders. In this way, the fight against injustice becomes an ethicopolitical exigency rather than an administrative issue – an impersonal dispensation of entitlement relegated to the state.

Levinas' emphasis on these categories affirms my argument in the next chapter that for him, these categories are fundamentally social; but it is a sociality that bypasses the particular–universal dialectic. Indeed, social relations capable of abstraction are always corporeal, and vice versa. Although irreducible to social relations, the face is already marked by social relations of oppression. In Levinas, the concrete is the concrete plus the abstract. So abstractions are corporeal, as corporeality can become abstract. The-one-for-the-other already encompasses my responsibility both for the singular other who is in front of me, and for all others – signified as the third – who are looking at me through the eyes of the other. As early as *Time and the Other* (1947), Levinas formulated this event as an "I–U collectivity" (TO 93). A political theory and praxis that approaches the other not in her singularity and uniqueness but in generality and universality – as a particular instance of a concept rather than its face – has not overcome the topography of alienation. Levinas, in "Freedom and Command,"[17] argues this point:

> The reality subjected to tyranny is an informed reality; it is already absent in the relationship the agent has with it. It is in the third person, hidden by that which represents it ... Its particularity is already clothed with a generality. It is correct to say, with Hegel, that in the world of knowledge and action nothing is strictly individual. But the direct relationship with a being is ... that which puts us in contact with a being that is not simply uncovered, but divested of its form, of its categories, a being becoming naked, an unqualified substance breaking through its form and presenting a face. (CPP 20)

Yet Levinas' text rarely engages directly with the political as an independent tradition of thought or as a project. Instead, he radically reshapes the question so that the political can no longer be considered in isolation from the asymmetry of one's responsibility for justice demanded in the face of the other. The question of the political arises in his texts through other trajectories, such as his discussions of justice and law, the subject, freedom and responsibility, peace and war, and the basis on which a state justifies itself.

Levinas posits a difficult relationship between ethics and politics. I see this as stemming from his profound criticism of the political status quo, especially that of the modern era. This does not mean that he creates a chasm between the political and ethical. Rather, his reluctance to explicitly formulate the political in terms of his ethics stems from important considerations. Primarily, he is attempting to avoid the spirit of ethical "saying" being reified and fixed in the "said." The ethical saying, for Levinas, is the very "signifyingness of signification," and not a statement about ethics or a program for political action. It cannot be thematized or comprehended, nor can it be reduced to the said, the unsaid, or the not-yet-said; therefore, it cannot be restricted to a fixed political project.

Yet the irreducibility of the saying to the said does not mean that we do not thematize and finalize our political praxis into sets of programs and projects. As Levinas insists, the structure of the relationship between the saying and the said is that of betrayal – the hold of the said on the saying, more than just attesting to the fall of the saying, testifies that in and beyond what the said conveys lies the motivating, orienting, and disrupting forces of the saying. The hold of the said on saying never becomes mastery; saying is never entirely subordinated to the themes of the said. As such, the said is always an open system, never a totality, even as it decides on plans and projects for a political praxis. In Levinas' terms, although the said always contains the traces of saying, saying is irreducible to the said. Therefore any fixed and finalized political project, which closes itself to the surplus of saying (be it past, present, or to come) – or in Derrida's terminology, to "undecidability"[18] – is suspect.

As previously mentioned, the politics of the modern historical era cannot be adequately addressed without confronting the fundamental problem of ethics. If political legitimacy, and all wars and violent political actions – be they espoused by imperial states or by liberatory movements – are already based on some moral justification, then it may be necessary to re-examine morality. But if, after Machiavelli, the political claims a divorce from morality and justifies itself in the sovereign authority of the individual or the polity (or both), then it is vital, in the face of past and present atrocities, to re-examine the ethical dimension that informs or is the basis of this individual and this polity. It is with this in mind that Levinas begins the preface to one of his most important works, *Totality and Infinity,* with these words: "Everyone will readily agree that it is of the highest importance to know whether we are not duped by morality" (TI 21). A re-examination of ethics and its place in inter-human relationship, rather than any concrete political project, becomes Levinas' lifelong priority.

Still, Levinas has a keen eye for detecting the place of, and the role assigned to, the other in liberatory traditions. He is also alert to the totalizing claims and outcomes of liberatory movements that, in the name of struggle against domination, have reproduced another form of totality. He does not hesitate to commend liberatory traditions that attempt either to escape totality, or to find political recourse to respond to the other's demand. For example, in a 1982 interview, at a time when the Eastern Bloc was distancing itself from Marxism and the Soviet Union was embracing Gorbachev's Westernizing reforms, Levinas, while clearly not a Marxist, discussed what he thought was redeeming about Marxism: "In Marxism, there is not just conquest; there is recognition of the other. Marxism invites humanity to demand what it is my duty to give it. That is a bit different from my radical distinction between me and others, but Marxism cannot be condemned for that. Not because it succeeded so well, but because it took the other seriously" (EN 119–20). Levinas holds that Marxism is not just about political mastery or a more smoothly integrated totality; it also entails hope that political power can be made to respond to the demand of the other. Levinas sees in Marxism an attempt to radically transform the meaning of political power – to reformulate it as the social concretion of the ethical response to the outsider, not just a rational peace established through a social contract among insiders. In the same interview, Levinas quotes Lenin (not a very popular figure among philosophers) as saying that "the day will come when the woman cook can lead a country" (EN 120). Levinas finds here the trace of a radical break with the given. He concludes that Lenin was trying to say that the day would come when our political problems would be posed in new terms, when a political impossibility would be seen as a real possibility (EN 120). The ethical, as understood by Levinas, is a move towards such a political future, one that seems an impossibility right now. In one of his later works, "Peace and Proximity,"[19] Levinas distinguishes his notion of an ethical peace from the rational peace proposed by the modern liberal tradition: "It would no longer be a matter of the bourgeois peace of the man who is at home with himself behind closed doors, rejecting the outside that negates him" (BPW 165).

Levinas' underlying political concerns are also apparent in his comments and criticisms of past revolutions and social movements. In an important footnote in "No Identity,"[20] Levinas suggests, if elliptically, that a radical political praxis should entail a definition of the subject based on its vulnerability, its radical passivity, and its irreducible responsibility towards the other, rather than on its self-satisfaction and its self-acquisitions – including its own rights and freedoms:

> It is interesting to note how among the most imperative "sentiments" of May, 1968 the dominant one was the refusal of a humanity that would be defined not by its vulnerability more passive than all passivity, by its debt toward the other, but by its self-satisfaction, its acquisitions, and its acquittances. Over and beyond capitalism and exploitation what was contested were their conditions: the person understood as an accumulation of being, by merits, titles, professional competence – an ontological tumefaction weighing on others and crushing them, instituting a hierarchized society maintained beyond the necessities of consumption, which no religious breath any longer succeeds in rendering egalitarian. Behind the capital of *having* weighed a capital of *being*. (CPP 150:fn:9)

Levinas, at a very important level, is preoccupied with the praxis of failed political social movements and revolutions. His undertaking speaks to those whose dreams of "the woman cook becoming the leader" turned into the horror of Stalinism; it speaks to the fighters of Paris in 1968 who witnessed their liberatory discourse being devoured and recuperated by the dominant politics. It speaks to millions who – in various revolutions around the world – have dreamed of a just society but have witnessed instead the miscarriage of their attempt to change the world. Levinas, who himself had high expectations for Paris 1968, admitted in an interview that for him, one of the greatest disappointments of the twentieth century was Marxism's disintegration into Stalinism (EN 120). In the above quotation, the italicizations in "the capital of *having*" and "the capital of *being*" are important. In highlighting the insufficiency of liberatory struggles that fight solely against exploitation in terms of material accumulation and distribution, he points at deeper workings of domination, ones that are rarely addressed by liberatory movements. He is, in effect, suggesting an "ethicopolitical subjectivity" that is one-for-the-other, a sense of subjecthood whose very individuation is initiated in responsibility for the oppressed other (OB 55).[21] Levinas' ethics, therefore, compels us to imagine a liberatory movement that struggles against both the "capital of having" and the "capital of being." If Levinas' insight is true – that exploitation does not bring passivity, but rather it is through one's passivity, one's exposedness to the other, that the subject can be exploited (OB 55)[22] – then this insight can perhaps help liberatory movements find new ways of conceptualizing the agent of social change, ways that are *not* based exclusively on self-enclosed individuals, each after his or her own rights and freedoms. It is also important to note that by posing this criticism, Levinas does not intend to advocate some organic solidarity based on the idea of "the people," "the community," or "the nation." Rather, his insight can help us go beyond the current dominant frameworks of social movements, frameworks that force such movements to compete for resources and distributive policies that benefit their members' interests while consolidating their political identity to the point of excluding a host of others. This outcome, Levinas tells us, is inevitable insofar as these movements did not originate in a radical openness of one-to-the-other. It is time to take the other, and one's irreducible responsibility for the other, more seriously.

What can be elucidated from Levinas, as I read him, is that the liberatory movements and revolutions failed, and continue to fail, because the political subject of these revolutions was not properly individuated so as to take its responsibility for the other seriously. In "Useless Suffering,"[23] he argues that the most profound adventure of subjectivity, the most upright relation to the other, to confront oneself in the other's suffering – to feel responsible for the suffering of the other – is the turning back of the I to itself; it is the most profoundly inward journey (EN 99).[24] Did the modern political subject emerge out of its suffering for the other's suffering? Or was it defined primarily in terms of parts of a whole, with each subject seeking to acquire its own individual *and* collective rights and freedoms? In each social movement, is it not that the subject is to struggle for her own rights and freedoms, for her own interests, and against her own oppression, rather than for the oppressed who is irreducibly other than her? Does the right-wing dismissal of social movements as "special interests" not entail a warning as to the orientation of many recent social movements? Is Levinas not accurate in his criticism of twentieth-century revolutions, that they were merely reactions to, and antitheses of, a liberal capitalism that held on to the "capital of being"? And as such, that these revolutions were prisoners to that which they aimed to negate?

The political saying of Levinas' ethics is therefore a reminder that recent social movements have missed, or halted prematurely, the inward journey that seeks the one-self and the other, expressed in Levinas' discourse as "me." It is this me who, before any calculation or rationalization of the situation, suffers for the suffering of the other and who thereby opens the subject to political struggle against injustice. In Levinas' words on revolution, *"the disalienation itself is alienated"* (CPP 143). As a result of this forgetfulness, the spirit of revolt is devoid of youth and sincerity, devoid of a pure praxis whose call to act comes from the face of the other who looks at me and demands justice, justice for which only I can be responsible. This sensibility is being forgotten – excluded from political consideration, branded as the naïvéte of the apolitical and the idealist. The-one-for-the-other is ethics itself, without which no revolt against injustice can succeed and no political arrangement can justify itself. We have witnessed the failure of so many revolutions not because they went too far but because they did not go far enough. They lacked ethical orientation as their constitution. They did not find the "me," and they did not seek the other; they were, for the most part, totalizing political projects.

(ii) An Alternative Reading of Ethics and Politics in Levinas

Even having addressed the above concerns, the relationship between ethics and politics in Levinas remains enigmatic. How do Levinas' ethics interact with the political? What are the implications of his ethics for the political? As Asher Horowitz rightly argues in "Beyond Rational Peace: On the Possibility/Necessity of a Levinasian Hyperpolitics,"[25] for most of Levinas' readers his ethics of one-for-the-other is simply a guide, to be added to existing political structures, and the effect of which, they claim, is the minimization of violence and the postponement of war. These readers argue that ethical and political order must live side by side, checking and balancing each other. In this view, the political is a fall, a necessary privation from ethics, imposed upon us by the requirements of being. As such, ethics is higher than the political and must remain separate.[26] In this reading, the ethical is that which reminds the political of its role as a public charity and that, whenever possible, corrects what is unjust. This reduces the ethical to an appeal to what remains of good conscience in politics.[27]

My intention is not to collapse the ethical into the political or vice versa. However, I believe that the above reading of Levinas' ethics (which Horowitz also sees as problematic) in relation to the political misses the transformative force of Levinas' ethics and thereby fails to explore the radical possibilities that an alternative reading of this relationship can offer. In the same article, Asher Horowitz proposes that the relationship between ethics and politics in Levinas is neither dialectical nor paradoxical. His point of entry is through Levinas' conception of the social bond, a conception that radically displaces the logic of sociality and by extension the relation between ethics and politics in political philosophy. In Levinas, as Horowitz has it, the primordial structure of sociality does not follow the formal pattern – the logic constituting the terms of the social relation is not a simultaneous union and distancing of the terms.[28] Instead, the terms maintain their distance without destroying the relation, and the relation, in turn, does not destroy the distance. In Horowitz's reading, therefore, the relation between the terms is not a dialectical one – it is not a prior step towards a final unity to which they must submit. He argues further that this move allows Levinas to avoid the assimilation of parts, and their relation, into the one. It also enables Levinas to access the idea of the "overflow of objective thought from a forgotten experience from which it lives,"[29] which is the one-for-the-other. Horowitz's reading, I argue, is consistent with Levinas' insistence that the self and the other – and the self with the other's other, the third – are absolutely separate yet intimately proximal and that their originary engagement, their sociality with one another, stems neither from their commonality nor from their similarity nor from their difference. Rather, their engagement originates in the exposure of the self to the absolute alterity of the other, the concretion of which is the subject's responsibility for the other's suffering. Therefore, although the proximity of the other opens the self to transcendence, the concretion of this transcendence is fundamentally both immanent and social and is expressed as the ethical task of one's substitution for the other's suffering and destitution.

Through this reading, Horowitz can propose that for Levinas, the relation between ethics and politics is not paradoxical. Their relation still expresses tension and conflict, but this tension is not due to a "reciprocal requirement and negation of the terms in tension."[30] None of the terms is a privation from the other, or from a totality. To suggest an alternative relationship between ethics and politics, Horowitz extends this analysis to Levinas' notions of saying and the said, exploring the structure of betrayal proposed by Levinas as the logic underlying the relationship between these terms. Although saying and the said correlate, this correlation "lives from exposure to another."[31] The relation of betrayal between saying and the said allows saying to appear in the said; but retained is "another meaning than the enunciation of the Said."[32] The relation of betrayal between the saying and the said, Horowitz suggests, is akin to the relation between transcendence and its concretion. The structure of this relation of betrayal is radically different from paradox, dialectical synthesis, or the relation between the one and its parts. In fact, there are two notable differences. First, whereas paradox requires mediation, in the form of either a synthesis or the one, the relation of betrayal requires "the unforgetting of, development of, and commitment to a meaning that was never constituted by the ego."[33] Second, the relation of betrayal is a matter of degree; therefore its reduction becomes the central task of ethicopolitics. For Horowitz, these two aspects of betrayal suggest that Levinas' ethicopolitics has the potential to transcend mere commerce and rational peace.[34] Hence, economic, social, and political domination and exploitation, and the philosophies of the neuter and the totality that justify them, are no longer deemed necessary privations from ethics, but rather betrayals of the ethical saying. Exploitation and injustice, then, are not ontological givens, nor is their existence a matter of the state's faulty distributive policies. They are instead the betrayal of ethics. The concretion of the ethical is precisely a political effort whose degree of betrayal is constantly subject to collective "unforgetting, development and commitment." In other words, the logic of betrayal marks the political as a debt – as a notion of politics whose debt to ethics must constantly be remembered, worked through, and compensated.[35]

In Levinas, in relation to the political, it is the entry of the third onto my scene that prompts the betrayal of the saying in the said. Therefore to arrive at the implications of Levinas' ethical relation for a radical political praxis, we must extend the logic of betrayal to the relationship that Levinas establishes between me, the other, and the third – that is, we must work through the problem of the other as both irreducible alterity and multiplicity, as well as the implications for political justice. Two interrelated questions need to be addressed. First, what kinds of changes happen in the ethical relationship when the third appears, especially as pertains to justice? And second, does this turn Levinasian ethics towards radical ethicopolitics or (as many readers of Levinas argue) towards an entrenchment of the existing liberal structure? In the following section, I discuss these issues surrounding Levinas' concepts of justice and of the third.

(iii) The Problem of the Third and Justice in Levinas

All Levinasian scholars agree that the appearance of the third raises the need for thematization, calculation, and judgment. Most scholars conclude from this that the third introduces the question of politics into ethics (and not vice versa). They view the entry of the third as the limitation of the subject's infinite responsibility; the third, they argue, demands formal justice – and, by extension, the law – as well as political violence as expressed in the state's institutions and hierarchy.[36] The third is seen only as the limit of responsibility and the birth of this question: What do I have to do with justice? Indeed, Levinas himself seems at times to argue along this line: "The self, the I, cannot limit itself to the incomparable uniqueness of each one … Behind the unique singularities, one must perceive the individuals of a genus, one must compare them, judge them and condemn them" (IRB 205).[37] Alternatively, regarding the need for the state, he argues that "the State, general laws, are necessary. Institutions are necessary to carry out decisions. Every work of politics and justice is necessary. This order negates mercy … Is this concern for reconsideration … not in effect the essence of democracy and of the liberal State, the sign of a mercy and charity that breathe there?" (IRB 230).

I, however, argue that there is usually more to what Levinas says than this when he discusses the third and its relation to politics and justice.

Most of his readers ignore this surplus or do not seriously consider it.[38] The first aspect of the surplus that must be emphasized is Levinas' repeated insistence that the state is required *by* ethics (i.e., not *despite* ethics), and furthermore, that the state must be oriented to concretize ethics in politics: "It is in the name of that responsibility for the other … that goodness to which the face of the other man appeals, that the entire discourse of justice is set in motion" (IRB 206). For Levinas, politics and the state originate in goodness, and moreover, goodness must be present in every working of politics. Levinas' sense of goodness *cannot* be reduced to charity or mercy, nor to a Kantian goodness that takes as its *a priori* the will of a rational being, concretized and expressed in reciprocity (TI 128).[39] In Levinas' thought, goodness originates in positing being as the anarchy of Desire, obsessing the subject to substitute for the other (TI 305–6; OB 57).[40] In this sense, goodness finds itself in society as prioritizing responsibility for the other over reciprocal exchange. As such, society – plurality – no longer means "the coherence of the elements that constitute plurality" (TI 306), but rather a genuine peace. The question Levinas leaves us with is whether political power (and its state) can reformulate itself to contain and become an expression of this an-archical goodness.

In Levinas' discussion of the third and its relation to politics and justice, the second aspect of the surplus is the resistance of the structure of betrayal to the formation of a political totality. The state must realize the incompleteness of its own formal justice, which is less just than the ethics that instigate it. Levinas states that "inspired by love for one's fellow man, reasonable justice is bound by legal structures and cannot equal the goodness that solicits and inspires it" (IRB 207). The third aspect is the possibility that the betrayal that stems from the fact of mediation can be minimized or reduced to bare necessity or public charity. This realization cannot remain at the level of formal recognition. Rather the state, whose legitimacy is derived from one's responsibility for the other, must reduce the impact of this betrayal. Formal justice – laws, institutions, and so on – exists to oblige the state to fulfil its social promise, which is "the possibility for a man to see the face of the other man" (LR 261).[41] In contrast to liberal readings of Levinas, the state is not merely the expression of this betrayal; rather, it points to the imperative of paying a debt, which remains a surplus to, and in excess of, politics. To put it differently, the call is for the state to intervene in inter-human relationships and to reduce the effects of this betrayal. Forgetting this important aspect, according to Levinas, amounts to sinking the state, and its justice, into a totalitarian and ideological deduction. More important, it leads to politics forgetting to invent new forms of human coexistence (IRB 206). We need to situate Levinas' citations regarding the need for the state, introduced at the beginning of this section, in this broader context. When we do so, the limitations of the reading, which describes the third as necessitating the existing state, and which justify the work of its formal justice, will become apparent. This reductive reading articulates both the political and its structures as ontological givens stemming from the unresolved paradox between ethics and politics.

Yet we are still left with the question of what, besides the limitation of one's responsibility, the third signifies. How can the third be read as enabling the human community to invent new forms of coexistence? I argue that there is a radical difference between the following two approaches to the third: one that articulates the third as an event that brings only the necessity of thematization, comparison, and judgment, and a second that views the third as a simultaneous call for ethics and politics while constantly questioning and challenging the same law and the totalizing effect that politics brings forth.

As Robert Gibbs states in *Correlations in Rosenzweig and Levinas*,[42] the third poses a serious challenge to the Western, modern subject. He argues that "it is an unfortunate heritage we have that mislocates ethics in individuality and sociality in totality."[43] If we take the third as society, it raises the question of what we are left to interpret in the relationship between the I and the other. Is it a non-society? A dyad? The relationship between the subject and the other cannot be reduced to a relationship between the ego and its outside, between two totalities – that is, to a dyad. Yet it is precisely this dichotomy between individuality and sociality, which forces them to read Levinas' ethical demand as contradictory or paradoxical, that drives many of Levinas' commentators, as soon as the third appears, to focus solely on "comparing, contrasting, and calculating" and by extension on the unfortunate necessity of the state, of hierarchy, and of violence. It has not helped that many of these commentators have repeatedly stated that the third, according to Levinas, is another to the other, present from the beginning and looking at me through the eyes of the other. It has become a truism that the third is not another who is added later to the sociality between the other and me – she has already expressed herself through the first in the scene. There is hardly a situation in which there is only me and one other. Indeed, the presence of all the others and their multiple demands on me signifies thematization, comparison, prioritization, and a decision. The question, however, is whether the social starts from these requirements, or whether sociality, and the question of the political, has already begun, originating in what Horowitz terms "the forgotten experience of the command of all the others."[44] The ethical is already in the sociopolitical – it has always been there and has made its expression. Although we can trap the terms "individuality" and "sociality" in a formal dichotomy, their concrete social expression need not instantiate ontological structures that perpetuate the same mutual exclusion. In reality, both terms, though separate, are constitutive of each other.

None of the relationships – between the self and the neighbour, between the self and the third, between the neighbour and the other, and so on – form a totality, either within or outside themselves. Each relationship is engaged with the other one in an infinite chain of responsibility of one-for-the-other. While it is true that the entry of the third means that the relationship of the neighbour with the third is hidden from me, that relationship concerns me nonetheless: "What then are the other and the third party for one another? What have they done to one another?" (OB 157). Here, Levinas is saying that the first on the scene is already all humanity, concretized in a face that demands a response, and acquires a different signification than mere statement of a paradox. This saying means that this relationship concerns me on two levels. At one level, where the relation hides itself from me but still concerns me, I need knowledge, comparison, and judgment; and in the relationship between the neighbour, the third, and myself, not only do they and we bear responsibility towards one another, but insofar as my responsibility for them is concerned, I must know what we have done to one another. This requires retelling: comparing, calculating, and judgment.

On the second level, my irreplaceable responsibility for the neighbour and the third gives rise to my concern for what they have done to each other. I am as much responsible to the other as I am to the third, fourth, fifth, and so on. The third limits my action, not the quiddity of my responsibility, which has been commenced with the first one on the scene. The entry of the first, the primordial experience of face-to-face encounter, does not imply a chronological order – the first does not refer to a quantity, but to a quality that is the condition of sociality, sharing its trace with all inter-human relationships. It is only within this chain that my judgment of what has gone between the neighbour and the third is still an ethical imperative and not merely a matter of formal law. Therefore the sociopolitical plane is a "curvature of social space," one that retains the asymmetrical relation between the infinite number of selves and the others – my concern for the relationship between the neighbour and the third is what obliges me to compare, calculate, judge, and even condemn.

The existence of both these orders at the level of sociopolitical life must be emphasized. Both orders enter into the social and the political; neither is left out. More important, they enter into the sociopolitical without forming a totality. We are confronted with a chain of face-to-face relationships, each infinitely exposed to the others. Without this conception, my concern to know what the other and the third have done to each other would become either obsolete or exclusively the subject of formal justice with its universal laws.

The Third and Justice: Two Conceptions of Justice in Levinas

If the subject should not be judged exclusively in terms of formal justice, the third then entails two intimately related notions of justice – the formal and the ethical. It is crucial to analytically distinguish these two notions and to explore their interrelation. I will focus on these two orders of justice as signified in Levinas' thought, and draw out some of the implications for the political.[45]

In Levinas, justice is sometimes the recognition of the other as my master: "justice is the recognition of his privilege qua Other and his mastery" (TI 72). Its work becomes the uprightness of the face-to-face, signifying the establishment of the ethical relation, as Levinas suggests: "The establishing of this primacy of the ethical, that is, of the relationship of man to man – signification, teaching, and justice – a primacy of an irreducible structure upon which all the other structures rest" (TI 79). When speaking of justice in this sense, Levinas usually uses terms such as "ethical justice," or, in more religious language, "divine" or "celestial" justice (see for example, BV 104, 107).[46] Sometimes (as in the above quotes), he simply uses the term justice, thus making the distinction between the two orders more difficult, and perhaps indicating his reluctance to separate the two.

At times, Levinas becomes even more specific about his conception of "ethical justice," suggesting that the third signifies two important and interrelated exigencies for "ethical justice." The first aspect is the irreducible responsibility for the other, the non-indifference to the suffering and death of the other (LR 244). The second is ethical justice as "tikkun olam," which means, literally, "to repair the world" (HO xxxvii).[47]

I will not immediately explore the implications of these two embedded aspects of Levinas' conception of ethical justice, or their significance for a radical political praxis. Suffice it to say that to view justice as non-indifference to the suffering and death of the other, as an obligation to repair the world, is to immediately open Levinas' ethics to a collective political praxis that aims at a non-violent rebellion against injustice committed against the other.

Returning to the second meaning of justice in Levinas, the Third, as many have already argued, brings the necessity of justice as thematization, equality, comparison of the state, hierarchy, and even violence. This meaning is especially apparent in Levinas' later work *Otherwise Than Being*, but it also appears in some of his early works such as "The Ego and the Totality" (see OB 128, 157–8; CPP 29–39).[48] In *Otherwise Than Being*, when discussing saying and the said, he argues that "justice is necessary, that is, comparison, coexistence, contemporaneousness, assembling, order, thematization" (OB 157). This quote, and others, have prompted many Levinasian scholars to argue that by the time of *Otherwise Than Being* Levinas had abandoned his former notion of justice – the notion of ethical justice – having recognized the limitation that the third brings into the anarchical responsibility of one for the other. For example, both Simon Critchley and Robert J.S. Manning[49] put forward such an exposition and argue along the same line. Manning argues that in *Totality and Infinity*, justice is within the face-to-face relation, but by the time of *Otherwise Than Being* Levinas has abandoned his original notion of justice and introduced a different justice – one that occurs only when the third party arrives,[50] that is, justice as thematization, comparison, law, and the state. Yet even within this second order of justice, these commentators reduce Levinas' notion of justice to formal equality, and they do so without seriously exploring his assertion that formal justice starts with economic justice – a point that Levinas never hesitates to emphasize: "equality among persons means nothing of itself; it has an economic meaning and presupposes money, and already rests on justice – which, when well-ordered begins with the Other" (TI 72). Although the demand for justice comes from outside economic relations, justice, in Levinas' words, "can have no other object than economic equality" (CPP 44). I will look more closely at this in the next section of this chapter, where I discuss liberal readings of Levinas. Manning's reading presents not only a reductive interpretation of Levinas' understanding of justice, one that creates dichotomies between justice and compassion and between formal and economic justice; but also leaves unexplored the significance of Levinas' conception of ethical justice for the political.

It is worth repeating here that in Levinas' ethical relation, justice does not arise to restore the reciprocity between the I and the other or to reinforce the stability of "rational peace"; it arises from the fact of the third who is "another other" to me (EN 229). Just because we are more than two, my responsibility towards the third is not diluted among the other's others among us. Instead, I am the one who is responsible for the other and for all the other's others – no one else, no institution, can take this responsibility. So the third makes my infinite responsibility a finite practice and raises the necessity of calculating, thematizing, and prioritizing. However, the social, the political, and the state are to emerge from this finite practice of the one-for-the-other and not from the limitation of violence. Levinas' insistence on my infinite responsibility for the other, therefore, does not merely imply the impossibility of meeting my responsibility. Rather, infinite responsibility functions as a measure of legitimacy for every social, economic, and political arrangement in every state. Accepting ethics as the first politics means that one-for-the-other should ground the constitution of the state. Levinas makes this distinction as "those who seek to have a State in order to have justice and those who seek justice in order to ensure the survival of the State" (LR 261). Though the third and its call to justice work within history, the state does not rely exclusively on the logic of formal justice. While most of Levinas' commentators start with the ethical and end with the state, Levinas, I argue, envelops formal justice within his conception of ethical justice. As such he radically disturbs and transcends the conception of the political and of the state whose legitimacy is derived from a reductive, liberal, and modern notion of justice, which according to Levinas "neutralizes the face into a totalized concept called equity" (OB 71).

Levinas therefore does not abandon his earlier notion of justice, even if he sometimes writes as though he has. Rather, in his later works, the third becomes a link between the two orders of justice and an embodiment of them. "In reality, justice does not include me in the equilibrium of its universality; justice summons me to go beyond the straight line of justice" (TI 245). The entry of the third, while it does not annul the command of the face that "you should not murder," adds another essential layer to my ethical task – namely, the concern for injustice done to this other, which since it is hidden from me compels me to compare, calculate, and judge. I now have two ethical tasks proper to the sociopolitical life: to defend the other, be it the neighbour or the third, against injustice done to her; and to obey the original demand of the face, which commands me not to murder. I will now elaborate on these two points as aspects of Levinas' conception of ethical justice.

In the first aspect of Levinas' conception of ethical justice – and here is where I differ from other readers of Levinas – before limiting my responsibility, before compelling me to compare and thematize, the third calls me to "demand justice for the other man" (LR 242). It is the third who awakens the subject to another aspect of the ethical relation, one that goes beyond the subject's private hospitality and goodness to the other. The existence, from the beginning, of the third marks the face-to-face encounter as both an ethical event and a political one, forever linking the meaning of the political to the circumstance of the other and not to a notion of the political that is preoccupied with the maintenance of one's own rights and freedoms, with a system of rights and duties, or with public charity. It exposes the ethicopolitical subject as an instant that appears in the political as a struggle against injustice done to the other. This is the meaning of Levinas' claim that I am always more responsible for the other, to the point that I could die for the other. In Levinas' language, the humanity of the human is awakened through the call for justice: "morality comes to birth not in equality, but in the fact that infinite exigencies, that of serving the poor, the stranger, the widow, and the orphan, converge at one point of the universe" (TI 245). Reducing this responsibility to acts of private or public charity, as in liberal readings of Levinas, simply will not do. Ethical justice demands that the subject repair the world (HO xxxvii). This demand, however, cannot be reduced to an individual struggle between good and evil. Rather, to view justice as immediately repairing the world opens Levinas' ethics to a radical and collective political praxis whose aim is to demand justice for others. Levinas states clearly that "rebellion against an unjust society expresses the spirit of our age. That spirit is expressed by rebellion against an unjust society" (LR 242). In an endnote to this quote, he points out that our age sometimes caricatures this rebellion; he then alludes to the many revolutions of the past century that ended up as dominant and dictatorial as the ones they rebelled against. However, he immediately adds: "But the caricature is itself a revelation from which a meaning must be extracted; a meaning that requires correction, but which cannot be ignored or disregarded with impunity" (LR 248n5).

Yet we already know that this situation is not straightforward. As soon as we think we have understood the command of the face, Levinas confronts us with another seemingly contradictory aspect of ethical justice. The third, the fourth, and the fifth – sociality – command me to fight against injustice. Yet the other and the third, and all the other's others, also command me: "you shall not murder." So, how should the subject simultaneously repair the world and refrain from the possibility of violence and murder? Any serious exploration of the relationship between ethics and politics in Levinas must somehow work through this apparent enigma. I will look closely at the issue of (non-)violence in Levinas' ethicopolitics in chapter 4. Suffice it to say that Levinas carries the full weight of both these primordial commands of the face in the political – the ethical demand to non-violence is in no way annulled by the entry of the third and one's struggle against injustice.

The problem with most of Levinas' commentators is that they attribute the demand "you shall not murder" to the ethical order and thereby reduce the demand to repair the world to the formal justice belonging to the order of the political, the state, and its impersonal administrative structure – or worse, to a private-individual sphere. Consequently, the third becomes the moment at which the ethical is abandoned in the political and not, as Levinas insists, "betrayed."[51] Hence, the question of collective political praxis becomes irrelevant, or seems to be far from Levinas' ethical preoccupation. That is, in the work of these commentators there exists a rift between Levinas' conception of ethical relation and sociopolitical liberatory movements, a rift that is impossible to traverse. In the same light, the issue of (non-)violence is discussed only as it pertains to Levinas' face-to-face encounter; because of this, his insistence on the insufficiency of rational peace as the social bond, and the implication of this for a collective, non-violent ethicopolitical praxis, is not seriously explored.

Me, the Other, the Third, and (In)Justice: Ethical Justice and Liberatory Political Praxis

In this section I explore the interrelation of these two aspects of Levinas' conception of ethical justice and its relevance to liberatory political praxis. If the third brings into human sociality the demand of justice for the other, then the subject is responsible for fighting against injustice done to the other, while fearing the death of the other more than her own. The force of the ethical command of one-for-the-other is at once peaceful and revolutionary. With the entry of the third, both these ethical commands acquire an added urgency; the commitment to both thus becomes the measure of the degree of ethical fulfilment, or of the betrayal in the political. I suggest that it is much more productive if, instead of employing the logic of abandonment, we read into Levinas' distinction between ethical justice and "earthly" justice and the entry of the third, what Horowitz suggests – the logic of betrayal. If the concretion of ethical justice in the political contains the two aforementioned aspects, then the fulfilment of these commands becomes the degree of betrayal in the political.

In this context, one important but underemphasized point is the relation between Levinas' discussion of the demands of the other and those of the third. As I read Levinas, the other not only calls me to be responsible for her suffering and death but also summons me to be irreducibly responsible for all others. This is the precise meaning of Levinas' emphasis that the third looks at me through the eyes of the other. Insofar as the other is irreducibly responsible for another, and all others, her call embodies the demands of all humanity. If the social originates in infinite numbers of asymmetrical and interrelated relations, then the entry of the third, who is also the first, summons me to rise against injustice and to strive for peace and non-violence. In this sense, the subject born in the social is not a neutral subject but rather an ethicopolitical one. A society that is born out of irreducible responsibility for the other's suffering and death, out of responsibility for the injustice done to the other, is already a society of ethicopolitical subjects who resist and rebel against injustice and violence at every instant.

But what does all this mean for a liberatory political struggle and for the subject involved in rebellion against injustice? What can Levinas tell us about the constitutive event of this agent and about the foundations on which this struggle can be imagined? In what ways, after Levinas' ethics, can one rethink the contours of liberatory struggle? On what basis can a society of resisters relate to one another and to others?

Levinas' ethical relation provides a more fundamental ground – if one can still use this term – for radical political praxis. He takes us beyond the concern for the formal (un)freedom of the individual against or for which the modern liberal subject is called to fight, and beyond the class bondage against which the Marxian subject is summoned to unite. Ethical justice in Levinas summons the ethicopolitical subject to fight for the rights and freedoms of another human and against the sufferings of the excluded and forgotten. That is to say that the primordial call to fight against injustice is not about the ethicopolitical subject regaining her "natural" freedom, but rather for the subject to justify her freedom – to "indict my arbitrary and partial freedom" (TI 245). Levinas not only surpasses the formal justice established by and through the liberal modern state but also shows the displaced origin of the call for justice in Marx, with significant consequences for liberatory political struggles in the twentieth century and profound implications for those in the twenty-first. In this sense, Levinas expands the notion of justice to include both formal and economic equality; he also shows that the origin of this human quest stems from the poverty of the face of another human being, who calls the subject to respond. To elaborate on how Levinas shows the limits of both liberalism and Marxism, I must briefly discuss Levinas' short essay "Reflections on the Philosophy of Hitlerism." Levinas published this extremely succinct essay in 1934, shortly after Hitler's rise to power in Germany. This brief article contains some of his most profound criticisms of the modern liberal tradition, the insufficiency of the Marxian break with liberalism, and the inadequacy of both discourses when faced with the claims of National Socialism.[52]

In this essay, Levinas states that political freedom does not "exhaust the content of the spirit of freedom" (RPH 64). Although Levinas does not elaborate on his conception of the "spirit of freedom" in this article, his subsequent works expand on this notion, formulating it as "created" or "finite" (see TI 147–8, 293–4; OB 121–9). Briefly, for Levinas, "created freedom" signifies humans' freedom, which, in *and* because of its absolute separation, simultaneously resists a closure into a totality and engenders the subject's radical exposure to the other, expressed in unquantifiable responsibility for the other (I discuss Levinas' take on freedom, in more detail, in chapter 3). Levinas describes the absolute separation involved in created freedom as "the power given to the soul to free itself from *what has been*, from everything that linked it to something or engaged it with something" (RPH 66). Therefore, although created, this liberation is fundamental and foundational; in other words, this is a "created and fundamental freedom" that signifies the absolute separation between the self and the other, making possible both disengagement with the world and the non-reciprocal relation with the other. Liberalism retains only one aspect of this freedom; in liberalism, the absolute alterity of the face is reduced to autonomy, emphasizing the sovereign freedom of reason in the autonomous individual. As such, liberalism places the human spirit on a plane that is superior to reality, creating a fantastic void between the human and the real world. Liberalism asserts the final sovereignty of spirit or reason over all earthly circumstances and beyond the very justice of this spontaneous freedom. It cannot accept the determination of human life by concrete history, and therefore it cannot comprehend the significance of the original and unnecessary bondage of the body to its concrete existence (RPH 69). As such, it cannot provide a notion of justice that addresses the surplus of economic exploitation. It is not truly just. Levinas concludes that when it focuses solely on individual political freedom and equality, autonomous reason cannot see the most fundamental aspect of liberation – the power bestowed on the soul to "free itself from *what has been*, from everything that linked it to something or engaged it with something" (RPH 66). Implicit in this paper is Levinas' insight into liberalism's inability to account for the absolute alterity of the other or to find freedom in one's ability to respond to the unconditional responsibility for the other. In a 1990 prefatory note to this essay, Levinas raises this point in saying that "we must ask ourselves if liberalism is all we need to achieve an authentic dignity for the human subject" (RPH 63). Implicit in this is the question of whether liberatory struggles, within the framework of liberal democracy, can fight for the singularity and absolute dignity of the other. In other words, the struggle to determine whether I am my brother's keeper continues and remains unresolved. Liberalism cannot sufficiently go beyond the individual quest for one's own rights and freedoms and therefore reduces the human struggle for liberation to formal justice. And because it does not recognize the originary bondage of the body and consciousness to material existence, it cannot alleviate the material exploitation above and beyond the original bondage. In the above-mentioned prefatory note, Levinas alludes to these criticisms:

> This article expresses the conviction that this source [the source of the bloody barbarism of National Socialism] stems from the essential possibility of *elemental Evil* into which we can be led by logic and against which Western philosophy had not sufficiently insured itself. This possibility is inscribed within the ontology of a being concerned with being ... Such a possibility still threatens the subject correlative with being as gathering together and as dominating ... that famous subject of transcendental idealism that before all else wishes to be free and thinks itself free ... Does the subject arrive at the human condition prior to assuming responsibility for the other man? (RPH 63)

Marx, according to Levinas, is right insofar as he realizes that consciousness, as perceived in modern liberal philosophy, cannot determine being. Marx was the first philosopher to recognize "the whole weight of matter in the present itself" (TO 62). According to Levinas, Marx is the only Western philosopher who does not view the human as pure freedom – who acknowledges the chaining of the body and its consciousness to a concrete existence that no reason can undo completely. In Marxism the spirit "is not longer a pure reason that partakes in a real of ends. It is prey to material needs" (RPH 66–7). Consequently, Levinas claims that Marxism "is opposed not just to Christianity, but to the whole of idealist liberalism, wherein 'being does not determine consciousness,' but consciousness or reason determines being" (RPH 67).

Yet for Levinas, Marx's break with liberal, Western tradition is not sufficiently radical (RPH 67). When he insists that being determines consciousness, Marx does not take the implications of the original freedom seriously enough. In Marxism, the consciousness is expected to liberate being from that which determines it. If consciousness is determined solely by being, how then is consciousness to free the being from that which determines it? How can an overdetermined consciousness free the being unless it is originally constituted through something beyond itself, through its openness to the idea of transcendence? Marxism ignores the fundamental sensibility at the heart of subjectivity, which inspires the subject to transcend its own being, and her thought to think beyond itself in such a way that liberation means something more than a resubjugation of one and the other to the domination of another totalized identity.

Marx realizes that economic justice is central to human dignity, and he opens philosophy to something beyond itself by acknowledging the other and her demand on humanity (EN 119–20). Even so, he is unable to open the fundamentally ethical dimension of liberation. Marx's foundational legitimacy of the liberatory struggle is still based on comprehension and identification of the other and on the equation of her suffering with one's own. Levinas' ethical relation suggests that for a radical political praxis, the legitimacy of a liberatory struggle is not based on difference, as proposed by new forms of social movements in liberal democracy. Nor is it based on a class consciousness that converts members of a class from a "class in itself" to a "class for itself."[53]

Levinas' ethical relation contains both formal equality and formal justice and, at the same time, transcends both. The liberal achievement of formal equality (equality of rights and freedoms) is welcomed, and a Marxian struggle for formal justice (economic equality) is demanded. Yet both are seen as insufficient to establish an ethical kinship based on an asymmetrical relation between me and the other, one that Levinas views as radically opposed to oppression (OB 177). The relation suggested in Levinas' ethicopolitics is a relation without a common ground, not one of difference or identity. Or rather, it is a relation of in-difference, difference here signifying a relation of non-indifference to the suffering and death of the other with whom I have no apparent ontological relations (LR 244).

Yet there is always the problem of how to interpret the other's call. That is, how do I "know" that I "know" the demand of the other? How do I know that what I take as the voice of the other is not my own voice? How do I know that what I am doing for the other is what she would want me to do? How do I differentiate my responsibility for the other that originates in the other's demand, from that which originates in my own benevolence and appropriation of the voice of the other? In short, if the subject, by its definition, is always an ontological category, how can it ever transcend that category?

Levinas' answers to these questions are multifaceted. One important aspect of Levinas' response is that he sees the relationship with the other as not originally having the structure of intentionality, opening onto or aiming at a known, identifiable object (BPW 16). This relation exists prior to knowledge and intentionality, and sometimes as a *different* intentionality, in the phenomenological sense. Here I use the term "intentionality" as Levinas himself does: "Hence intentionality, where thought remains an adequation with the object, does not define consciousness at its fundamental level. All knowing qua intentionality already presupposes the idea of infinity, which is preeminently non-adequation" (TI 27). The other, before being represented in or out of a totality, summons me to my responsibility. One rushes to help another person in distress – sometimes a total stranger – without reflecting on the danger to one's own life. And sometimes one loses one's life in such non-reciprocal acts. It is easy to find these events daily in the media, even more so in times of social upheaval and revolution. The media's representation of these non-reciprocal acts is problematic in that they are depicted as the "ultimate act of sacrifice." Still, their occurrence forces political theory to articulate the implications of this ethical reality, which occurs outside the system of reciprocity and reveals the limit of this conception of the political. In this sense, Levinas' ethicopolitics surpasses the liberal project, which takes thematization, totalization, calculation, and reciprocity as the basis of political praxis.

Yet, since most of Levinas' commentators view his ethicopolitics as a continuation and a deepening of the liberal political tradition, we must delve deeper into liberal interpretations of Levinas and into Levinas' relationship with liberalism. To this end, I undertake two tasks: first, I suggest that Levinas' ethics cannot be exhausted in liberalism; and second, I offer an alternative reading of Levinas' ethics beyond liberal democracy through his conceptions of the "individual," "peace," and "economy."

(iv) Levinas and Liberalism

Richard A. Cohen is an important proponent of reading Levinas within a liberal framework. Cohen rightly distinguishes Levinas' political orientation from that of Machiavelli. According to Cohen, in Machiavelli political power is sovereign, deployed for its own sake; whereas in Levinas' utopian politics, political power must justify itself in ethics.[54] He goes even deeper, differentiating Levinas' utopian politics from those political projects that use utopian rhetoric, such as Stalinism, religious fundamentalism, and so on.[55] In fact, Cohen, in the introduction to his book *Ethics, Exegesis, and Philosophy: Interpretation after Levinas*, rightly reminds his readers that Levinas rejects the entire experience of the past century in relation to the political state yet does not explore the implication of this radical insight in his own works. Cohen's definition of politics as "rule over society and resources ultimately sanctioned by coercion," and justice in such a polity as "equitable law, equal access, fair play apropos politics,"[56] radically departs from Levinas' definition of the political. Levinas, as discussed in the previous section, sees the inherent violence in such a liberal construction of politics and justice. In "Transcendence and Height,"[57] he offers a profound criticism of the state, including the liberal state:

> For me, the negative element, the lament of violence in the State, in the hierarchy, appears even when the hierarchy functions perfectly, when everyone submits to universal ideas. There are cruelties which are terrible because they proceed from the necessity of the reasonable Order. There are, if you like, the tears that a civil servant cannot see: the tears of the Other (Autrui). (BPW 23)

Nevertheless, Cohen sums up this position thusly: "Clearly, then, what Levinas is defending, namely, a state regulated by justice, and justice guided by morality, and morality understood as that of independent individuals in social relation, is what has been known in modern political theory as *liberal* politics, 'liberal' in the classic sense first articulated by John Locke."[58] For Cohen, Levinas' ethics is ultimately a foundation for a deepening of liberal ethics and politics. In this section I discuss three central points in Cohen's reading of Levinas that demonstrate how Cohen falls short in his insight into what Levinas' ethics could mean for the political.

Levinas and the Liberal Conception of the Individual

Since I elaborate on this theme and its political implications in chapter 2, I discuss it here only briefly. Levinas is a defender of subjectivity – not the subjectivity that is founded in Cartesian cogito/ego, but one that is predicated on the idea of infinity. Cohen, in several places, addresses this issue at length.[59] Yet in discussing Levinas' critique of modern subjectivity and its implication for politics, he keeps the separation and non-relation between the sovereign authority and supra-political ends intact and unchallenged. The sovereign authority – be it the individual or the state – remains within the liberal construction and undergoes only minor modifications. Furthermore, only the supra-political end (in the form of moral guidance) is added to the liberal political construction. So, although he agrees that Levinas' subject is based on one-for-the-other, he locates this construction firmly within the classical liberal tradition, albeit without "the individualism of monadic subjectivity."[60]

Cohen does not go far enough. Levinas' objection to the subjectivity of the liberal, modern individual is a critique of the history of Western ontology, with its persistence in essence, its at-home-ness with itself, and its totalization of both the self and the other. This is not a small change or some minor modification. One cannot simply add, as Cohen does, moral considerations and Levinas' ethics of responsibility to the modern liberal subject. This addition does not produce a subject who is open to transcendence and hostage to the other, nor does it produce a state that is founded on the irreducible responsibility of one for the other. This misreading of Levinas' ethicopolitics is mainly due to the exclusion of Levinas' meta-phenomenology of the face, of radical passivity, and of fundamental asymmetry between the self and the other, and their implications for a different politics.[61]

Cohen conflates Levinas' insistence on the subject's interiority with the autonomy of the liberal subject. He claims that in defending the integrity of the individual, Levinas adheres to the classical liberal tradition, since both perspectives defend the "inalienable rights" of humanity.[62] Indeed, respect for individual dignity appears to be a commonality between Levinas and the classical liberal tradition. Both argue that the state – and by extension all of its political institutions – must respect the individual *qua* individual. However, the defence of individual dignity proposed by Levinas clearly shows the limits of the liberal defence of individual dignity. For Levinas, individual dignity must be respected and protected not because it possesses natural or divine rights, but because each individual is irreducibly responsible for the other "with whom initially I have nothing in common" (BPW 27). Levinas states: "The I that I defend against the hierarchy is the one that is necessary for going right to the Other" (BPW 23). The liberal framework ends with a defence of the individual dignity that the impersonal state and its bureaucratic institutions are charged to protect. For Levinas, defining the "individual" in this way disregards the surplus of being, that is, "me" being infinitely and uniquely responsible for the other (BPW 17). As such, he surpasses liberal ontological borders and opens the possibility of radically reconstructing the individual and her relation to the political. In the structure of liberalism and its limited focus on the rights and freedom of the same, Levinas sees a "hypocrisy" (BPW 24). The politics, the state, and the institutions that result from this orientation alienate that which they were supposed to maintain. He argues this point as follows:

> But war and administration, that is to say, hierarchy, through which the State is instituted and maintained, alienate the Same, which they were supposed to maintain in its purity ... The Same does not recognize its will in the consequence of its vote. The mediation, which should have assured the triumph of the Same, is the source of a new alienation of the Same. (BPW 15–16)

Levinas and the Liberal Peace

Levinas provides one of the most fundamental criticisms of band-aid solutions to violence and war. Cohen himself argues that in contradistinction to political utopianism, Levinas' messianic politics claim only a few absolutes. The first and perhaps most outstanding feature, according to Cohen, is that there should and will be a time without war.[63] However, Cohen does not seriously explore the role of violence and war in maintaining liberal politics. Nor does he seriously pose the question of whether the liberal state is able to create the conditions for what

Levinas calls "ethical peace" (see BPW 166). This issue, however, is central to Levinas' thought, and through it he offers a radical critique of, and an opening beyond, the liberal state and its violence.

Levinas repeatedly claims that Western morality is based mainly on contracts among self-interested individuals, its workability guaranteed by the spectre of violence. Peace in the liberal state is an armed peace, and its justice arises to preserve peaceful commerce among members of that society. But does Levinas also claim that liberal justice can break with the structure of violence and war? Does his justice correspond to, or is it a modality of, the logic of war? My answer to both questions, contra Cohen, is no. If Levinas' justice is grounded in infinite openness to the command of the other, then the difference between an ethicopolitical order that rests on the responsibility of one-for-the-other and a state that is based on limiting the freedom of autonomous individuals is more than a theoretical or philosophical difference (BPW 111, 168–9). Levinas is not simply revealing the deeper justification for, or another limited critique of, the liberal state. By revealing the ways in which liberal politics is founded in violence, and concurrently limits that violence with further violence, he is making clear distinctions among different societies, politics, and states.

Therefore, the problem with liberalism, its politics, and its state is that its constitution can only be based, in Walter Benjamin's terms, on the power of law-preserving violence, maintained by the threat of lawmaking violence.[64] In liberal states, power is merely the power of self-continuation, passed from one master to another. According to Benjamin, law-preserving violence is the mechanism through which the state maintains its hegemony, permitting only recuperable forms of excess and revolt that do not threaten the present arrangement of commerce.[65] Law-preserving violence – the threat of punishment, functioning as a deterrent – is founded in mythical violence, which is in turn is based on the spectre of pure destruction. Benjamin holds that although the ostensible purpose of law-preserving power is the non-violent resolution of political conflict, "this remains, however, a product situated within the mentality of violence ... because no compromise, however freely accepted, is conceivable without a compulsive character. 'It would be better otherwise' is the underlying feeling in every compromise."[66] Compromise, here, alludes to the social contract, which results in the creation of the modern state, whose end is not justice but the establishment of law through a state monopoly on violence. That is, lawmaking violence is the founding myth upon which all social contracts are created and maintained. As such, the state must forever rely on lawmaking and law-preserving violence, while also forgetting their origin. This forgetting produces a cycle through which the legitimacy and life of the modern liberal state is established.

In the context of this forgetting, Levinas describes liberal society as hypocritical in two senses of the word. First, as Levinas argues, "to tell the truth, ever since eschatology has opposed peace to war the evidence of war has been maintained in an essentially hypocritical civilization, that is, attached both to the True and to the Good, henceforth antagonistic" (TI 24). The good, one's responsibility for the other, does not belong to the order of the true; rather, it precedes the true–false distinction. If liberal politics finds, as it has found many times in history, a truth for war and violence, this does not mean that war and violence are justified. To justify war, humanity must appeal to the good, which according to Levinas is excluded and forgotten in times of war. Although war may contain a truth, and may impose itself as a terrible moral unavoidability in an exceptional circumstance (a theme I will explore in detail in chapter 4), morality cannot justify war; war and violence do not belong to any justifiable order. In other words, war is devoid of justice. In one of his commentaries on the Talmud, "Judaism and Revolution," Levinas comments on Rabbi Eleazar's suggestion that in order to get rid of the thorns in the vineyard (read corruption), violence is needed:

> If I am violent, that is because violence is needed to put an end to violence ... The vine's corruption has produced violence which, through violence, Rabbi Eleazar will bring to a halt. He will clean up society. By fire and steel; but then the only grapes there will be will be those that produce a wine which never turns into vinegar. (NTR 114)[67]

This quote has been cited repeatedly as Levinas' acceptance of violence[68] and as evidence that he gives the same weight to violence as to non-violence. Yet I think this quote has more to offer: it reveals Levinas' acknowledgment of the self-defeating nature of war and violence. If, for Levinas, wine's ability to transform itself into vinegar implies fecundity and ethical transcendence, then peace is the condition of both, and war – even unavoidable war – deprives humanity of these two principles. Furthermore, Levinas immediately after this quote offers one of his most succinct warnings against political violence and makes one of his most shocking claims – that the persecuted is responsible for everyone, including her own persecutor:

> To bear responsibility for everyone and everyone is to be responsible despite oneself. To be responsible despite oneself is to be persecuted. Only the persecuted must answer for everyone, even for his persecutor. Ultimate responsibility can only be the fact of an absolutely persecuted man, having no right to a speech that would disengage him from his responsibility. In Rabbi Eleazar's acceptance of the political action in which revolution takes place, Rabbi Joshua bar Karhah saw a danger. (NTR 114–15)

The second sense in which the liberal state is hypocritical is that because its politics are founded in a totality – be it the notion of the individual's inalienable rights and freedoms, or of citizenship – and because it totalizes the disenfranchised as a "minority," it is permanently threatened by the ontology of war. Totalization gives rise to war, and the ontology of war issues from totalization. Yet war establishes an order that turns against the totality to which it has given life. If totality establishes the identity of the same through the exclusion of all that inhabits its outside, then the order of war destroys everything that is external. As such, the totality of war is so extreme that it eventually destroys the identity of the same (TI 21). Insofar as the individual is signified through the fall and/or separation of a particular from the universal, the subject appears in the world as a deficiency, in need of reassimilation into some form of totality. Therefore liberal peace is the colonization of, and the disappearance of, alterity. This "peace," paradoxically, must be enforced through violence so that individuals, in their freedom, tranquility, and identity, can maintain their reciprocal relations of exchange. Liberal politics and its state have not overcome violence and war and may never do so. Therefore the structure of liberal capitalism cannot posit justice as its end, not only for the reasons Marx offers, and not only because in it there is a permanent subjugation of the majority, but because to maintain peace, the liberal capitalist state must increasingly rely on lawmaking and on law-preserving violence.

Taking peace seriously, as Levinas would, means taking the absolute otherness of the other as that event in which "Thought" is awakened not as a "thought of," but as a "thought for" (BPW166). It means taking the moral height of the other seriously: the obligatory presence of the unique other, in proximity, awakens me to my responsibility, which is, foremost, peace and welcome (BPW 161). It is no wonder that Levinas starts the preface of *Totality and Infinity* with the question of war in relation to politics and morality (TI 21). Here lies his important claim that politics is the art of winning war: "The art of foreseeing war and of winning it by every means – politics"; therefore, "politics is opposed to morality, as philosophy to naïveté" (TI 21). In the same passage he equates being, as posited in Western philosophy, with war: "We do not need obscure fragments of Heraclitus to prove that being reveals itself as war to philosophical thought" (TI 21). Based on quotes like these, many commentators have argued that Levinas equates politics with war and that therefore politics, by definition, cannot escape violence. So this question must be posed: Is Levinas describing the *de facto* situation – the logic of what-is – or is he outlining his own position in regard to politics, war, and morality? My answer is that he is describing what has taken place so far, especially in the Western philosophical and political tradition. Remember, this quote is in the context of a challenge posed in the opening lines of *Totality and Infinity:* "it is of the highest importance to know whether we are not duped by morality" (TI 21). Levinas immediately poses his own answer to this question. For him the answer depends on whether we can posit a new relation, both originary and unique, with another existent. This new relation must issue from the asymmetrical relation of the self to the other and proceed from the approach of the other (TI 22–3). Levinas equates politics with war where he talks about politics as it is. Even if he seemingly fixes his own saying in a said that views violence as an inevitable possibility of ontology,[69] his ethical relation implies that politics need not be defined as the calculus of war. To open Levinas to such a possibility – the traces of which can be found in his ethics – we have to take more seriously his repeated ethical affirmation of non-violence, his notion of "eschatological/messianic peace," and his claim of the "nonviolent approach of the other," as the grounds for both society and its politics.

Political war and violence have always found some form of moral justification. Wars, whether by states or by liberatory movements, have been waged in the name of a "just" cause or in the guise of a fight against another violence. In this spirit, Levinas argues that

> the true problem for us [other[70]] Westerners is not so much to refuse violence as to question ourselves about a struggle against violence which, without blanching in non-resistance to evil, could avoid the institution of violence out of this very struggle. Does not the war perpetuate that which it is called to make disappear, and consecrate war and its virile virtues in good conscience? One has to find for man another kinship than that which ties him to being, one that will perhaps enable us to conceive of this difference between me and the other, this inequality, in a sense absolutely opposed to oppression. (OB 177)

Levinas and the Liberal Economic Arrangement

In the above quote, Levinas poses his vision of ethical asymmetry as a new kinship that is absolutely opposed to oppression. This new kinship, as discussed previously, contains both liberal formal equality (equal rights and freedoms), and Marxian formal justice (economic equality) yet also reveals the limits of both. Here I focus on Levinas' emphasis on economic equality as (what he sometimes calls) "first freedom."

I do see an important difference between Levinas' notion of "first freedom" (freedom from economic exploitation) and his conception of "created and fundamental freedom"[71] discussed in the fourth section of this chapter. For him the former is crucial for the realization of the latter as well as for the concretization of ethical relation in the social. Remember that "created and fundamental freedom" can be abstracted, but this abstraction must commence in and through the concrete.[72] This means that human beings need freedom from economic exploitation in order for the ethical asymmetry of non-reciprocal relation to become a viable alternative to the existing social relation. Without first freedom, non-reciprocal relation remains an exception, witnessed only in individual acts of goodness. The formal equality of liberal society, even with its redistributive policies, cannot by itself oppose the violence of economic oppression. Economic oppression is not merely depriving a person of access to material resources necessary for a dignified life; it also denies her the "first freedom" that is crucial for concretization of ethical relation in the social. Levinas supports this interpretation when he says that "the daily run of our everyday life is surely not a simple sequel of our animality continually surpassed by spiritual activity ... economic struggle is already on an equal footing with the struggle for salvation" (TO 61). Economic struggle, then, is the first freedom, the freedom of beginning.

The problem with liberal readings of Levinas is that they reduce economic responsibility for the other to private charity and that the social and political dimensions of this responsibility are ignored – ethics becomes an ultimately private righteousness (NTR 188).[73] Cohen rightly argues that Levinas' one-for-the-other requires one, say, to visit the sick, feed a hungry person, provide shelter for the homeless, and open one's home to a refugee.[74] Indeed, as Cohen reminds us, spending one hour of our time reading for a blind person is a noble charity, one that is "both to be and to be beyond being."[75] But the spirit and the force of Levinas' ethics cannot be limited to these personal, albeit important, acts of kindness. Is Cohen not reducing Levinas' ethics to a merely private affair? What of the environmental pollutants that have made the sick person terminally ill? Or the economic exploitation that has deprived the other of food and shelter? Or the war and colonization that has made another a refugee? Indeed, one-for-the-other is a deeply sensuous, embodied, and "private" awakening, but it is an awakening that, at its core, is already a call to go beyond a capitalist economy. Levinas' ethical demand does not stop here: it invites us to ask how society can "tear away the human from economic determinism" and restore the original dignity and freedom of each individual. In what ways can the economic arrangement preserve the singularity of the face of each and every one?

Robert Gibbs correctly points out that Levinas' ethics includes a materialist demand of economic justice beyond "fair exchange."[76] Levinas offers the most persuasive ethical argument for such an economic justice. For him, one of the ways in which ethical responsibility for the other manifests itself is in the economic arrangement of a society. Although the demand for justice comes from outside economic relations, justice, in Levinas' words, "can have no other object than economic equality" (CPP 44). Cohen's interpretation of Levinas' ethics, however, does not account for this central aspect of Levinasian justice: "it is an illusion or hypocrisy to suppose that, originating outside of economic relations, it [justice] could be maintained outside of them in a kingdom of pure respect" (CPP 44). This is a clear allusion to the limits of Kant and liberalism. To eliminate oppression, formal and legal equality are necessary. But Levinas contends that formal equality is not enough. The social must be seen as a curvature of social space, with each human approaching from an absolute height, carrying both peace and a command. Formal equality can be neither the ground nor the destination of human sociality; its danger lies in its ability to turn the other into an instrument, an object, or an equally changeable part of a whole. As such, ethical justice cannot be reduced to formal equality. Ethical justice is not exhausted in equalities of opportunity, or even in so-called equalities of result, or in relationships among equals. Rather, justice opens the social horizon to transcendence, to one's substitution for the suffering of the other, to liberating her from the bondage of economic exploitation.

Ethical justice embodies more than equality of rights and freedoms. Cohen, however, tries to superimpose Levinas' ethics – and then only as a guiding principle – on the unjust and exploitative structure of liberal society.[77] In this sense, I agree with the general assertion of Annabel

Herzog, who, in "Is Liberalism 'All We Need'? Levinas' Politics of Surplus," argues that whereas the liberal state is for those who already are representable, Levinas' politics proposes a state and a society for the excluded and disfranchised.[78] For Levinas, only a society grounded in the asymmetrical relationship between the self and the other and in the curvature of social space is able to aim for economic justice. The other, who comes from height, calls me to attend to her suffering, the most basic form being suffering from lack of food, shelter, clothing – the material necessities for a dignified life. More than a century ago, Marx echoed – but only barely – Levinas' fundamental criticism of formal equality and formal justice by demanding that in life after capitalism, it must be "from each according to his ability, to each according to his needs!"[79]

Usually the answer to these objections is met by an argument that Levinas himself admits: that as saying is always betrayed by the said, so too the irreducible responsibility for the other must be rectified by justice, which in turn necessitates the state, its hierarchical and bureaucratic structures, and even economic inequality. Indeed, Levinas consistently repeats this when confronted by questions about the impossibility of his ethical demand. He reminds us that saying is always betrayed by the said, by thematization, calculation, and prioritization. But betrayal is *not* inevitably translated into exploitation, oppression, and poverty, all of which are tolerated and justified in the liberal tradition and the liberal state. As Horowitz argues, almost all of Levinas' readers interpret the relation between saying and the said, between ethics and politics, as paradoxical, viewing the political and the said as necessary and inevitable privations from the ethical relation, imposed by the requirements of being.[80] Such a reading, Horowitz continues, confines Levinas within the liberal framework, from which position he accepts rational peace as the limit in politics and conveniently forgets that abolition of economic domination and exploitation are to be put as the first ethical task.[81] For Horowtiz, as discussed previously, the relation between ethics and politics, between saying and the said, is not a paradox but a betrayal that can be reduced. But why cannot those scholars who, much like Cohen, interpret Levinas in such a way as to justify the liberal state and its institutions, address and expand on these central themes in his ethics? Levinas argues that underlying his philosophy is a concern with reducing this betrayal to the extent that "one can at the same time know and free the known of the marks which thematization leaves on it by subordinating it to ontology" (OB 7). Levinas sees the possibility of freeing the other from the scars that thematization leaves, above liberating her from the economic exploitation and class structure inherent in liberal capitalist societies. In fact he considers the tearing away of the human from economic bondage as the meaning of a revolution, suggesting that "revolution takes place when one frees man, that is, revolution takes place when one tears man away from economic determinism. To affirm that the working man is not negotiable, that he cannot be bargained about, is to affirm that which begins a revolution" (NTR 102). Therefore, beyond the objectification necessary to the human condition, bondage and suffering are unnecessary and avoidable, and the struggle against them is central to Levinas' concept of one-for-the-other.

Conclusion

In the interrelation of ethics and politics, the logic of betrayal can function as the structure that helps situate ethical relation within, and not above, beyond, before, or after, politics. The logic of betrayal, spanned in degrees rather than dichotomized into two poles, can provide us with a viable mechanism for judging the degree of the concretion and fulfilment of ethics within politics. This is a significant step towards establishing the necessity of rethinking the contours of a liberatory political praxis that resists totalization and violence, one that is capable of extending its horizon beyond the set framework of liberal democratic values.

Far from being an event through which ethics is abandoned in politics, the third is the simultaneous, and tenacious, embodiment of two different orders of justice. The third transfigures the conception of the political from a mere administrative order, from a war of all against all, from the postponement of war so as to establish and maintain peaceful commerce among autonomous individuals, into an ethical construct that originates in the irreducible responsibility of one-for-the-other and that aims at establishing ethical peace. This is true insofar as the third, by holding on to the primordial commands of the face-to-face relation, is the moment of concretion of one's responsibility for the other – the responsibility to demand justice for the other and to approach the other in non-violence and peace. These two demands of the face are the meaning of what Levinas, often in a nuanced way, calls ethical justice. The second order of justice in Levinas, concrete justice, embodies formal equality and economic justice. These two aspects of concrete justice are significant for what Levinas terms a "freedom of beginning," without which no ethical justice can be achieved or sustained in the real world. Yet contrary to the claims of liberalism that limit the horizon of its discourse to formal equality, this cannot be the ultimate goal of a politics whose aim is ethical peace.

Levinas does not unequivocally negate liberalism, but insofar as his notion of ethical justice remains a surplus in liberal ethics, his ethicopolitics remains incommensurable with liberalism. This is evident, among other places, in his criticism of the liberal discourse of rights. In applying and expanding on Levinas' critical approach to liberalism, my goal has been to demonstrate the indispensability of ethical justice to ethicopolitical praxis – a significant lacuna in liberal ethics and politics.

It is imperative that we analytically distinguish between the two notions of ethical and concrete justice, implicit in the works of Levinas, for this distinction helps us think of alternative ways to approach liberatory political praxis. Insofar as ethical justice constitutes the subject as one-for-the-other, peacefully demanding justice for the other, we must find ways to incorporate these imperatives into liberatory movements. In the effort to actualize these demands, an effective liberatory movement cannot reduce its framework to a struggle for its members' rights and freedom, oblivious to its own exclusionary practices and totalizing effects. Instead we need to conceive of an ethicopolitical subject whose constitutive moment is non-violent struggle against the oppression of the other.

2
Radical Passivity, the Face, and the Social Demand for Justice

In order to describe the passivity of the subject, one should not start with its opposition to a matter which resists it outside of it ... Nor should one start with the opposition between a man and a society that binds him to labor, while depriving him of the products of his labor. This passivity is, to be sure, an exposedness of the subject to another, but the passivity of the subject is more passive still than that which the oppressed one determined to struggle undergoes. The most passive, unassumable, passivity, the subjectivity or the very subjection of the subject, is due to my being obsessed with responsibility for the oppressed who is other than myself. Due to it the struggle remains human, and passivity does not simulate essence through a recapture of the self by the ego, in a will for sacrifice or generosity.

Levinas, OB 54–5

I start this chapter by repeating, albeit in different words, Levinas' question in *Otherwise Than Being*: "What meaning can community take on in difference without reducing difference?" (OB 154). How can we account for the idea of the subjective in Levinas? In what ways does Levinas' exposition of radical passivity signify subjectivity as a demand for the other's justice? Who is this other in Levinas for whom I must be infinitely responsible? What are the contours of my responsibility for the other? Moreover, what is the subject's relationship to the other, and what is it in the other for which I am infinitely responsible?

Thus far, Levinasian scholars have not explored Levinas' account of radical passivity as a central investigative theme in examining the relation between his ethics and his politics. Discussions of Levinas' radical passivity and its relation to politics remain cursory at best.[1] Levinas' readers have, for the most part, explored this concept as it pertains to the relation of ethics to phenomenology;[2] comprehensive works that engage with this concept are mostly in the fields of the phenomenology of communication and literature.[3] Even Robert Bernasconi, who in "What Is the Question to Which 'Substitution' Is the Answer?"[4] provides an insightful exposition of Levinas' substitution, hardly addresses the role of radical passivity in the subject's substitution for the other. To my mind, it is radical passivity that makes possible the condition of being hostage to the other; substitution as the-one-for-the-other is possible by virtue of a primordial passivity, of a susceptibility, and of an exposure to the other's suffering and death. In other words, this radical passivity is what makes the other's plea for justice and its reception by the subject a fundamentally sociopolitical event rather than a merely private one. Moreover, perceiving the subject as radically vulnerable to the other grounds political praxis in something other than the totalizing individuality of the subject.

(i) Oneself: Subject as Radical Passivity of the Sensible

In "Philosophy and the Idea of Infinity,"[5] Levinas outlines his central criticisms of the self as usually imagined in Western philosophy, stating that if it is not to remain a solipsism, an adequate – read *non-idealist* – account of the subjective must get beyond the concern for the self. For Levinas, a philosophy that posits "consciousness," "ego," or "the self" as the constitutive moment of subjectivity is still caught within the discourse of the "same" – an idea of the same as an identity that is self-referential and complacent within itself. Levinas, in several places, calls this idea "egology" (CPP 50). Two characteristics can be inferred from Levinas' description of egology. First, philosophy of the same posits subjectivity as a soul in dialogue with itself; and as such, that which stands outside is reduced to its echo, or to its alter ego, or to the same (CPP 49). Second, because this philosophy founds the subject on a ground that is fundamentally solipsistic, it, in its encounter with the other, has no choice but to resort to neuters – either in the form of an abstract essence or as a third term. In this way the intrigue and the trauma of the face-to-face-encounter are denied; the other is reduced to an object for the subject to grasp, to comprehend, and to thematize (TI 42). For Levinas, this is a fundamentally unethical construction of subjectivity; but more important, it is one that does not stand up to phenomenological scrutiny. Egology, or the philosophy of the same, only maintains the supremacy of the same and its persistence in being;

the idea of the same-identity remains as both the centre and the horizon of the subject's everyday experience; and as such, whatever is perceived as exteriority is destined to function as the object of perception, thought, and comprehension. The collective struggle for social equality and justice is thereby denied.

Levinas' idea of "otherwise than being" aims to offer a non-solipsistic and non-consumptive account of the subject and its relation with the other. He finds in Descartes's idea of infinity a moment in Western philosophy that points to the capacity of thought to be more than it thinks and to contain more than it contains (see TI 48–50, 196–7; OB 146–7). Yet he insists repeatedly that otherwise than being is neither "being otherwise," nor "not to be"; rather, it is a difference over and beyond that which separates being from nothingness. Otherwise than being is the idea of transcendence that points to the irreducible other, to beyond the same; it points to the surplus that overflows the thought and that marks a being with the trace of that which exceeds the thought. Yet this trace is not merely a metaphysical occurrence; it is also, without being trapped in a substantiality, an embodied event. The trace is a "this-worldly" event insofar as it is expressed in the face of another human being (OB 3–4).

Contrasting his position to Western ontology occupies a central place in Levinas' thought. He posits the subject as the intrigue of the other in the same. So it comes as no surprise when in the preface to *Totality and Infinity* he declares that "this book then does present itself as a defense of subjectivity, but it will apprehend the subjectivity not at the level of its purely egoist protestation against totality, nor in its anguish before death, but as founded in the idea of infinity" (TI 26). To Levinas, that which begets subjectivity is neither the question of being, nor the Sartrian question of the subject's anguish, nor a Heideggerian anxiety with regard to death. These moments merely reflect the movement of being within the grounds of its own self-same. The originary question confronting a being is whether one is "one's brother's keeper." In other words, "why bother?" So the primordial event, as Levinas would see it, is the encounter with the other whose arrival at one's scene induces a response, here and now, in proximity to my flesh and my blood. From this vantage point, which is far from neutral, the relationship with the other is not first practical, empirical, perceptual, or pragmatic (although it makes all of these possible), but ethical. In other words, the ability to respond to the other is the core principle of individuation (EN 108). As such, at some level, the question of the ethical is the question of the constitution of subjectivity, and vice versa.

The subject, born in responsibility for the other, is the individual proper – what Levinas calls the "oneself."[6] It is important to distinguish Levinas' oneself – an enigmatic term in his ethics – from the individual of Western philosophy. The latter emerges out of the possession of a form of self-consciousness, through which the subject is only able to identify with that which remains exterior to it. Levinas' notion of oneself – the individual proper – connotes a singular event that is irreducible to self-consciousness; in other words, oneself is conscious without being merely a consciousness. I call Levinas' oneself "post-individual individuation" and elaborate on this reading in relation to four trajectories: exilic experience the structures of heteronomy, consciousness, and intentionality.

First, Levinas' idea of "oneself" is anti-foundationalist insofar as he views individuation as the instant of un-grounding rather than of grounding; it is the event of exile itself. Unlike Heidegger, whose philosophy is one of enrootedness, Levinas describes his as a philosophy of émigré: "But he or she who emigrates is fully human: the migration of man does not destroy, does not demolish the meaning of being" (EN 117). For Levinas, Heidegger's idea of "nomad" is still trapped in a foundationalist framework; nothing is more enrooted than the nomad, wherein the concept of "homeland," as Levinas reminds us, is merely multiplied. To signify the human as an émigré is to testify to uprootedness as the basis of individuation. Levinas' notion of oneself is akin to the experience of exile; oneself is the principal event through which one is exposed to both the significance of "home" and the realization that there has never been a home. Levinas' oneself never rests in being; one is always a guest, a quasi-stranger in one's home:

> To revert to oneself is not to establish oneself at home, even if stripped of all one's acquisitions. It is to be like a stranger, hunted down even in one's home, contested in one's own identity and one's very poverty ... It is to be emptied even of the quasi-formal identity of a being someone ... to the point of no longer having any intention, exposed over and beyond the act of exposing oneself, answering for this very exposedness, expressing oneself, speaking. It is to be an indeclinable *One*, speaking, that is, exposing one's very exposedness. (OB 92)

Therefore, and this is the second point, identity is not the primary event of the subjective. The primordial occasion of oneself is a unicity that is continually self-splitting – like breathing. One is always inside then out, a unity without totalization.[7] Levinas signifies this quiddity with the word heteronomy – a filial tendency, and a primordial susceptibility and receptivity to the outside. Levinas' heteronomy stands in sharp contrast to individuality as the experience of an autonomous subject, one whose power to grasp is her ultimate authority. Heteronomy reveals that the reduction of the subject's interiority to autonomy is a fictional formalization. That is, Western philosophy focuses on the abstract formal structure of the subject without rigorously examining the content of its form, which for Levinas is heteronomy. Although it seems a banal point, it is important to emphasize that Levinas' heteronomy is not a return to blind submission to an external authority, nor is it a situation of slavery or bondage, or a state of undifferentiation. Rather, heteronomy is the modality in which the absolute alterity of the other weighs infinitely upon the subject, continually disrupting the order of identity without diffusion. It gives rise to a unity without totalization and to an interiority more radical than autonomy. Levinas posits heteronomy as the following: "It is in a certain sense atomic, for it is without any rest in itself, more and more one, to the point of break up, fission, openness. That this unity be a torsion and a restlessness" (OB 107). Heteronomy testifies to the fact that the most sincere interiority is only accomplished via the subject's movement towards an outside, and not in the sense of absorbing the subject into exteriority, nor of opposition to the inside; exteriority is not about the negation of an inside, but about the obsession with the marvel of the face.

Moreover, this marvel of the other's face separates Levinas' heteronomy from being a merely phenomenological event; in Levinas, heteronomy is an ethical instant. The truth of exteriority and heteronomy resides in the fact that it is "produced in a positive mode as me" (TI 290), as a question that only "me" is capable of answering: "Are you talking to me?" As such, heteronomy signifies not a purely formal relationship but the infusion of that formal structure with the concrete content of an encounter, of a command from the other. Levinas is quick to insist that A commanding B is *not* a formula for B's non-freedom and servitude; rather it is an elevation, a reception of subjecthood:

> If B is the human being and A is God, the subordination is not servitude; on the contrary, it is an appeal to the human being. We must not always formalize ... If A command B, B is no longer autonomous, no longer has subjectivity; but when, in thinking, you do not remain on the level of form, when you think in terms of content, a situation called heteronomy has a completely different signification ... It is "ordered" and the word

> "to order" is very good in French: when you become a priest, you are ordained, you take orders, but in reality, you receive powers. (EN 111)

This takes us to the third aspect of Levinas' conception of subjectivity – that is, subjectivity cannot be reduced to consciousness. The very positioning of the word consciousness in a sentence, always appearing in conjunction with the preposition "of," signifies that consciousness is the consciousness "of" something; hence, it points at something other than itself (OB 65–6). Levinas writes: "Humanity, to which proximity properly so called refers, must then not be first understood as consciousness, that is, as the identity of an ego endowed with knowledge or (what amounts to the same thing) with powers" (OB 83). Consciousness is not the origin of itself; it is the signification of something beyond itself. In other words, consciousness does not exhaust subjectivity but instead refers to something beyond, above, and/or beneath it; it is already marked by the trace of something immemorial. Consciousness, in its referentiality to that something, already refers itself to the trace of alterity at its horizons. However, consciousness can only know the other when the other has already been brought into light, thematized, and fixed under the grip of the same. As such, subjectivity becomes the consciousness of being when the other is exhibited and manifested to the self by the power that the same exerts over the world. Therefore consciousness, as distinct from the oneself of subjectivity, is always "correlative with a theme, a present represented, and a theme put before me, a being which is a phenomenon" (OB 25). Still, the "of," through which consciousness is fatefully linked to an exteriority, the "of," without which an outside cannot even appear in language, functions as a reminder of the irreducibility of consciousness to itself. The "of" of intentionality refers simultaneously to the propertied (and hence intentional) relationship that consciousness establishes between itself and the other, and to a non-recoupable exteriority. As Levinas puts it, the fact that consciousness cannot exist without an "of" testifies to another modality in which "the same has to do with the other before the other appears in any way to a consciousness" (OB 25). So, as an irreducible trace, the alterity of the other remains at the horizon of consciousness, out of reach of the power that structures a purposeful aim. The primordial approach of the other is older than its appearance in consciousness; it incessantly disrupts the coincidence of the ego with itself, and as such breaks up the ego's essential structure – it undermines the ego's essence as its principal structure. In other words, consciousness arises from the inevitable arrival of the other on my scene. So, before philosophical consciousness there is an ethical one – or better said, consciousness presupposes oneself.

Ultimately, what situates Levinas' conception of the subjectivity radically outside the subject of Western philosophy is the fourth aspect, which is, his claim that oneself is prior to the subject forming an intention or a purpose, and that as such, it is not primarily grounded in reflection that arises out of intentionality, which is understood by Husserlian phenomenology as structured through appropriation and correlation. As will be made clear later, this move enables Levinas to break the subject free from the hold of totality. For Levinas, reflection is the identification of the ego with itself, which, at the end of a temporal journey, observes and discovers itself in a theme. For Levinas, reflection is merely "dispersion into phases, exterior to one another, in a flux of immanent time ... retaining the past and biting on the future" (OB 105). For him, the subject exists prior to intentionality, in the modality of the passivity of exposure to the proximal other. Of central importance is that the subject originates in passivity of obsession and not in intentionality, whose primary function is to aim at the visible and/or an idea (OB ch. II; OB 91–2). For Levinas, even Husserlian pre-reflective consciousness maintains a relation of intentionality, even if only as a deprivation of the structure of intentionality. Understood in this sense, Husserlian pre-reflective consciousness is a lesser consciousness, or a privation of theoretical consciousness. For Levinas, this description does not go far or deep enough. Consciousness, at the fundamental level, is not only pre-reflective but also non-intentional. This non-intentional consciousness is the modality of radical passivity (OB 23–34). Therefore, prior to the intentional structure, there is an involuntary openness at the heart of the subject that exposes her being to the other and to the other's alterity.[8] This openness is neither an openness to the world (as Heidegger would have it) nor an openness that is willing; it is not that the subject opens herself to the world and as a consequence realizes the existence of alterity. Rather, as Simon Critchley puts it, it is sensibility that opens itself.[9] This involuntary openness is precisely the impossibility of arresting the subject's outward movement towards the other. Such impossibility is the contour of subjectivity – the subject is radically passive in the approach of the other and in her own move towards the outside.

Phenomenologically, Levinas describes this sensibility as the simultaneous movement of inwardness and overflow, a recurring without rest. Oneself is not "a representation of the self by the self – not a consciousness of self – but prior recurrence that alone makes possible all return of consciousness to itself" (EN 59). The recurrence of oneself is the swelling, which, once shrunk, is not equivalent to consciousness; rather, it shows the irreducibility of the subject to consciousness. It testifies to the existence of a modality beyond the dimension of intentionality. In this sense the "oneself," as an event, never occurs; it is an event without a fixed origin – an-archical – whose modality is an involuntary recurrence, in passivity and despite itself:

> The oneself comes from a past that could not be remembered, not because it is situated very far behind, but because the oneself, incommensurable with consciousness which is always equal to itself, is not making for the present. The oneself, an inequality with itself, a deficit in being, a passivity or patience and, in its passivity not offering itself to memory, not affecting retrospective contemplation, is in this sense un-declinable, it is the identity of the singular ... It is unsayable, and thus unjustifiable. (OB 107)

We can argue that oneself is not issued from its own initiative, nor can its origin be traced to a purposeful intention. Its event is the passivity of recurrence (OB 105). Levinas tries to signify this recurrence through the metaphors of breathing, of heartbeat, and of the passivity of obsession. This simultaneous movement of inwardness and overflow recurs without rest, like breathing or the heartbeat. Sometimes he describes this passivity in recurrence as a sound that would be audible only in its echo. This echo signifies passivity as an "underside without a right side" (OB 106), lacerating the inside and opening it to alterity, making "oneself" a refugee within the self. This ineluctable recurrence, devoid of intervals, does not lead to relaxation; the recurrence of oneself does not end in identification, rest, or repose. Rather, this recurrence, the heartbeat, sends oneself into a refuge, "exiled in its own fullness, to the point of explosion or fission, in view of its own reconstitution" (OB 104). Therefore, recurrence of the oneself in the same signifies both an excess and an absolute alterity; this for Levinas is interminable and prior to the will and intentionality.

The exilic nature of oneself signifies subjectivity as an expulsion outside of being but inside itself, without recourse, without a "fatherland," already sent back to itself but unable to stay there – there I am one, and irreplaceable in my responsibility for the other who has always been gestating in me (OB 103). A nomad uprooted in the instant of un-grounding. It is through this recurrence of the oneself in the subject that oneself signifies singularity and uniqueness. In other words, my irreplaceable responsibility for the other is the constitutive of the oneself of the same:

> The oneself has not issued from its own initiative ... The oneself is hypostasized in another way. It is bound in a knot that cannot be undone in a responsibility for others. This is an anarchic plot, for it is neither the underside of a freedom, a free commitment undertaken in a present or a past that could be remembered, not a slave's alienation, despite the gestation of the other in the same, which this responsibility for the other signifies. In the exposure to wounds and outrages, in the feeling proper to responsibility, the oneself is provoked as irreplaceable, as devoted to the others, without being able to resign, and thus as incarnated in order to offer itself, to suffer and to give. It is thus one and unique, in passivity from the start, having nothing at its disposal that would enable it to not yield to the provocation. It is one, reduced to itself and as it were contracted, expelled into itself outside of being. (OB 105)

So, in Levinas, the subject is signified not in agency but in vulnerability – agency in both its meanings: power over, and wilful action. The radical passivity at the core of subjectivity is "having been offered without any holding back, a not finding any protection in any consistency or identity of a state" (OB 75). For Levinas, this exposedness to the other is unlimited sensibility at the core of the subjective, more passive than passive–active dichotomy. Robert Bernasconi is correct that insofar as the passive–active dichotomy already points at a principle or a foundation, Levinas is anxious that his radical passivity not be interpreted as one pole of this bipolarity.[10] This means that exposure as sensibility and receptivity is more passive than the generosity of offering oneself, which is still an intentional act. And receptivity is not a comprehension of that which is received; rather, it is to be altered by that which obsesses, it is the inability to let go. In other words, it is a passive receptivity that initiates movement in the form of offering oneself without one's initiative (OB 140–6). Non-initiative service, older than a past–present, points to vulnerability itself, to subjection out of which the subjective arises. To be offered without one's initiative – ethical subjection – is not servitude; it does not come out of being grasped by another's power (OB 54). This service does not signify freedom or non-freedom – it is older than the freedom–necessity couplet: "In the proximity of contact arises every committed freedom, which is termed finite by contrast with the freedom of choice of which consciousness is the essential modality" (OB 76). This is a service arising out of the obsession of a contact with that which is proximal.

Levinas' notion of radical passivity as the core constitution of the subject has posed a radical challenge to the Western philosophical conception of the individual, but it has also presented his readers with the difficulty of how this primordial constitution signifies itself in the sociopolitical realm. Levinas' radical passivity opens a space in which one can think of subjectivity as an economy without totalization; his account of subjectivity as radical passivity of proximity and contact presents us with an individuation – one for the other – whose initial demarcation is not within the economy of self-enclosedness and power-over. Yet at the same time, the subject's an-archical beginning in the radical passivity of his exposure to the other can be translated neither into lack of power nor into agency; rather, its power to act is marked by its concern for the other, by its for-the-otherness. One way that Levinas distinguishes the radical passivity of the subject from "inability to act or lacking power" is by situating radical passivity as the "yes-saying" of a welcome. For Levinas, the radical passivity through which the contour of subjectivity acquires its form and content is the ethical Good, which is an animated modality. Subjectivity, despite its original passivity, or because of it, is neither a lack nor a negativity. The affirmative movement of the primordial responsibility does not originate in a need that must be fulfilled or satisfied; this would still assume intentionality. This "pre-intentional" yes-saying does not unfold in the horizon outlined by need – rather, it is the initial affirmation of a welcome; it is the positivity of a response. This is the filial tendency of the order of desire that precedes and conditions the possibility of all human sociality (TI 33–42). For Levinas, it is only when desire is situated in the dimension of power and intentionality that it signifies itself as a need. Therefore the primordial yes-saying is the affirmative moment of desire that only intensifies with each response; there is no intention and hence no end or prospect of satisfaction. It is itself continually self-splitting – like breathing. An increase in the affirmative means only an increase of the affirmative response. It does not convert, nor does it fall back to, any "opposite," since this primordial affirmation is not in the same dimension in which positivity and negativity establish their dialectic. That dimension is termed "desire" and is described by Levinas as "a hunger that nourished itself not with bread but with hunger itself" (TI 179). Therefore the radical passivity of the response does not coincide with an unsatisfied need; it is situated beyond satisfaction and non-satisfaction (TI 179). Indeed, far from being a state of passivity, stasis, or negativity, radical passivity is the foundation of affirmative praxis, a never-ending desire to respond.

This exposition is an important instance of imagining the ethicopolitical subject, for it signifies the production of the subject in an instance other than the intentional satisfaction of a need that must be fulfilled, even if that need is formulated as an obligation towards the other (as liberal ethicists argue). Therefore it radically departs from formulating responsibility as mutual obligation, altruism, benevolence, one's commitment to service, or one's need for service. Levinas signifies subjectivity as an event of the passivity of infinite responsibility for the other, infinitely uncontainable in any given instance, originated in the an-archy of goodness, beyond the activity of my power, and irreducible to intentionality. This is a movement prior to decision; it is a disinterested movement. In one of his Talmudic commentaries, Levinas describes this affirmative yes-saying of an ethical response: "This undoubtedly indicates that the doing which is at stake here is not simply *praxis* as opposed to theory but a way of *actualizing* without *beginning with the possible*, of knowing without examining, of placing oneself beyond violence without this being the privilege of a free choice" (NTR 43).

To conclude, radical passivity is the vulnerability of a response before knowing, a praxis prior to planning, and the-one-for-the-other before questioning.[11] The Levinasian subject arises out of this radical passivity at the core of the an-archy of responsibility for the other. This pre-reflective, non-intentional, and animated openness is what makes possible all subsequent knowing, planning, and questioning. This is the event of diachrony, of the subject's experience of a temporality that is not hers but that of the other.[12] By virtue of its immediacy, the radical passivity of one's vulnerability to the approach of the other precedes consciousness and knowledge. Instead of knowledge, or the universal idea of truth, or agency as the onset of the subjectivity, the Levinasian subject arises out of this radical passivity at the core of the an-archy of responsibility for the other. Levinas calls the radical passivity at the core of subjectivity the powerlessness of power itself.

Maternity as a Praxis Grounded in Radical Passivity

For Levinas, maternity is a structure that reveals radical passivity at the heart of creation. This is why he so often signifies radical passivity as gestation and as the principle of maternity (see, for example, OB 75–81; NTR 181–3).[13] Levinas uses the metaphor of the womb to signify a praxis that is not primarily based on the agency of an intentional subject, but rather is instigated in the radical passivity of one's responsibility for the other. Here, I elaborate on this moment as one example through which Levinas attempts to convey the implications of conceiving radical passivity as the inspiration for a praxis that is not grounded in virile subjectivity. As discussed before, Levinas' view of radical passivity as testifying that beyond the negation of being lies the affirmative moment of creation, and beyond the modality of power, there exists a passivity and a positivity in incarnation – a body in fear for the death of the other, flesh embodying the contact of the other in the same, of subjectivity in its disinterestedness. Incarnation presupposes a fundamental affirmation that is *not* based on the agency or the power of the subject, but rather rests on the fundamental passivity and involuntariness of oneself in the same.

In his Talmudic reading "Damage Due to Fire,"[14] Levinas elaborates on a Hebrew word for merciful justice – "Rakhamim" – which is connected to the word for womb – "Rekhem." According to Levinas, Rakhamim conveys the relation of the uterus to the strange other whose growth takes place within it. The word represents the principle of giving and sustaining life, which Levinas calls the principle of maternity. This principle, he argues, transfigures the notion of virility to encompass what the maternal element may signify – a passivity and a vulnerability at the heart of creation. It disturbs the notion of virility versus inactivity implied in the passive–active dyad and testifies to its limits insofar as virility claims to be the foundation of creation and praxis.

Many feminist theorists have picked up Levinas' notion of maternity, which has enabled them to challenge different aspects of the construction of the Western subject. Luce Irigaray is one of the most notable who has formulated a "placental relation" in order to signify an economy, beyond the reciprocal relationship of exchange, as that which gives rise to the subject. Irigaray explores the mediating role that the placenta plays during inter-uterine life. Her argument is that traditionally, Western discourse's representation of the relationship between the mother and the child in uterus suggests one of fusion and oneness. However, the placenta is a mediating organ, one that belongs neither to the mother nor to the child yet has simultaneous traces of both.[15] Irigaray's placental economy makes two important interventions that are relevant to our discussion. First, the placental mechanism demonstrates that the differentiation between the mother and the child is already in place well before its signification in ontology and/or speech. For the maternal body to produce the placenta, it must first acknowledge the existence of the other within itself. This recognition triggers the body's production of the organ, which in turn serves both the mother and the fetus. Irigaray demonstrates that from the beginning, there is a separation between the child and the mother in their intimate proximity.[16] In other words, the interiority of the mother's body is already outside of itself. Second, placental economy is organized simultaneously around both the recognition and the responsibility of the-one-for-the-other. The responsibility of the subject, which is born in the radical passivity of the sensible in proximity, ensures the growth of the fetus within itself; it recognizes its absolute otherness and its irreducibility to her own body. So the placental economy is based not on exchange but on a one-way relationship of the-one-for-the-other. This economy is based on a radical intimacy in which the other is always irreducible to comprehension and sameness. In short, this event exposes creation and praxis as primarily the work of a passivity more radical than the passive–active dichotomy.[17]

From Levinas' insistence on the maternal principle (which has exposed him to much criticism from feminists), it can be inferred that radical passivity as the constitutive event of subjectivity offers a different impetus for praxis than the one founded on the wilful virility of the autonomous subject. Insofar as radical passivity is an-archical vulnerability and exposedness to the other and all others' others – insofar as it opens the self, so to speak, and allows the outside to be inside – radical passivity can be imagined as the source of the communal praxis. Radical passivity allows for a sense of subjectivity that is part of a collective whole without either closing itself to, or being dissipated in, that whole. This structure is communal because it allows the imagining of a different form of "coming together," one that is founded in yes-saying to responsibility for the other. The Western construction of agency only permits a certain mode of praxis based on the gathering of individuals around a universal truth; but it falls short of articulating a communal praxis that insists on a face-to-face relationship, a form of actualization that emanates from one body in unicity, in openness and vulnerability.

In radical passivity, Levinas insists, totality and totalization are betrayed, side-stepped, or suspended as the ground upon which the subject finds herself as a doing agent. Radical passivity denies that the subject and her relation can be perceived as a totality, which keeps this relation profoundly open to alteration by the absolute alterity of the other and its demand for justice. The suspension of totality in the modality of radical passivity is crucial insofar as it allows us to think through Levinas' ethicopolitical project as radically distinct not only from the modern conception of collective sociopolitical praxis but also from a blind return to a traditional mode of collectivity. This, I argue, is the radical moment of Levinas' ethics in terms of addressing the issue of violence, and specifically political violence, which stems from totalization. The traditional and modern conceptions of communal praxis can both easily engender violence, albeit from different grounds and for different reasons. Both conceive of the structure of totality as the ground and *telos* of communal praxis. Within this structure, violence towards, or the murder of, the other, or the "sacrifice" of another for a higher cause, can be easily legitimized and accepted. Levinas' radical passivity allows for a communal political praxis without falling into the idea of the one; the coming together creates a body in unicity, not in totality. In this sense, political praxis is still provoked by a higher ideal – justice – but the locus of this "ideal" is not at a distance, nor is it faceless; rather, it is within the immediate experience of the subject's suffering for the other's suffering. In this sense, the ethicopolitical subject can only demand her own sacrifice and not the sacrifice of another. There is no symmetry between my responsibility and that of the other; I cannot demand of the other what I must demand from myself.[18]

To reiterate my argument, Levinas' ethical relation provides us with an alternative modality to imagine the ground of political praxis based not on the power of agency but rather on the radical passivity of the subject in proximity to the other. This is not to obliterate the "self" that constitutes itself in its persistence in being. Rather, it is to emphasize that Levinas posits the ethical relationship between the same and the other not as one of power and/or superior power, but as a non-allergic involvement and engagement in proximity. This articulation radically disturbs the framework that imagines the origin of the relationship between the self and the other as an intentional and purposeful encounter of one power with another greater or lesser power. For Levinas, this indicates one of the fundamental reasons why the West predominantly conceives the relationship of the self with alterity as an allergic relationship – a perpetual state of war. Radical passivity as the core constitutive modality of ethical subjectivity is the basis of human's praxis, of her transcendence and its radical transformation. It is in essence the expectant mother as praxis, her radical intimacy a lesson in radical passivity. Levinas' exposition of primordial passivity can serve as a bridge between an ethical conception of subjectivity and the radical subject of political praxis. As a consequence, it rewrites our understanding of radical subjectivity, whose basis in political praxis emanates from the irreplaceable responsibility of the-one-for-the-other. Levinas was the first philosopher to posit the subjective as an event without this event ending up as the mirror image – or as the inversion – of that which is the same.

Levinas' conception of the subject as this primordial openness takes us further in imagining a new ethicopolitical praxis. The oneself of the subjectivity is radically open to the other's suffering and death – a theme I will return to in more detail later in this chapter. This radical openness to the other's suffering and death signifies itself in the demand of the other's face, in the subject's demand to do justice to the other "man." This is a significant moment in Levinas' ethics. The Levinasian subject arises out of a response to the call for justice for another human, and as such, it does have an intimate relationship with the political in general and with political praxis in particular. The subject, as the sensible, cannot but respond to the call of the other who demands justice. As such, that which initiates the subject's entry into the sociopolitical scene is not to escape the brutality of the war of all against all by signing into a social contract. Nor is it to secure her own rights and freedoms against another's aggression. It is not to be a witness to the historical unfolding of the Spirit of which she is supposed to be a part, nor is it for the reason of postponing the spectre of war and violence through their sublimation into an equal, reciprocal commerce among autonomous individuals. Rather, her entry into the space of the social and political is already marked by her responsibility for repairing the injustice committed against the other. Levinas offers an ethicopolitical subjectivity, one that makes possible a perpetual openness to political critiquc, as well as a rebellion against injustice, without this being reducible to the political projects of any given time.

Levinas' attempt to break with totality is not limited to his reconceptualization of the subject; he extends the same analysis to that which is deemed as exteriority. Egology and totality cannot be transcended without marking exteriority with an ethical significance, and in order to accomplish this, Levinas names this irreducible alterity "Face." In what follows, I discuss my reading of the face, and I elaborate on how the face initiates in me an obsession with justice, and how this obsession, although profoundly an individual event, is far from an individualistic one.

(ii) The Irreducible Other: The Face as a Social Demand for Justice

Levinas insists that the face is not a phenomenon. In fact, he defines it with negatives: it is not a plastic form, it cannot be grasped or represented, it resists adequation, and so on. Almost all Levinas commentators have pointed out these negations, and some have concluded that Levinas' face cannot offer anything concrete or affirmative. Others attribute Levinas' emphasis on the non-phenomenality of the face to the "infinite process of othering."[19] Yet in equating, even implicitly, the significance of the face with the endless process of deconstruction, these readers ignore the sociopolitical significance of the encounter between the subject and the other's face. Underemphasized is that Levinas' phenomenological approach to the face, and his insistence on the absolute alterity of the face, are accompanied by his argument that this absolute alterity is not merely theoretical, philosophical, and phenomenological, nor is it an ethical reality alone; it is also a sociopolitical event.

Indeed, Levinas posits the face as non-phenomenal and as an absolute alterity. The face cannot be reduced to substantiality, actuality, or phenomenality – or to a mere essence. The face is also irreducible to manifestation, comprehension, and presentation. The alterity of the other is absolute insofar as it cannot be reduced to a substantiality in itself. It is not that the alterity of the other is a substantiality that escapes comprehension; the other's alterity is the non-substantiality of its nakedness. To describe the alterity of the other as another essence is still to assume the other as another totality or as another autonomy: "The alterity of the other does not result from its identity, but constitutes it: the other is the Other" (TI 251). For Levinas, the construction of the subject and the other as totalities is at the root of their allergic relationship. Reading the alterity of the face as another essence means that its demand can be read as a deed that limits the subject's comprehension and, consequently, its freedom. This configuration – defining the alterity of the other as another essence – imagines the escape of the face, its passive resistance to comprehension, and its ethical demand as the function of its autonomy and a sign of war. As such, the face connotes an obstacle, a barrier, or a limit to one's freedom. Levinas' approach to the other as a face makes his theory immune from fixing the other as an essence, a totality, or a general, universalizable idea.

Yet Levinas' originality does not lie simply in his delimitation of the other as irreducible to a theme or a totality. According to him, Western philosophers and Greek metaphysicians – namely Descartes and Plato – have, at a minimum, already noticed that the ideas of infinity and the Good lie beyond and surpass totality and as such are unquestionably inadequate to idea and thought. Yet only Levinas articulates this beyond as an absolute alterity expressed in the face of another human being. He insists that the other is not "absolutely other"; this, he states, is ultimately another totality in itself. Describing the other as another totality or another ego subordinates the alterity of the other to a totality, to a substantiality, and hence it is still caught within the economy of the same. For Levinas, the alterity of the other is absolute. This is to say that the other is neither derivative of me nor equivalent to me and that, as such, its separation and strangeness from me is absolute.

So Levinas' offers his strange claim that the self is not involved with another entity, that the alterity of the face is not a force whose power to escape is greater than my power to comprehend. Absolute alterity of the other is not an actuality, nor is it a substance with power. How, then, can the other escape or evade gripping the power of the same, if not by its own power? The escape of the face, as Levinas would have meant it, disturbs the ego's cohesion in its spontaneous movement in the world. The "escape" cannot be taken in its literal sense; the other's escape and/or withdrawal is, in fact, the obsession of contact. In other words, its escape is its demand. The other does not elude the power of manifestation because of its own power; it eludes this power because it has a demand on me. As such, the other's approach invests the subject with responsibility. The approach of the other addresses me and singles me out, and as such, "I" finds itself without a double and with an ethical burden that is hers and hers alone. It is in the approach of the face that the questions of politics and ethics intersect.

Insofar as the face is irreducible to an impersonal exteriority or formulation, it signifies what Levinas calls "the idea of infinity," that which remains in excess of manifestation. The face is irreducible both to the manifestation it brings forth and to my representation of it. This means that the subject is exposed to transcendence, through which the face of the other is concrete and not merely an idea. The face of another human being is the modality or the event of this revelation. Hence responsibility does not originate in an abstract idea that is later universalized and applied to others through the power of thought. Rather, responsibility is issued from the face of another concrete human being who summons me to my obligation. After all, to posit the origin of responsibility as an impersonal, universal idea is to reduce ethics to a view from nowhere. For Levinas, the only modality that can signify the ethical relation as an "ethical optic," and not a universal gaze, is in positing the ethical relationship as the responsibility for the singular other.

For Levinas, the face manifests two seemingly contradictory expressions: it is expressed as both an extreme poverty[20] and an indeclinable authority. The face is naked and, as such, defenceless: "The skin caressed is not the protection of an organism, simply the surface of an entity; it is the divergency between the visible and the invisible ... the ambiguity of a phenomenon and its defect, poverty exposed in the formless, and withdrawn from this absolute exposure in a shame for its poverty" (OB 90).

Phenomenologically speaking, the nudity of the face is not a surface that lacks a covering; the nudity *is* its covering. The nakedness and destitution of the other constitute its inaccessible alterity through which my power loses all mastery. In its approach, the nudity of the face disrupts and shocks the identity of the same, inspiring a desire that is for-the-other. At the same time, there is a concrete "authority" in the face to which the subject must respond – or stated otherwise, the face derives its authority from its extreme fragility, which is its suffering. In other words, the unsubstantiality and non-phenomenality of the alterity of the face is her destitution, exhausting my attempt to thematize and comprehend that suffering. Yet ironically, for Levinas, as I read him, it is precisely through this fragility that the concrete and the non-phenomenal intersect; the face of the other is its suffering and destitution, and as such, it comes forth real and embodied. In other words, the true face of the other is a "concrete abstraction" (OB 91). Levinas does not transmute the face into an abstract exteriority; rather, he introduces transcendence into the "this-worldly" face without reducing its worldliness to immanence. So the face is the locus where the concrete and the abstract congregate. This exposition enables Levinas to overcome the seemingly irreconcilable gulf between immanence and transcendence.

The face, in its irreducibility to my universe, in its opposition, resists me without having a resistance; the face tells me that "reality is opposed to me" (CPP 19). This opposition does not signal the threat of war, but designates the weight of responsibility. As such, the absolute alterity of the face introduces the subject to "ethical resistance," which is a peaceful, non-violence resistance. In Levinas' words, the opposition of the face to me is "the resistance of what has no resistance – the ethical resistance" (TI 199). The ethical resistance of the face is not an opposition to my freedom, nor is it a hostility; it is prior to both freedom and violence: "it opposes itself to me insofar as it turns to me" (FC 19), and in turning to me it demands a response. As Levinas reminds us, the face is "a demand; a demand, not a question ... That is, it needs something. It is going to ask you for something" (PM 169).[21]

Although the alterity of the face escapes my comprehension, its concreteness is an expression of a command. In other words, the concreteness of the face comes forth in the expression of the face: "A face does not expose, nor does it conceal an entity ... A face is an expression" (CPP 19). Even as the expression of the face reaches and touches me, it denies me the ability to translate this event into a universal idea, including the idea of truth and non-truth; before and beyond relating to the other through the power of thought, I am held hostage by the other through her expression that transcends normative judgment. Expression does not give up the other's interiority; the fact that in expression she can either lie or not lie reveals the absolute dignity of the face. This situates the face outside the modality of truth and untruth. In the face, the expression of the other does not have the status of a value, nor is it primarily about a universal truth. The expression of the face is in fact an invitation. Levinas presents this idea in the following:

> What is expressed is not just a thought which animates the other; it is also the other present in that thought. Expression renders present what is communicated and the one who is communicating: they are both in the expression. But that does not mean that expression provides us with knowledge about the other. The expression does not speak about someone, is not information about a coexistence ... Expression invites one to speak to someone. The being that presents itself in expression already engages us in society, commits us to enter into society with him. (FC 21)

Speaking, before and beyond the concrete content of that which is "spoken," points at a face who demands "me" to be-for-the-other; it is sociality, but a sociality that is ethical from the beginning. The face speaks to me prior to speaking about something.[22] As such, its expression takes the form of an appeal, a forceless authority, a demand. This demand is the demand for justice – the phenomenology of the face reveals its poverty. The face demands justice even if it does not speak to me, and exposes the humanity of the human as demanding justice for the other (TI 213).

While it is true that justice arises because of the third, my concern with justice originates from the ethical, not the formal sense of justice. An ethical sense of justice that is not only an origin but also an envelope that embraces formal justice from inception to execution. The anxiety for justice is because of the other that has a face, and because of all the other's others that have faces – everything, though, begins and must continue "as if we were only two" (PM 170). My response to the appeal of the face, even when I disregard it, is immediate; this (non-)response short-circuits the ontological structures that function as mediations among me, the other, and all the other's others. The economic, social, legal, linguistic, cultural, and political orders must be created in response to the face of the other who demands justice. Therefore the face is not only, as Simon Critchley argues, "the condition of possibility for ethics,"[23] but also a fundamentally sociopolitical event.

(iii) Self and the Other

While Levinas' phenomenology of the face is deeply social and political, his conception of radical passivity relocates the nucleus of the subject's relation with the other from the modality of knowledge to the order of proximity. Proximity implies neighbouring; hence the metaphor of the neighbour becomes a crucial signification: "A neighbor concerns me outside of any a priori ... This is the notion all our inquiry means to bring out, so as to reach the concept of an absolute passivity" (OB 192n20). The neighbour stands beyond my power of grasp because she is neither similar to me nor the reverse of me.

The ethical resistance of the face signifies the powerlessness of my ability for power. The relation between the subject and the face is not described by the extent to which another power can overcome my power; rather, it introduces the powerlessness of my ability for power and exposes radical passivity as the an-archic modality of the subjective. Insofar as the face of the other is present in its refusal to be contained, it cannot be comprehended; instead, it introduces an involuntary openness as the structure of the subject's relation to the face. The face's resistance to the subject's power to grasp does not signify the other's insurmountable power; the expression the face introduces into the world does not oppose my power. There is here a relation not with a great resistance but rather with something whose otherness is absolute. Levinas argues: "The expression the face introduces into the world does not defy the feebleness of my powers, but my ability for power ... The face speaks to me and thereby invites me to a relation incommensurate with a power exercised, be it enjoyment or knowledge" (TI 198). This insight is, in Western philosophy, either ignored or branded a negation. The approach of the face in its nakedness is not conditioned by the negative; Levinas' ethicopolitics means that my relation with the face must be approached as an affirmative event. The affirmative moment is the face speaking to me and, as such, soliciting and demanding my response (TI 66–7).

Jacques Derrida describes the relation between the self and the other as "non-relation as relations."[24] The enigmatic nature of the relationship between the self and the other is located in its relation of non-relatedness – absolute separation. To be exposed to the other's death is to be in proximity to an absolutely separate universe that is not accessible to my ability to exercise power. Such exposure obeys the structure of the passive approach of death and the passing of time – aging – in the face of which the subject is stripped of all its power and is exposed to the absolute alterity of the other. As in the passing of time and in the advance of death, the absolute separation is an approach irreducible to an arrival. This structure establishes proximity as the modality of the relationship between the self and the other even while it maintains the absolute separation between the two. Within this structure, absolute separation is an un-relating relation, one that does not fill the abyss of separation but confirms it. Levinas sees the concretization of this structure in events such as speech, teaching, and a face-to-face encounter (see TI, Section III, "Exteriority and the Face"). Levinas' writes that "here the relation connects not terms that complete one another and consequently are reciprocally lacking to one another, but terms that suffice to themselves. This relation is Desire" (TI 103). Absolute separation in proximity is not the neighbouring of two autonomous entities equal with and contemporary to each other. Absolute separation in proximity is irreducible to the principle of correlation and comparison; it must be called an enigma.

Walter Benjamin, as though anticipating Levinas, describes the nature of human relationships as enigmatic.[25] Benjamin describes his approach as different from Greek philosophy, which views relationships as based on similarity and hence on identity. For Benjamin, only substances can be similar, and as such they are subject to analogy and conflation with one another. The irreducible un-substantiality of the face makes the structure of human relationships irreducible to the Greek moment that posits causal connection as the primary characteristic of relatedness. Benjamin describes the insufficiency of the Greek's conception:

> Thus, children are not related to their parents *through* their similarities (here there is a failure to distinguish between analogy and similarity!), nor are they related to them *in* their similarities. Instead, the relationship refers undivided to the whole being, without the need for any particular expression of it. (Expressionlessness of relationships). Nor does a causal nexus form the basis of a relationship any more than of an analogy. A mother is related to her child because she has given birth to it – but that is not causal connection. The father is related to the child because he has begotten it, but certainly not by virtue of that aspect of the act of begetting which is, or seems to be, the cause of birth. That is to say, what has been begotten

(the son) is determined by the begetter (the father) in a manner different from the way an effect is determined by its cause – not by causality, but by relationship. The nature of a relationship is enigmatic.[26]

For Levinas, this enigma is the effect of the proximity of the sensible to the alterity of the other, irreducible to any causality in relation or in correlation. The enigmatic nature of the non-relation as relation, then, signifies the infinite distance of the other in proximity. For Levinas, this reveals the relationship between the self and the other as an experience that is both binding and absolutely separate. The absolute separation in Levinas does not make the self and the other autonomous entities; rather, it signifies the nature of their relation as a binding in separation.

Proximity in absolute separation offers us some clues to other aspects of the enigmatic relation between the self and the other. The infinitely separated nearness of the sensible to the other is the de-phasing of a moral subject who comes to signification as a hostage to the other. In its proximity to the subject, this radical passivity of the other's approach disposes the subject of its "self," alters the self, and invests it with inspiration, all at the same time. So, subjectivity is summoned or provoked in response to the call of the other, before it exists as a site designated for its own manifestation. In other words, the affirmative yes-saying is possible since my relationship to the other is marked by the intrigue of proximity in absolute separation.

To the extent that desire is instantiated in absolute separation, it obeys the structure of non-indifference, rather than one based in a vested interest or in indifference. Levinas' use of "non-indifference of the same to the other in proximity" is crucial insofar as it signifies disinterested responsibility; the subject, the expectant mother, in her radical separation from the other, is nonetheless open to the other's suffering, and as such, she cannot be indifferent. I am non-indifferent to the other's suffering, though it has nothing to do with my "being." This odd formulation radically departs from articulating the relationship between the self and the other as reciprocal between two different, autonomous, but equal entities – a relationship that must be maintained through a mutual correlation and investment in each other.

Levinas' framework reveals the limits of the modern conception of the social as founded in symmetrical relation; for Levinas, the structure of symmetrical relation is fundamentally inadequate to sociality insofar as it cannot transcend the logic of utility and of exchange. This structure reduces sociality to an equal, reciprocal, and calculated give-and-take among individuals. For Levinas, the social, from the beginning, is a "curvature space,"[27] which although it includes the equality of human rights, also transcends that equality: his conception of the social bond acknowledges the absolute alterity and the singularity of all individuals as irreducible to their lowest common denominator – their measurable, calculable, and comparable rights and freedoms.[28] The curvature of social space is neither a return to hierarchy nor a blind submission to an authority; it is the original positioning of the subject as both deficit and surplus. It is a deficit, since the face comes from a dimension of transcendence and height, and summons me to my obligations and judges me on the measures to which she demands my response. In this sense, the other is the first teaching. The subject is simultaneously a surplus because its position as a subject is produced concretely in its ability to alleviate the essential poverty of the other, to welcome the other in hospitality and generosity.

For Levinas, insofar as sociality is engendered in the asymmetrical relation between the self and the other, it is marked by a peace prior to war – before the discovery of one's capacity to wage war, and before its congealment in the idea of the political, there is the state of peace, of welcome, and of the-one-for-the-other. The presentation of the face is non-violent; and while the face remains terrestrial, it does not negate the same. The other invests and weighs upon the same because her approach comes from her break with power; in other words, the other's approach is pacific and therefore denotes the principle of non-violence (hence the question of the possibility of violence, a theme I will elaborate in later chapters). Levinas' insistence on peace before the spectre of war does not stem from his political naïveté – he does not intend to hide the possibility of tension and violence in the approach of the other. Rather, his insistence stems from the fact that it is only by appealing to something older and pre-originary – peace with the other – that the regimes of war can be avoided and/or disrupted, and their totalizing effect transcended.

Peace with the Other as Being Responsible for the Other's Suffering and Death

What does the face invite me to, or make me responsible for? Levinas, as early as *Time and the Other* (1947), acknowledges the centrality of the other's death in the formation of the subject. It is banal to observe that one can only witness the other's death and never one's own; only through this exposure can one acquire an idea about and hence an anxiety over one's own death. But unlike philosophers before him, this observation leads Levinas to insist that this witnessing, which is simultaneously a sensibility and an involvement, occurs not in knowing but in proximity. A self who is exposed to the fear of the other's death is forever held hostage by the other (OB 100). The one to whose suffering and death I am the witness, and to whom I must respond, is not me, but the other. Following this line of inquiry, I ask whether the other's suffering and mortality is not the limit of my power, knowledge, and understanding. Is this witnessing not a transmutation from the plane of knowledge, power, and negativity, to that of affirmative exigency of for-the-other in responsibility? The suffering and death of the other exposes the subject to the idea of infinity, mystery, and enigma. The one-wayness of this experience, of death – unlike all other experiences, which involve a going and a returning – testifies to the "ex-ception" (ex-ception: to seize and put outside of the series) and the singularity of the other's suffering and death. For Levinas, this primordial non-indifference to the other's suffering and death is the expression of oneself for the-one-for-the-other.

The-one-for-the-other reveals itself in the singularity of the expression of the face, which exposes one to the suffering and death of this one person. Therefore the expression of the face is simultaneously a prohibitive command and an affirmative provocation. To the extent that the alterity of the face provides the unique event for total negation (TI, section III), it is also the instant that carries the first prohibition: "Thou shalt not kill." The oneself-for-the-other is already about my fear for the other's suffering and death. The subjective is signified in one's fear, in one's sensibility for the other's suffering and death, for which I am always responsible and accountable. But the other's death, of which I am fearful and for which I am responsible, is not "someone's death." It is the unique suffering and death of a singular person.

As Levinas argues, the alterity of the other is precisely the reason for murder; I can only wish to murder an absolutely independent being. Murder is possible only in relation to a face whose incontrovertible meaning is "You shall not murder." Strictly speaking, the only thing that can be murdered is a face; murder is not the exercise of power over another power. It is the attempt to annihilate that which infinitely exceeds my power, to remove that which paralyses the very power of power. Indeed, it is always possible to kill, but it is only in ethics that killing signifies murder. Otherwise it would merely be, in Adorno's words, the natural withering away of the weak. "Killing" is always murder; it cannot be anything else but murder because it is already the annihilation of a singular, unique face, and not of an impersonal exteriority. But as Levinas insists, "to kill is not to dominate but to annihilate; it is to renounce comprehension absolutely" (TI 198). The other is the only being I can wish to murder. Although this desire introduces the principle of negation into being, it is not the originary event. The face exposes me not to a greater force contemporary to me, but to the very transcendence of an alterity that is infinitely stronger than murder. Therefore, paradoxically, when I murder, I acknowledge the pre-originary command of "thou shall not kill." This command is already expressed in the face, whose nudity and destitution is its infinite alterity. This prohibition of murder points to a fundamental event at the core of the ethicopolitical subjectivity, that is, one's fear for the other's death. How could one be exposed to the wish to murder the other without first being exposed to the meaning of the other's death, and to the fear for that death? The original event of subjectivity is not the desire for violence or murder, nor is it the fear for one's own death. Rather, it is to be exposed to the fear of, and the responsibility for, the other's death to which I am a witness. Levinas emphasizes this point when he writes that "the subjectivity of the subjection of the self is the suffering of suffering, the ultimate offering oneself, or suffering in the offering of oneself. Subjectivity is vulnerability, is sensibility" (OB 54). In other words, the desire to murder – war – does not represent the meaning of the pre-originary encounter; it is instead derivative of a prior instant.

The prohibition to murder the one who is in front of me penetrates and touches me because of my passive exposure to the suffering of the other. In Levinas, however, this penetration evades my consciousness; it comes to me as "useless." To be able to suffer for the other's suffering is not an event of a consciousness that comes to know and/or understand the suffering and the destitution of the other. Neither does it occur through identification with the suffering of the other. Rather, the event of suffering for the other's suffering – despite one's inability to create meaning out of that suffering – is called "substitution." In "Useless Suffering," Levinas characterizes the suffering of the other as both unjustifiable and useless:

> The just suffering in me for the unjustifiable suffering of the other opens suffering to the ethical perspective of the inter-human. In this perspective there is a radical difference between the *suffering in the other,* where

> it is unforgivable to *me,* solicits me and calls me, and suffering *in me,* my own experience of suffering, whose constitutional or congenital uselessness can take on a meaning ... in becoming a suffering for the suffering of someone else. (EN 94)

The other's suffering stands outside and evades knowing and intentionality; it opposes "the assemblage of data into a meaningful whole" (EN 91) – the other's suffering is always useless to consciousness. Consciousness can ascribe meaning to one's own suffering, making it thematizable, comprehensible, and knowable; however, it reaches the limit of its knowability and its power when it comes face to face with the other's suffering. The other in suffering prohibits consciousness from making meaning out of it. In other words, the other's suffering is never my suffering, it is not mine to have, nor is it accessible to my comprehension. The suffering of the other concerns me in a non-cognitive sense – it is mine insofar as I am responsible for its alleviation. This dimension is not one of comprehension, understanding, or identification, but of response. To think otherwise is to equate suffering for the other with identity, which is to suffer with someone. To suffer for the other's suffering is to be exposed – in passivity – to outrage "in-spite-of-consciousness"; it is to suffer for a suffering that I can neither understand nor make sense of. In contrast, to identify with the other's suffering is to bring to light, to narrate, and to represent that suffering, and hence to have a closure that in effect creates yet another form of totality. To bring to light the suffering of the other necessarily requires a reasonable form beneath which the meaninglessness, the absurdity, of that suffering is situated. It is this absurdity, this trauma, that conditions the possibility of representing the other's suffering. Every representation points to the limit and the excess of its own working and thereby reveals its own inability to comprehend the suffering of the other, so that it becomes an object of self-knowledge. And this is where the dignity, the non-objectifiable quality of the other's suffering, resides.

From the beginning, the subject is the oneself-for-the-other of the ethical responsibility, as though she comes to the scene already accused (OB 106). This accusative form evokes anxiety, but not the Heideggerian anxiety of a being towards death. Rather, it is an anxiety that emanates from responsibility: "anxiety as the tightness of the going forth into fullness is the recurrence of oneself; but without evasion, without shirking, that is, a responsibility stronger than death" (OB 195n10). The singularity of this event is brought to bear on the subject who is being chosen to respond without the possibility of evasion. Levinas uses terms such as the soul, sensibility, vulnerability, materiality, and maternity to describe this pre-original responsibility of the-one-for-the-other. This responsibility, however, is not for everything and anything in the other; it is, rather, my responsibility for her suffering and for her death, a responsibility that assigns the self to be an ethicopolitical subject (OB 106).

But for Levinas, responsibility for the other's suffering and death means that the question of who inflicts that suffering, although important in many ways, is not the primary determinant of my responsibility for the other. I am responsible for the suffering that is not even my own doing. After all, in questioning whether I am my brother's keeper, I am not asking who inflicted the suffering. Rather I am asking why I, and I alone, am responsible for alleviating the other's suffering. This question points at the impossibility of evading that responsibility; hence Levinas' claim that there exists an "irreducible anarchy of responsibility for another" (OB 76). It is in this sense that Levinas argues that the proximity of the other is binding insofar as it occurs prior to all decision and intentionality; the person is chosen – prior to all decisions, even prior to finding the perpetrator – to expiate for the other. The first one on the scene bears all the responsibility for the suffering that is not her doing. Therefore the proximity, which envelops the ethical relationship, gives rise to my responsibility-for-the-other, even for the wrongs of the other(s).

Conclusion

Levinas' approach to the ethical subject presupposes a radical passivity at the heart of the subjective. The subject is constituted through two events: on the one hand, as a radically passive exposure to the other's suffering; and on the other, as a response to the other's plea for the alleviation of that suffering. This conception is crucial for a rethinking of an ethicopolitical subject whose praxis emanates not from the wilful virility of self-interestedness, but rather from a sensibility to the other's mortality and suffering, which is akin to maternity. This formulation allows thinking of "the-one-for-the-other" – justice – as peacefully revolutionary yet non-totalizing.

As Levinas argues, "moral consciousness is not an experience of values, but an access to exterior being" (DF 293). This approach to sociality as a fundamentally ethical event requires Levinas to propose an alternative conception of the subject, of the other and of their relation, different from that of modern Western discourse. This has subjected Levinas' ethics to variety of criticisms, most notably the charge that his construction of the ethical subject cannot be relevant to political praxis. Indeed, Levinas' ethics may not provide us with a system of values, or detailed rules and principles that would guide current political praxis. However, it furnishes the political with the condition of its possibility. Furthermore, part of the reason Levinas' ethicopolitics cannot provide us with a blueprint for political action is his insistence on one's irreplaceable responsibility. Levinas' ethics does not, in the guise of universal laws and principles, provide us with an escape route through which we may evade the burden of difficult decisions and the responsibility for our choices. The fact that his ethics leaves us uncertain about what decision to make, or which course of action to follow, speaks to his insistence that ethicopolitical life is about my singular responsibility, which I cannot shirk.

One implication of Levinas' radical passivity is that it reveals the dangers of understanding the subject, the other, and their relation as forming a totality. Radical political praxis cannot be reduced to the virility of a self-interested modern individual, even if and when this individual defines her relationship with the other through rational means. That is why I have emphasized Levinas' insistence that the ethical relation break with reciprocity and the expectation of a return; it is also why I highlighted and elaborated on his conception of ethicopolitics as an endeavour that must demand justice for the other in a non-totalizing way. This emphasis can perhaps help us see more clearly how so many sociopolitical deeds performed in the name of justice, or in the name of fighting against injustice, are unjust and unethical. In other words, it can guide us in finding the ways in which we imagine and actualize our political ends and means. Radical passivity of oneself can be simultaneously imagined as a transcendental and corporeal condition through which the subject can substitute itself for the other's suffering and mortality, without totalizing and erasing the face of the other. Substitution is the ground of radical political praxis, and the most intimate link between ethics and politics in Levinas; substitution enables his ethics to be a driving force and an inspirational guide for liberatory social movements.

3
Substituting Praxis and Political Liberation

... in the substantiality of the subject, in the hard core of the "unique" in me, in my unparalleled identity, of a substitution for the other; to conceive of this abnegation prior to the will as a merciless exposure to the trauma of transcendence by way of a susception more, and differently, passive than receptivity, passion and finitude; to derive praxis and knowledge in the world from this nonassumable susceptibility – these are the propositions of this book which names the *beyond essence.*

Levinas, OB xlvii–xlviii

(i) Substitution in Radical Passivity

Substitution is one of the central themes in Levinas' conception of ethical relation. Indeed, his second major work – *Otherwise Than Being or Beyond Essence* – is marked by his discussion of substitution. In terms of its weight and its centrality, Levinas himself tells us that the chapter on substitution is the "centerpiece" of this work (OB xli). For Levinas, the modality of radical passivity leads to substitution – from "me for the other" to "me in suffering for the other." It leads not in a chronological sense, but in a fundamental sense. Substitution is finding oneself sensing, and feeling for, the other's suffering without being able to make it fully meaningful or to bring it into a system of representation. Substitution starts with one's exposure and sensibility to the dignity of the other's suffering, to its absurdity and its meaninglessness (EN 91–4). This is to say that substitution testifies to the limit of meaning-making; insofar as the other's suffering, being an excess over meaning, reveals the "frontier of sense and non-sense," her suffering fundamentally disturbs my order. This disturbance does not occur through a universal idea appearing to my consciousness, as when the "I" happens to discover an exteriority other than its ego. It is much more fundamental and elemental; it strikes, and is expressed as, an immanent and deeply corporeal occasion. Confronted with the other's suffering, the body-mind-sense is scarred and split open.

Before the conscious ego congeals this sense into a meaning, the subject is already affected and scarred. Levinas maintains that however transitory, provisional, and insignificant this moment may be, this event signifies something important. Indeed, for an ego, whose life is lived through the linearity of the past–present–future continuum, this moment becomes meaningful as it thematizes itself in the consciousness, and as such is already a thing of the past. Yet Levinas tries to revive the traces of this immemorial past-but-not-completely-forgotten incident to explain the an-archic origin of substitution. Substitution begins in suffering for the suffering of the other, which thrusts itself forward as a sensible quality; the subject is jarred by the singularity of the face that suffers. As such, substitution presupposes one's involuntary exposure and sensibility to the other's suffering, which is irreducible to a system of meaning; it is to encounter, to face, the absurdity and meaninglessness of this suffering. Therefore substitution is the concretion of the subject's non-indifference to the other's suffering. For Levinas, it is only through this event – substitution – that the abstract idea of exteriority gains ethical relevance. Substitution means that the subject finds itself as a "me" – me as an addressee. As such, the psyche from the beginning is the substitution of me for the others, not in assuming the other, nor in knowing the other, but in *being responsible for* the other.

Strictly speaking, there is no ethical subject, no "here I am," prior to substitution. Although the here I am of substitution can be reduced to an announcement of identity, it is not uttered primarily by a being as such. Before all this, "here I am" is spoken in order to welcome and respond to the other's call. In other words, signification in its signifyingness is substitution; substitution presupposes a breakup of essence and of identity by the other's call (OB 14). This breakup of identity is the ego's subjectivity; it is its subjection to the other in susceptibility, vulnerability, and sensibility (OB 14). This subjectivity finds its ethical signification in its passive exposure to and substitution for the suffering of the other.

Indeed it is true that substitution, as me-for-the-other, is only possible by virtue of a radical passivity, of a fundamental susceptibility, and of an exposure to the other's suffering and death. In other words, to suffer for the suffering of the other is the nucleus of substitution. Yet substitution signifies much more than what happens to sensibility; its meaning exceeds a description of an affect that gives rise to pity or compassion. Its signification even surpasses mere description of an ethical subjectivity or an ethical instant. Substitution structures the subject's ability to move "outside" herself, a deed primordially marked by one's concern for the plea of the one who suffers. Substitution, as a structure, is already saturated with a deed, or a praxis, that emanates from the yes-saying of one's responsibility for the other. This means that substitution can be read as the ethical structure of social and political praxis. Levinas claims that "toward another culminates in a for another, a suffering for this suffering" (OB 18); substitution is the ethical constitution of social response. Consequently, I read substitution as a transformative praxis in which "being able to die" is subordinated to "knowing how to sacrifice oneself" (NTR 50).

(ii) Substituting Praxis as a Liberatory Struggle

Other readers of Levinas have attempted to read substitution as that which conditions the possibility of an ethical praxis. For example, in "Levinas, Substitution, and Transcendental Subjectivity,"[1] Philip J. Maloney draws on Levinas' substitution to address Derrida's much-debated criticism of Levinas in "Violence and Metaphysics." Briefly put, Derrida argues that only through foundational characteristics of subjectivity can we encounter the other; without this foundation, it is impossible for the alterity of the face to appear for an ego. Therefore, he insists on the necessity of an ego in the subject's encounter with the other. Maloney argues that Levinas' description of subjectivity as substitution effectively addresses Derrida's concern. He contends that Levinas' description of subjectivity as recurrence – as a primordial uneasiness in one's own skin, to the point of being responsible for all others, to the point of substitution – undermines Derrida's warning that the subject cannot "evade the return to the economy of the verb to be."[2] For Maloney, insofar as the Levinasian subject is "in itself only for others," insofar as substitution signals a recurring of one-for-the-other, the subject evades its entrapment in itself for itself.[3] Although Maloney limits his interpretation of substitution as a description of subjectivity, in his analysis he clearly indicates that the meaning of substitution includes a form of action expressed in the shape of a response: "substitution signifies this address by unfailingly responding, by being unavoidably responsible."[4] By unfailingly responding, substitution becomes the event through which the subject responds to the other's address.

Robert Bernasconi, in "What Is the Question to Which 'Substitution' Is the Answer?,"[5] points in the same direction when he argues that at one level, to address substitution is to situate it within the concrete, to view it as an event that has already happened. Bernasconi's insightful exposition is valuable since it demonstrates clearly that substitution is not an event that occurs in thought – it is not a property of consciousness, nor does it possess an intentional structure. For Bernasconi, substitution signals a "movement towards" and "a passage from."[6] Rather than being a mere displacement or interruption of my identity, substitution indicates a response, a behaviour, or an act. In this regard, Bernasconi quotes Levinas as saying that "the passage of the identical to the other in substitution … makes possible sacrifice."[7] And in another place, he cites another well-known passage from Levinas: "It is through the condition of being a hostage that there can be pity, compassion, pardon and proximity in the world – even the little there is, even simple 'after you sir.'"[8]

Maloney and Bernasconi both confirm that substitution signifies a form of response; yet both conflate Levinas' description of substitution with his articulation of ethical subjectivity. Their analysis still describes substitution as primarily the interruption of identity by the alterity of the face. For example, although Bernasconi claims that substitution can mean nothing if it does not "impact on our approach to concrete situations so that we come to see them as ethical,"[9] in the last instance he still reduces substitution to an activity of thought, describing it as a "reorientation of thinking," one that gives ethical meaning to concrete situations.[10] Thus, he stops short of exploring substitution as that which structures the subject's ethicopolitical praxis in the world. I contend that however important it is to find ethical meaning for concrete situations, substitution cannot be reduced to an interpretive activity or to an activity of thought. Not only does this reading maintain the traditional dichotomy between knowledge and praxis, which has been the subject of Levinas' tireless critique, but it also fails to establish the relevance of ethical thought to the concrete sociopolitical situation. Bernasconi's take on substitution is valuable, for it explores the ethical meaning-making praxis; even so, we need to explore the question of what are the social and political expressions of a thought that thinks ethically.

It is significant that in his prefatory note on *Otherwise Than Being,* Levinas accounts for both praxis and knowledge, in this world, as being driven by substitution for the other. He views this accounting as the central proposition of his book (OB xlviii). Indeed, unless we view substitution as an event through which ethical praxis is accomplished in the world, the social and the political remain irrelevant to ethics, except in its individualistic form of expression. Furthermore, when we confine the impact of substitution to the ways in which our knowledge of this world is produced, we reduce ethical relation to an abstract idea whose relation to ethical meaning in concrete situations, again, must be sought within formal relation. Bernasconi rightly argues that Levinas does not want to construct a transcendental or quasi-transcendental notion of substitution, nor a notion of substitution as a description of experience.[11] Indeed, for Levinas, substitution is not a description of experience but the ethical condition of its possibility. For the sake of developing the empirical and the concrete, Bernasconi makes a notable effort to elaborate on Levinas' substitution, maintaining that "Levinas' claim here is that if one asks how sacrifice or giving is possible, one will ultimately be led ... to substitution."[12] Yet he immediately adds a curious qualification: "But his thought remains directed toward the concrete, which is where the encounter takes place. The point is not just to show that such acts are impossible for an existence that is concerned only for its own existence ... Nor is the point to build the ethical into the very structure of subjectivity on the evidence of such actions."[13] It seems that Bernasconi, almost in a brush of a pen, has here reduced that which is real to one's concern for one's own existence, and in the process has conflated the concrete with egology. In other words, he seems to reduce the real to (using Levinas' term) gnoseological adventure. As such, it is obvious that these actions – giving and sacrifice – seem an impossibility not only in the ego's life but in concrete situations as well. For Levinas, this conflation of the real and the being exists only in and as a formal structure, as in the formal logic of Reason. For him as well, it is obvious that a human who gives her life for the other is unreasonable; the question is whether Reason is all that constitutes the reality of her life. Hence, he insists that substitution – as gratuity and sacrifice – occurs in the concrete and is part of the real. The saying is in the said, the transcendence is in the immanence. They do not lie beyond life; rather, they are expressed in the real without losing their quiddity, which is their "out of life-ness," or "otherwise than being-ness." I read substitution as a concrete event, one that exposes the irreducibility of the real to one's persistence in being, revealing a radical distance between the concrete and egoism, and exposing the arbitrariness of this conflation.

Bernasconi stops short in his own attempt to elaborate on the relevance of substitution to the concrete; he concludes that the significance of substitution is in showing that "a transcendental account that is not oriented on the ethical situation as the locus of meaning would be open to a series of serious challenges where alternative meanings and alternative experiences would be proposed."[14] This is a very conservative reading of Levinas' substitution, one whose primary concern, perhaps, is to avoid alienating those readers who are imbued with the Western philosophical tradition of individualism. In Bernasconi's approach to substitution, then, the important redeeming moment in Levinas' ethics is when it gives ethical legitimacy to the transcendental account.[15] Indeed, one of Levinas' most important contributions was to situate the transcendental account within the concrete, inter-human ethical relation. Yet Levinas' substitution far exceeds this exposition. The radical implication of Levinas' ethics is not merely, as Bernasconi concludes, that concrete situations can be seen as ethical.[16] Rather, it is that substitution reveals the possibility of altering the concrete to heighten the possibility of experiencing me being for-the-other in the concrete. In other words, substitution reduces the distance between the concrete and the ethical relation; it reduces the degree of betrayal of the latter in the former. It is unfortunate that Bernasconi has moved so far from his more radical readings of Levinas, such as in his early 1990s article "The Ethics of Suspicion,"[17] in which he calls for a reading of Levinas' ethics in a way that opens the possibility of a praxis that alters concrete situations. I offer a long but passionately insightful quote by Bernasconi to prove my point. Reflecting on the extraordinary claims of Levinas' ethics, he argues that

> it seems that only a responsibility as far-reaching as this ... of those who have done nothing, would be sufficient to break though the all pervasive individualism of modernity to the point that institutional injustice, whether based on race, caste, class or the division of the world into rich and poor countries, might cease to appear as simply given. Only the recognition of such a responsibility enables me to acknowledge – but for how long and to what effect? – that I am responsible for the suffering created by a system of which I am also the beneficiary. I am all too ready to assume as my own the advantages this system has given me. Should I not also assume as my own the suffering it perpetuates? *It would seem therefore that*

> *there is a call for this conception of responsibility not just within ethics, where it tends to relapse into preaching* ... but at the point where ethics intersects with politics, *where it might lead to protest against the complacency and indifference that surrounds institutions.*[18]

But in 2002, Bernasconi concludes that "there can be no 'deduction' in the conventional sense of ethics and politics from 'substitution.'"[19] I rather agree with Critchley's suggestion that Levinas' phenomenological reduction can be taken up to explore the ways in which "the said can be unsaid, or reduced, thereby letting the saying circulate as a residue or interruption within the said."[20] Perhaps a way to overcome the impasse of Bernasconi's approach is to start from where he ends. Perhaps, to address substitution, we must start from the concrete sociopolitical given, not in order to find a foundational ground for substitution in thought, but in order to disentangle and reveal the gap that exists between the real and gnoseology.

Unless we investigate the ways in which substitution radically reconceptualizes the social and political praxes, ethical relation and political praxis remain within their formal relation with each other, so that it appears as though there is unbridgeable gulf between the two. Substitution for the other's suffering opens the possibility of another relation between the ethical and political praxes, a relation that is undertaken for the other's demand for justice. Levinas describes the structure of this relation as inspiration of an obsessional proximity of the other in the same (OB 114). This ethical structure can effectively prevent the experience of political praxis as liberation from one alienated form leading to imprisonment by another. It reveals that political praxis is not an event merely added to the psyche of an already self-possessed ego, as if political praxis is taken up only after one finds the egoism of a virile subject. Substitution signifies the conditions of the possibility of a "me-ontological and metalogical" (OB 102) relation between the subject and the outside; it also exposes the existence of a more fundamental orientation underlying human praxis. This structure, which is radically different from the logic of comprehension and devouring, points towards a praxis that cannot be explained by the function of a hand that extends itself to the world in order to grasp. Therefore, although substitution presupposes the alterity of the other's face, Levinas' substitution (whether he wanted this or not) is more than merely an interruption, or the challenge of identity; this is where his ethics can be related to radical political praxis. While radical passivity signifies the modality of an ethical subjectivity, substitution expresses the structure of an ethicopolitical praxis. As such, substitution is not merely a description of the ways in which the subject approaches the ethical, or merely about an ethical relation confined in thought; it structures the contours of the sociopolitical response to the other's plea for justice.

A principal obstacle to reading substitution as an occasion in which ethicopolitical praxis is initiated, and from which it is transpired, is that whenever Levinas describes substitution, it seems to be accompanied by hyperbolic terms such as "an-archy of passivity" (OB 113), or with an insistence that substitution is not an act: "Substitution is not an act; it is a passivity inconvertible into an act" (OB 117). As Bernasconi rightly argues, Levinas' insistence on substitution as an-archical passivity is due to his deep concern that substitution not be reduced to a new principle, or foundation, which then can be easily subjected to thematic analysis.[21] Indeed, these hyperboles of passivity and inaction save the structure of substitution from disappearing into formal logic and offer a description for substitution that is different from foundational metanarratives.

But that is not all. Levinas is anxious about the possibility of substitution disappearing into mere action, for he equates certain forms of action with unlimited freedom of the ego and with violence. This action is not, however, all that we call praxis. Levinas describes this form of action as "the act of thought – thought as an act ... The notion of act involves a violence essentially" (TI 27). In other words, Levinas' hyperboles of passivity serve two functions. First, they express his deep criticism of reducing the real to unlimited freedom of thought – to rational freedom. This criticism helps him reconceptualize freedom as created rather than as the creator; it also helps him offer freedom as one's responsibility rather than as one's unhindered spontaneity, which serves merely to extend one's self-same into the world (discussed in chapters 1 and 2). It is not then surprising that he spends much of the section on substitution criticizing the freedom of ego (see OB 114–18). Second, the hyperboles highlight the role of radical passivity – not the virility of an autonomous will – as the inspirational ground of substituting praxis. These hyperboles are motivated by Levinas' conscious attempt to distinguish responsibility in substitution from the passive–active bipolarity that constitutes the contours of the morality of a free ego. These hyperboles serve to locate substitution as launched in radical passivity and not in the virility (or the pacifism of indifference, for that matter) of the subject. Thus, rather than being an attempt to divorce substitution from the possibility of an ethical praxis that alters the concrete, his insistence on the an-archy of passivity at the heart of substitution is an effort to signify that substitution is a structure that evades the passive–active dichotomy – a structure that is most readily accessible in formal analysis. So, insofar as the "break-up of the I" occurs in one's substitution for the other's suffering, substitution can be read as the link between Levinas' formal description of ethics and the concretion of this experience.

Substitution is the name of that structure through which the cry of the other both concretely appears and is responded to. In this sense, substitution signals my response to the call of the other that demands me to act. This is where Levinas' substitution is potentially the condition of a sociopolitical praxis that is not based on a fixed principle or on a thematic identity, and that is not caught in the passive-active dichotomy, but rather presents us with an ethical structure of human response instigated by sensibility and vulnerability to the other's suffering. Substitution is the account of the ethical agency in the moment and of the immediate response to a plea. In other words, substitution is not the point of view of a neutral spectator witnessing the other's suffering as though from nowhere. In this sense, substitution can be read as the sociopolitical expression of what Levinas means by ethical relation.

Yet substitution cannot simply be reduced to suffering for the suffering of the other. Substitution finds its expression in a liberatory praxis that takes up the responsibility for the other's suffering and injustice by taking charge of relieving the suffering and exploitation of those who are deemed strangers. If substitution is a response to the other's plea for justice, this response also amounts to one's responsibility to rebel against injustice done to the other. Although Levinas does not address this issue directly, there are scattered moments in his writing where he points in this direction. In an article published in 1973, he contends that "rebellion against an unjust society expresses the spirit of our age." And he immediately adds that "spirit itself is expressed by rebellion against an unjust society" (LR 242). For him, substitution is not just a good liberal gesture of avoiding the infliction of cruelty; rather, it signifies an active response to end the cruelty, the exploitation, and the suffering of the other. It is a rebellion against injustice done to the other. This responsibility extends even to the cruelty and injustice that is not my doing. In some ways, his conception of the spirit of rebellion is a deepening of what he already finds in Marx. Before it was congealed in what we came to know as Marxism, Marx recognized the other as the other, and his call to fight against injustice was aimed towards the eradication of the indignity and suffering of the oppressed other. Although he is clearly not a Marxist, Levinas describes this spirit as "a prophetic cry, scarcely discourse; a voice that cries out in the wilderness; the rebellion of Marx and some Marxists" (LR 238).[22]

My attempt to relate Levinas' notion of substitution to social and political praxis may seem to be stretching him too far, but I argue that the saying that allows such an elucidation already exists in him. He himself argues that in substitution, "the possibility of every sacrifice for the other, activity and passivity coincide" (OB 115). To me, this passage is very important, for it supports my claim that there is a mode of praxis that lies outside poles of passivity and activity. Substitution is the moment of radical praxis wherein the ethicopolitical subject, in its radical openness to the other's suffering, comes to respond to the other's demand for justice. This movement cannot be explained by the traditional account of activism. Substitution, as an explanatory framework, finds the origin of human generosity, sacrifice, and hospitality – however little there is – neither in egoism nor altruism, but rather in radical openness of the sensible to the suffering of another human. It further signals a mode of praxis in the world that lies beyond one's attempt to extend one's being in the world – such as in labour. It is, rather, the act of being for-the-other and all others without expectation of salvation; it is me-for-the-other with neither expectation of a return nor hope for redemption.

This introduces non-reciprocity, asymmetry, and inequality into the concrete reality of human praxis; without these, Levinas' insistence on the "curvature of social space" would remain hollow rhetoric. It is a crucial point here that the asymmetry of substitution is not articulated in contradistinction to equality. Nor can it be translated into a denial of formal equality. Asymmetry is about *my* responsibility, for which no one else can be substituted; it expresses the fact that I am infinitely more demanding of myself than of others, and as such there is no equality between what I take as my responsibility and what I think the other's responsibility should be. I cannot expect anyone else to do what I must do. For Levinas, only this asymmetrical relation can guarantee equality: "For equality to make its entry into the world, beings must be able to demand more of themselves than of others" (DF 22). I am responsible for everyone else, even for their responsibility for me; substitution expresses the fact that the subject is uniquely chosen to respond. Here, being chosen does not constitute an identity in its traditional sense: being chosen does not define me, but responding to the call of the other elevates me to subjecthood. This is not a symmetrical situation – it occurs outside the symmetry of reciprocity, and the burden is on the shoulders of the one who has been uniquely chosen to respond. Substitution, in this sense, is the "praxis" of bearing "the wretchedness and bankruptcy of the other, and even the responsibility that the other can have for me" (OB 117). I am responsible for it all. This assertion cannot be generalized; I cannot ask substitution and sacrifice from anyone else. Levinas expresses this as follows: "No one can substitute himself for me, who substitutes myself for all" (OB 136). Because it demands unique responsibility, substitution is accomplished not in preaching but in my acting for-the-other. That is to say, substitution cannot be expressed except through a praxis in this world, through ethical action in this life. In this sense, praxis signifies a radically different sense than that of a political action that is congealed in a project or a political program; substitution is the condition of the possibility of political praxis. Substitution, as praxis, is the ground of one's entry into radical political action, but it is irreducible to any particular political program.

Levinas insists that substitution is a response to the other's suffering. The absolute alterity of the face has no substantiality, yet it is precisely this lack of substantiality that renders the face vulnerable and naked. In its nakedness, the other's demand for justice does not oppress me; rather, it obsesses me and compels me to substitute myself for her suffering. This is crucial, since it presents Levinas' substitution as the structure of a praxis that emanates not from my power or my agency, but from the passivity of the obsession of oneself-for-the-other. It is a praxis that is less for my rights and freedoms – and even less for an abstract notion of justice – than for a call to ethical justice. As such, substitution signals radical praxis not so much as the possibility of consciousness awakening to justice, but as the constitutive event of a collective response to the other's suffering in liberatory praxis.

Central to this constitution are the ways in which substitution retains the corporeality and immediacy of the call. In substituting praxis the subject responds to the others as if she is responding to one unique and singular plea. Substitution proclaims the other's call for justice as if it is not issued as an abstract, or from a universal plane, even if it later gives rise to a formal notion of justice. In substitution, the call for justice is neither universal (devoid of a face) nor particular (issued from a part that belongs to a whole and hence is replaceable with another particular). The call for justice, while it retains its singularity and irreplaceablity, encompasses all of, and possibly more than, what we know or thematize as humanity. Substitution extends my responsibility to all those who suffer from injustice; in being substituted for the other's suffering, I am substituting myself for everyone, close or far. Even with the third, who looks at me through the face of that singular other and who compels me to compare and calculate the two ethical demands with each other, I cannot replace one for the other. The two ethical demands – and oneself is always faced with at least two simultaneous ethical demands – are irreplaceable.

(iii) The Contours of Substituting Praxis

So far I have discussed substitution as a new approach to praxis, one that emanates from the radical sensibility and the response to the other's plea for justice. This structure takes the political struggle for justice beyond its current definition as the struggle of a virile subject (or subjects) for its own rights and freedom; this activity is then extended to cover the rights and freedom of all others who share the same goal, same border, same citizenship status, same blood, same religion, and so on. In this section I attempt to explicate the contours of what I earlier coined as substituting praxis. More specifically, I will build on Levinas' insight to extend and explore the implications of such a praxis as an alternative approach to liberatory struggle. To illustrate the fundamental differences between substituting praxis and traditional liberatory praxis, I discuss four distinct contours of substituting praxis: pre-intentional proximity as the basis for social mobilization, freedom actualized in responsibility, the spirit of sincerity and youth, and, finally, the role of (non-)violence in substituting praxis.

Substituting Praxis: Liberation in Pre-Intentional Proximity

Part of Levinas' criticism of Husserl's phenomenology is that the latter is still caught within the ontological horizon with its intentional structure. In Husserl, the structure of *noema* and *noesis* assumes a correlation between an intentional act and the object of that intention. Within this schema, no relation that exceeds the horizon of Being – one's persistence in his or her own being – can be understood. Substitution initiates a movement for the other in me before I thematize the other into an object. As such, substitution does not primarily express reflection on someone's plea, nor is it an intentional and coordinated plan of action involving thematization, comparison, and calculation. Rather, it is an affirmative engagement in a non-assimilative response to the cry of the other for justice. Insofar as it instantiates a response to the other's suffering (a suffering that cannot be totally subsumed by my understanding), substitution exceeds this horizon. This excess is not about discovering a world beyond this world; rather, it indicates the irreducibility of the "real" to being. As such, it expands the real beyond one's persistence in being with its intentional structure. Therefore, substitution can be taken as the structure of a praxis that resists – even if fleetingly – falling back into the subject–object divide. This means that substituting praxis can offer to radical political praxis, as its order, not simply an abstract call for justice but the proximity of the face-to-face.

Praxis that emanates from substitution signifies a command to act prior to knowing, experimenting, or even believing. Substitution is the strange proclamation that, as Levinas suggests, is necessary "to do in order to understand" (NTR 42).[23] This form of praxis does not claim to possess a goal, nor is it enacted in order to comprehend or to understand; it is not that "we do and we will understand" (NTR 42). Here, a reasonable person might ask, "But how can one act before knowing?" For Levinas, this alternative relationship between praxis and knowledge, between doing and understanding, signifies a realm beyond the rational that is neither intuitive nor impulsive and that is not reducible to the laws of priority. The unconditionality of the "here I am," which one utters in substitution, is not that of "an infantile spontaneity" (OB 122), nor is this yes-saying a naive reaction. It is not naïveté, for naïveté, as Levinas reminds us, "is an unawareness of reason in a world dominated by reason" (NTR 38). For him, substitution, expressed as sacrifice and gratuity, has already occurred in the world, and this in turn indicates the existence of a modality that is beyond the rational calculation of an ego striving for identity. Rather than being simply blind faith, naïveté, or childish trust, substitution is a mode of praxis that makes possible the signification of inspiration, through which all inspired acts emerge (NTR 42–3).

According to Levinas, one can act prior to knowing only in relation to the true; it is only a direct relation with the true that excludes the prior examination of its terms. It is only my substituting for the suffering of the other and all "other others" – justice – that holds a truth independent of my thought, attesting to the existence of an order prior to knowing. This order, for Levinas, is pure praxis, or what he calls "pure undergoing" (OB 79): pure not in terms of perfection and precision, but rather in pointing to the source of its inspiration – the destitution and nakedness of the face of the other – which needs neither justification nor total comprehension. Understanding (and even the impossibility of its achievement) is already subject to retrospection and recollection. Substitution for the other, rather than imposing a truth with a specific content or law, signifies a demand on me to act for the other, a demand that does not begin with the knowledge of the possible. It is this spirit that Levinas tirelessly tries to reinscribe into the ethicopolitical undertaking and into the struggle for justice.

I take the affirmative yes-saying of a response in substitution as a point of departure for an affirmative praxis. This affirmation is one that breaks away from the economy of negation. I do not mean to deny the sphere of action based on negation. Rather, I want to emphasize that this sphere cannot, by itself, be the horizon of liberatory struggle, nor can it be its foundation. For an ethical liberatory struggle to not be the function of what it fights against, it must find itself in an-archic passivity of substitution, which is affirmation at the heart of oneself-for-the-other. The original response to the other's suffering does not emerge out of a truth or a value system inscribed in the self; as such, while the response remains outside the economy of power, it nonetheless remains as the possibility of mobilization and praxis – in other words, it retains, in the face, its promise of rebellion. Insofar as substituting praxis situates the inspiration for liberation somewhere beyond the logic of power, its affirmative yes-saying can exceed the limits that domination imposes on liberatory political struggle, and in the process overcome the overdeterminations that frame political praxis within a fixed totality.

Substituting Praxis: Liberation and Freedom

Substitution offers a radical critique of rational freedom. In 1964, three years before he wrote his text on substitution, Levinas mentioned the concept in one of his Talmudic commentaries, "The Temptation of Temptation." In that lecture he describes the subject as a point that "substitutes itself for the whole" (NTR 49). This substitution, he continues, evades the intentional structure of the ego and its freedom. He then humorously adds that the time taken for the suffering to be "assumed" by the freedom of an ego demonstrates clearly the extent to which this freedom has leisure time at its disposal (NTR 49–50). Responsibility cannot afford the time of an ego, assuming that the other's suffering cannot adequately describe the ethical relation. Substituting praxis proclaims a radically different notion of freedom than the rational freedom of a virile agent. Although rational freedom enables the subject to find compassion for and solidarity with the suffering of others, for

Levinas, this freedom falls short of initiating an ethical relation, a non-subsumptive relation, with the other and her destitution.

My reading of substitution does not deny the significance of freedom in Levinas' thought. I am suggesting, rather, that substitution indicates a redefinition of freedom in terms of its beginning elsewhere. Rational freedom – the egoistic freedom of the I – is not the origin of one's ability to respond to the other. Substitution suggests a radical transformation in the approach to freedom; freedom is not the first, and does not need to be perceived as the first, to claim dignity – dignity being a state in which one can free oneself from what has been, from everything that links with or engages one (RPH 66). The subject's response to the other's cry for justice is not established through the freedom of an ego, but through a freedom more fundamental and more an-archic. This freedom is revealed in the ability to disengage from one's own economy and be for-the-other; the concretion of this freedom is expressed in the ability of the subject to demand justice for the other. In opposition to the liberal claim that autonomy is the source of freedom, and contrary to the Marxian claim that the recognition of working-class consciousness amounts to the realization of true freedom for all humanity, Levinas suggests that it is in being for-the-other, in substituting praxis, that the subject can tear itself from that which conditions it. In other words, responsibility for the other is the condition of the possibility of freedom. Therefore freedom is neither the first nor the second; rather, rational freedom and the rights of human beings are inseparable from one's responsibility for-the-other. Substituting liberatory praxis is the concrete expression of this fundamental freedom.

Substituting praxis contends that rational freedom is not a radical enough ground for a liberatory political praxis. Political praxis that originates in rational freedom starts from the totality of a freedom and hence forms another totality, closing itself up to the face of the other at some point. As such, this freedom approaches the other not face-to-face but from "an indirect angle" (CPP 19). This freedom already contains the seeds of tyranny, violence, and domination. Levinas insists on this point, writing that "when one sets up freedoms alongside of one another like forces which affirm one another in negating one another, one ends up with war, where each limits the others. They inevitably contest or are ignorant of one another, that is, exercise but violence and tyranny" (CPP 22).

To realize freedom, in substitution for-the-other, is a paradoxical situation. To actualize her fundamental freedom the subject needs to acknowledge and embrace her "bondage," her radical susceptibility to the approach of the other. For Levinas, one of the problems of the liberal approach is that it reduces this fundamental freedom to the rational freedom of reason, anchored in an autonomous ego. To isolate the subject within the illusory walls of its own identity as to treat freedom as though it involves some essential attribute found only within the autonomy of the self. Freedom of an ego, perceived as an origin, whose construction assumes a gulf between the human and the world, cannot but construct and perpetuate itself through imperialism and ever more expansion of the same. For Levinas, the fragility of our bodies testifies to the illusion of such a reduction of freedom to "the man as absolutely free." For him, this conception of human freedom is "essentially unheroic. That one could, by intimidation, by torture, break the absolute resistance of freedom ... that an alien order no longer hits us in the face, that we could accept it as though it came from ourselves, show how derisible is our freedom" (CPP 16).

Liberal tradition tries to guarantee rational freedom of thought through law, institutions, and the state. Absolute freedom of thought is by definition the unlimited power of refusal; it is precisely that which refuses to be subjected to action. Hence the impersonal laws of institutions, which are established in order to defend and guarantee the freedom of the ego, become alien to the will. One cannot identify the will with the order of impersonal reason (CPP 17–18). Hence what remains free is one's capacity to witness one's own degradation, along with the incompetence of the machinery that is supposed to defend against that degradation. Paradoxically then, servitude and un-freedom amount to one's inability to be jarred and scarred. Un-freedom comes to the fore in the spontaneity of an ego that, in its effort to realize its freedom, keeps itself separate from the concrete situation that conditions it; that is to say, the ego anaesthetizes itself to the plea of the other. Social institutions and laws that are built afterwards function as structures that protect the ego's freedom from being scarred by the approach of the other.

It is in this sense that Levinas claims that un-freedom, paradoxically, is the inability to be commanded, to be moved by the demand of the other for justice:

> We know that the possibilities of tyranny are much more extensive. It has unlimited resources at its disposal, those of love and wealth, torture and hunger, silence and rhetoric. It can exterminate in the tyrannized soul even the very capacity to be struck, that is, even the ability to obey on command

> ... To have a servile soul is to be incapable of being jarred, incapable of being ordered. The love for the master fills the soul to such an extent that the soul no longer takes its distances. Fear fills the soul to such an extent that one no longer sees it, but sees from its perspective. (CPP 16)

The rational freedom of an unhindered ego is not the original inspiration of a subject who attempts to liberate herself and others; it is, as Levinas would say, the consciousness of a tyrant. An unhindered movement of ego, in its autonomy and its absolute freedom, is tyranny. With a tyrant, "there is no one in front of him. The tyrant has never commanded, has never acted; he has always been alone" (CPP 17). A freedom that is not radically called into account by the other gives way to tyranny or becomes complicit with it. Here, a cautionary note is necessary. Levinas is not proposing what liberal ethicists would suggest, that consciousness needs a "good conscience." He is not suggesting that freedom be merely tempered by a sense of care and responsibility for others. He is proposing a much more radical postulation – that the origin of tyranny, and one's complacency and silence in the face of it, lies precisely in positing rational freedom as the origin. Therefore both the modern conceptions of freedom, and the mechanisms to defend it, not only intensify the problem of human alienation but are also insufficient in their defence against tyranny, violence, and cruelty.

Levinas claims that there exists a more primordial order than freedom of reason, which inevitably gives rise to institutions such as law and speech. Prior to impersonal reason, there exist the conditions of speech and law; prior to a discourse is the persuasion, the persuading of one to enter a discourse – a discourse before discourse. Prior to freedom being institutionalized within laws, there exists another freedom that enables humans to freely understand one another (CPP 18). So Levinas proposes one of his most radical and troubling theses – that subordination is the formal structure of one-for-the-other:

> The formal structure of the presence *of one to another* cannot be put as a simple multiplicity; it is subordination, an appeal from one to the other ... Beings which present themselves to one another subordinate themselves to one another. This subordination constitutes the first occurrence of a transitive relation between freedoms and ... of command. One being commands another, but this is not simply because it embraces a whole, a system, nor is it already an exercise of tyranny. (CPP 21)

Substitution is the concretion of this structure. Justice cannot be sought outside this structure: "Political theory derives justice from the undiscussed value of spontaneity; its problem is to ensure, by way of knowledge of the world, the most complete exercise of spontaneity by reconciling my freedom with the freedom of the others" (TI 83). As it reduces freedom to rational freedom, justice becomes the art of finding harmony and balance among different freedoms. Indeed, the political condition for freedom requires that we impose external commands, yet insofar as rational law and/or the categorical imperative call the subject to its rational obligation, they cannot be a radical answer to this condition; the command must come from the other who commands me to command myself to rise to my responsibility.

Substituting Praxis: Liberation and the Spirit of Sincerity and Youth

Two concepts are central to my readings of Levinas as they pertain to an articulation of a liberatory praxis that assumes substitution as its point of departure. These two concepts are "sincerity" and "youth." I contend that these two concepts establish an alternative relationship between on the one hand, the substituting subject and the logic of utility, and on the other, the substituting subject and time. I argue that this reconceptualization is significant, for it affects the contours of radical liberatory praxis. Both these concepts are central to Levinas' own saying and, I believe, inform his ethicopolitical undertaking. He uses *sincerity* to connote a praxis that defies the logic of utility, and *youth* to refer to the possibility of a flight from linear time and, as a result, the revelation of diachronic time.[24] I elaborate on his scattered comments on sincerity and youth in order to elucidate their implications for liberatory struggle – or what he sometimes calls the spirit of rebellion.

To be sincere is to *be* in spite of oneself. It is to initiate a response without first calculating the outcome or the result, or better said, without "utility" being the primary determination for one's response to the plea of the other. Sincerity opens the horizon of liberatory praxis to the uniqueness of the face and disturbs the praxis in its attempt to form a totality. Sincerity, in Levinas' phenomenological language, marks the subject with an interruption that reverberates in the subject and closes off the self as a place of indifference and rest. The disjunction of the oneself with itself in the sincerity of youth is neither the effect of an internal call, nor an external call that after being absorbed by the ego results in the restoration of identity. Sincerity and youth compel the self to seek beyond itself infinitely. At one point Levinas alludes to Nietzsche's prophetic words as an example of such a spirit: "this youth is the break in a context, trenchant, Nietzschean prophetic word, without status in being. Yet it is not arbitrary, for it has come from sincerity, that is from responsibility for the other" (CPP 151).[25] In the same article, Levinas characterizes sincerity as belonging to "thoughts out of season" (CPP 150–1), independent of every evaluation of the forces in the present (CPP 92).[26]

Sincerity is expressed in the "uprightness of the welcome made to the face" (TI 82). Sincerity of substitution pronounces ethicopolitical praxis as a "facing" and not as a "togetherness."[27] This facing constitutes political struggle as neither a unity (togetherness) nor as the struggle against power by a higher power. Acting together for a shared cause, although a necessary aspect of political struggle, is not the original event through which liberatory praxis comes to be. Sincerity of facing the other shifts the attribute of (in)justice from being merely an abstract, universal concept, to the immediacy of one's concrete existence. As such, sincerity situates the oppression of the face as the underlying inspiration for one's rebellion against injustice in the world. Sincerity points to an orientation that finds responsibility again and again under the heavy layers of totalized discourse that reify it. This sincerity, for Levinas, already refers to vulnerability; it is to be obsessed by the other and to suffer for the other's suffering; it is to be hostage for everyone. For Levinas, the sincerity is no longer a transition and passage. It is to be, in his words, "man's humanity" (CPP 151). Even when liberatory praxis must fall back into the discourse of universality, this humane sincerity prevents the forgetting of the singular face who demands her justice. Sincerity, in other words, scars the subject, fracturing the self and introducing into one's life the inability to shut oneself off.

To be unable to shut oneself off is to be displaced in both temporal and spatial senses; one becomes a host–hostage–refugee uprooted in one's home and time. The spirit of youth presents to Levinas a structure that makes possible the flight from linear time. This is important insofar as in substitution the subject ceases its usual relationship with linear time and enters a temporal zone that is not formally hers. In the economy of self-preservation, the self experiences time as temporalized – what Levinas calls "the time of essence," or synchronic time – the past is assumed to be knowable for what it was, once and for all, and the future is taken to be the logical continuation of this essence, which unfolds itself in a comprehensible configuration. So the time of essence is understood by Levinas as "presence" – manifestation of being – and the present. In this modality the past is only a recollected present and the anticipated future is a present to come. In this linear progression the other is always destined to be comprehensible, available to be used as a means and to be absorbed into the economy of the same. Linear time is confined between the birth and the death of the subject; in this temporality, the other is your product who is born with you, dies with you, and, more important, is "for you." In this temporality the other is revealed to me as ossified and masked; she is understood in the said and is not encountered through the traces of saying. Confined to the said, the other's irreducibility is covered up. Saying is the possibility of one-for-the-other, a sign that simultaneously signifies the irreplaceability of one's responsibility and the incomprehensibility of the other. Translated into concrete political praxis, the other and her oppression only concerns the self as an event that happens "out there," as if time and space have collapsed into each other and have created layers of mediations between the subject and the other's pain and suffering.

The time of essence is the work of temporalization, through which time is experienced as the linear progression of past, present, and future. This linearity stems from the economy of self-preservation in which the self continues within the economy of the same, preoccupied with the work of its own being. The linearity of synchronic time is crucial insofar as it relates instances of past, present, and future to one another. Yet this linearity can only present these instances in a structure that is already reified; the past is assumed to be knowable – in principle – for what it was, once and for all, and the future is to be the logical continuation of this essence, which unfolds itself in a predictable and controllable configuration. The cumulative aspect of synchronic time, at one level, is the piling up of memories over time in which nothing of the past gets lost. Everything is presented as synthesizable and assemblable into substance; the subject is presented with an illusion of redemption–salvation. In this scheme the subject, through a subjective recuperation (what Levinas calls "retention" [OB 32]) of its past movement, clings to the past instant in order to simultaneously undo what has been done and make the future possible. The subject is to retain the past so as to make it its own. Retaining is modifying without changing, so that the past is changed without modifying its identity, differs from itself without letting go of itself; one merely becomes older and sinks deeper into a past (OB 32).

In synchronic time neither the subject nor the present moment in which she lives gets out of phase; rather, in it my ego is drawn out, confirmed, exhibited, and consolidated – the ego establishes its boundaries and solidifies its relationship with the world while recuperating the idea of exteriority. This is the reason for Levinas' assertion that in this modality the subject is only a project in the search for self-identity and self-coincidence (OB 99). This project involves the self possessing itself, knowing itself in knowledge, leading itself to sovereignty. In other words, synchronic time allows for the continuation of the same; it is the inability of the ego to will anything but the same. And to the extent that the same is the presence of intentionality, it is to will the will (BPW 50). This articulation suggests that in the synchronic time the other cannot be expressed as the other; her suffering and her plea for justice are understood in the order of knowledge and thematicity, arousing in the subject sympathy, compassion, and benevolence for the other, but not substitution.

What occurs in my time is not substitution; to substitute one for the other I need to enter into an order of temporality that is not mine, a temporality that is formally unknown to me. That is how sacrificing for another person, another generation, or another time-to-come becomes a possibility. Levinas means to convey the same message when he argues that the subject's experience in synchronic time is not "adventure"; rather, it is "the detour of identity" in which the subject has returned to its own ego from the start. In it, plurality already ends in unity (OB 99). To illustrate his point, he opposes the Greek experience of the subject, such as Ulysses' return to his island, to that of Abraham's journey towards the unknown with no possibility of return to his land (see TI 102, 176–7; OB 79–81; BPW 48). Levinas' brief reference to Ulysses, in many ways, is parallel to Max Horkheimer and Theodor W. Adorno's discussion in their book *Dialectic of Enlightenment*. For the three of them, unlike Abraham, whose journey is towards an unknown destin(y)ation, Ulysses' adventure starts from "home" and ends with his triumphant return to it; in other words, his voyage leads him back to the solace of the familiar, the origin. His detour starts with the memory of what he was in the past and of where he wants to end in the future. Both origin and destination are known, and the unknown is categorized as either that which awaits discovery or, if it resists thematization, as that which must be discarded as untrue and misleading.[28] In this sense Ulysses' voyage is the autonomous and triumphant procession of the same towards fusion with the One. This journey, for Levinas, demonstrates the limit of the temporalized, closed circle wherein the self finally realizes that which it thought it was always destined to be. Ulysses' voyage, therefore, is the return of the subject to a past that embodies the true and lost origin. What awaits the subject in this "detour of identity" is the self fusing with the One, leaving nothing unfamiliar, comprehending all that stands outside of the self – the archetype of totality. In other words, the ego remains content in its constructed totality, reducing that which stands as exteriority to the ego's theme/universe. As such, the work of totality is made possible in synchronic time. This work does not entail a realization of the new, but is merely the becoming of what has been anticipated by totality. In the order of synchrony, then, every human endeavour and every collective praxis is understood as a project, a projection of the same into the future.

Synchrony is the time of rational order; subjects experience one another as presence, synchronized and synthesized (OB 34), and as a result their relationship with one another is one of side by side – Heidegger's "being with" – which for Levinas is still caught within the economy of being and is not concerned with the relationship of one-for-the-other. Being "with" the other in synchronic time is, at best, a relationship of peaceful reciprocity between the self and the other, who for the sake of exchange are equally present in the presence of each other – that is, between two contemporary selves capable of retaining reciprocity (TO 40–1). Although the synchrony of reciprocity is crucial for formal equality, it is not the order in which substituting praxis occurs. The responsibility for the other is marked by its uncontainability in any past–present–future instance. I am responsible for all that has happened and for all that will happen, even if this sensibility occurs to me in a fleeting moment or in the most banal fashion, as when one feels personally injured, offended, and responsible by reading about past human genocides or their possible occurrence in the future. This infliction is the breakup of the subject's essence and its time, making possible the condition of liberatory praxis (OB 14). Ethicoliberatory praxis does not originate in synchronized time, but rather in the diachronic relationship between the subject and the other.

Levinas suggests that in substitution of one-for-the-other, a temporality emerges in which the dimensions of the past and the future have their own signification (EN 115).[29] In diachronic or ethical time, which Levinas contrasts to the time of essence, the future is not an event already awaiting me as if it had already happened, nor is it that which never arrives, as it is always to come. Rather, the diachronic dimension of time is a shattering "pro-phecy," an imperative, a moral command, an inspiration coming from "beyond" me and my life; it comes from a time without me (ibid.). In ethical time, the past of the other – or of all humanity – is not my present, and I have not participated in it. Yet it concerns me. Although the past of the other is incommensurable with mine, I am nonetheless implicated in that past. Therefore, substituting praxis is marked with my crossing the threshold of linear time and encountering another modality of time, for even though I did not participate in the past suffering of the other, I am still responsible to that past. This means that in substitution, one finds oneself outside of linear time and inside the diachronic dimension of time that does not necessarily concern the life of one's ego. This dimension is where I am chosen, prior to all decision, to be substituted for the other, to bear all the responsibility for all the suffering that is not my doing. Levinas suggests that the temporal attribute of the relation between the self and the other in substitution is signed by a fundamental asymmetry. The time of the other is never my time; there is a diachrony between my time and the other's. The ethical or diachronic time has already passed without ever having been present. Diachrony is not a negation of synchronic time but a positive diversion, interruption, and laceration of the ego's continuous time. In this dimension, past and future have their own signification – that of sociality.

Liberatory praxis is instituted in sociality, and sociality cannot realize itself simply in the gathering of individuals in exchange and commerce. Society is realized in response to the other, from greeting her in speech – "here I am" – to demanding justice for her, even to dying for her. Responding to the other in substitution introduces the subject to the time of the other and, as such, presupposes a fissure in the synchronic continuity of time. The sociality already attests to a dimension of time that is not mine. Seen in this light, the principal instant of liberatory praxis is the fecund time: renewal, resurrection, and incarnation in the here and now and in each moment; it is the possibility of a new birth (TO 4–10). What I have argued so far is not that we should posit a transcendental ground for liberatory praxis, or a formal description of the experience we call liberation. The response to the other's appeal, as contingent as it is, can be taken neither as a sovereign foundation nor as a transcendental ideality. Nor is this a theoretical postulate of an impossible demand; it is, rather, an explication of an order whose traces already exist in the human world. These traces reveal the possibility of a different modality in which the work of liberatory praxis can be realized, one that is neither founded in nor confined to the identity, rights, and freedom of its own members. As such, liberatory praxis cannot conceive its foundation in philosophy, or ideology, or identity, or even in politics. Even though these discourses constitute different modes of relation through which liberatory praxis reveals and expresses itself in the concrete, it also takes as its task carrying these discourses to their limits.

Disalienation, if it is not be another alienating process in which oppression is presented as a reified abstraction, requires a relation of facing as its structure. This face-to-face relationship obeys a different structure than that of an amalgamation of individuals who join, side-by-side, to work towards the completion of a project. The demand of justice for the other requires a time beyond the rational time of synchrony; this dimension cannot provide a justification as to why I must join the other to alleviate someone else's suffering; it can only appeal to my self-interest or to the promise of a return in my ego's time. Substituting praxis is formally excluded from this rational order, for it cannot represent sacrifice as anything but "irrational," "unreasonable," "psychotic," or at best an act of altruism or some form of solidarity with others. As such, the work of ethicoliberatory praxis stands beyond the order of synchrony but not outside of time. Rather, this praxis is inspired by the time of the other, and its point of departure is the face of the oppressed and excluded, who approaches me from beyond the time of the ego. This requires the asymmetry of the diachronic order, in which the subject substitutes herself for the one who suffers. Only in this modality can political praxis, which is traditionally defined as work for one's own rights and freedom, be turned into ethicoliberatory praxis – that is, into a praxis that aims at annihilating the suffering, injustice, and subjugation of the other without the expectation of a return or the hope of salvation in its own time – be it in its present or its future.

The ethics of liberation starts with substituting praxis – with substitution of one-for-the-other, of suffering for the suffering of the other – and with a response to the other's demand for justice. The contours of this structure are sincerity and youth, which establish a new relation with the workings of economy and time. This relation, I maintain, refuses to either disappear into the construction of the concrete as an economy of self-preservation, or dissolve into the time of the ego. The work of liberation occurs in the midst of the contingency of concrete human life. As such, an ethical response in the sincerity of youth takes the form of an affirmative possibility and an enabling horizon for liberatory struggle.

So that disalienation does not to turn into another alienating totality, it must choose ethical relation – as infinite responsibility of one-for-the-other – as its point of departure. This relation, as previously argued, cannot be reduced to compassion, sympathy, altruism, or benevolence, nor can it be made equal to the liberal notion of "good conscience" that articulates ethical relation primarily as avoiding the infliction of pain in its personal–public relationships. This avoidance, I have argued, necessitates the mediating structures that prevent the sociality from being conceived as a relation of facing. Part of the work of liberation is to ponder over and reveal the subject's alienation from, or her anaesthetization to, the other's suffering. This point cannot be brought to light through universal reason – it has to take the form of an appeal that is initiated from beyond universal reason; it must be issued from the absolute alterity of the face of another human being. For to establish this appeal from within the logic of universal reason would be to revert to that which is the other of this logic; it would be to fall back on a transcendental idealism whose break with egoticity is through its appeal to the particularity of one's belonging to a blood, to a nation, to a history, to a god of a religion, and so on.

Substituting Praxis: Liberation and Non-Violence – The Third as Persecutor

As Levinas mentions repeatedly, no serious deliberation on the demand for justice, or rebellion against injustice, can avoid the "third" party. As I argued in the first chapter, accounting for that third party is the most difficult task in establishing a relationship between Levinas' ethics and liberatory political struggle. It is much easier to address Levinas' notion of the third when the third merely signifies the need for thematization and comparison. It is much more difficult when the third represents people situated within inhuman structures that are responsible for exploitation, violence, and injustice. Note that here I am not using the third as a single person; rather, I am treating the third as the structure of an event in which a struggle may arise (see TI 199). Therefore the third can be me, the neighbour, or the third person, but the term always already inhabits some form of social and historical composition. Furthermore, insofar as the third signals all the humanity that looks at me through the eyes of the other, this third – who is in me, in the other, and in the other's others – is already the sign of sociality present in the face-to-face relationship. In contrasting violence and exploitation vis-à-vis thematization, I do not intend to construct an oppositional relation between these two categories. Thematization and comparison cannot be reduced to violence and exploitation; however, the latter is made possible through the former, making violence and exploitation one possible function of thematization.

With all of this in mind, we can see that the difficulty is compounded when the third party is the one responsible for inflicting injury on the other. In fact, the demand for justice at some level already implies that there is a third party who inflicts injury and who perpetuates injustice. Yet we already know that the third is another neighbour to me, one to whom I also have infinite responsibility. We already know that defending the other's justice would not change my infinite responsibility for the third, even if the third were the one who persecutes the other or me. This means that none of these ethical demands annuls the other; I am simultaneously responsible for the other *and* the third.

What is important in the context of my argument is the question of the limit, if any, of my infinite responsibility to the other – that is, whether my infinite responsibility to the third stops if and when this other is the cause of injustice to my neighbour. Or perhaps the question itself needs rewording; perhaps the more specific questions to ask are the following: In order to fight against injustice inflicted on the other, can I disregard my infinite responsibility to the third who is the cause of this injury? Can I disregard the face of the one who perpetuates violence? If not, what does my infinite responsibility to the persecutor amount to? Why is it important for a liberatory praxis to care about the fate and the face of its enemy, over and beyond what is already established in the formal law of liberal democracies?

Let me elaborate on the problem we face here. Levinas' conception of ethical relation – that I am infinitely responsible for the other – is read primarily as obedience to the command "you shall not murder"; it is to avoid infliction of pain and injury on the other. Yet we already know that Levinas' ethical relation does not stop here. For if his understanding of ethical relation had stopped at this point, his ethics would have been a merely private affair. Or at best, it could easily have been read as complementary to liberal etiquette as to how we must behave in our private and social relationships with other fellow humans (although I believe his ethical relation does also radically reconceptualize these spheres). The other also demands that I respond to her plea for injustice committed against her and that I defend her against perpetrators, meaning that there is always a third on the scene who may be responsible for exerting violence. The impossibility of Levinas' ethical relation (beside my infinite responsibility for the other) is located in the idea that I have the same infinite responsibility towards this third who is another neighbour to me. Therefore at some level the third party raises the fundamental question of violence in the social and the political, of how to approach the one who inflicts suffering and injustice on the other, and of the use of (non-)violence in the liberatory struggle. This issue is especially pertinent in our time, for so much violence and aggression is committed against some category of others in the name of defending another and her freedom.

As discussed in chapter 1, Levinas' commentators have generally stopped short of elaborating on this dilemma. Most literature on the third reiterates what Levinas repeatedly argued: that the third brings onto the scene the necessity of thematization, comparison, justice, law, and the state.[30] I contend that limiting our analysis to the necessity of thematization, comparison, and so on once again turns Levinas' ethical relation into a private affair. It does not answer the question of what my responsibility is after I (or we, for that matter) thematize, compare, and arrive at a judgment. In other words, what is my responsibility after I prioritize the demand of one over the other and arrive at a judgment as to who is the perpetrator? When we stop short at this juncture, the work of justice is relegated to the law of the state or to the jurisdiction of a universal history, so the implications of Levinas' ethical relation for liberatory movements are disregarded.

Furthermore, this reading cannot provide insight in a situation where the perpetrator is the state and its laws. What if the perpetrator is the same system of law that is supposed to bring justice to the other? And here I am not talking about an abstract system, one that by its invisible hand oppresses, subjugates, and violates the other. I am talking about real people in real sociopolitical contexts who act as the consolidators, maintainers, and perpetuators of these unjust systems. Levinas refers to these people collectively as "the persecutor." By reducing ethical relation to either the work of formal justice or the realm of private goodness, the above reading forecloses a serious analysis of the implications of Levinas' ethical relation to the sociopolitical reality of injustice. A reading that takes the entry of the third to mean the reduction of ethical justice to formal justice also reduces the entry of the third to mean the acceptance of and necessity for violence in the social, be that violence by the subject or by the impersonal apparatus of the state.

At this point one might ask how the third raises the question of violence in the social and the political. First, I must explain briefly what Levinas means by violence. In a fundamental way, Levinas' entire ethical project is a treatise against violence: it is to unmask the violence at the heart of ego's effort in existing, sustaining, and projecting itself into the world, in the process of which it not only reduces, appropriates, and devours the other into the same but also moulds the social as an extension of this same projection. This project calls for violence in all its shapes and forms. It follows that violence, while it is expressed in different modalities and forms, ultimately is an intentionality that aims to efface the other's face. Violence, the effacement of the face, moves from grasping, comprehending, objectifying, and thematizing, to tyranny, and finally to murder – especially as it is expressed in political violence. The ultimate form of violence is murder; to kill is not to dominate anymore, but to drive away the other from existing (TI 172). Therefore, Levinas' approach to violence is broad, fundamental, and acute. It is not difficult to see the fundamentality of (non-)violence in Levinas' ethical relation. The ethical relation and the social bond begin with my demand to call violence into question. But again, there are degrees of opposition here, from challenging the violent ontic structures to rearticulating liberation in order to bring an end to this violence. Levinas' ethical relation reveals the violence in totality and totalized systems towards those who are constructed as exteriorities – be they the poor, the orphan, the widow, the stranger, or, increasingly, the "citizen." That relation unmasks this violence even in totalities that seem to work as smoothly as a liberal democracy.

The cruel and nefarious nature of this violence is found in the ways in which it manifests itself. The workings of violence increasingly resemble what Levinas attributes to the phenomenon of light, which makes everything else visible while itself it is hidden – every other social relation thereby becomes a function of this violence. In other words, violence has been the structure through which our economic, social, and cultural spheres are managed, without being visible itself. Violence, especially in its economic and cultural forms, is increasingly visible, having long been utterly invisible under the guise of universal law. We witness this in liberal democracy more than in any other social regime, even if it sheds little blood directly.

Returning to the question I raised at the beginning of this chapter, I am claiming here that the work of justice does not stop after I go through the agony of thematization, comparison, and judgment; I am also responsible for alleviating the oppression and subjugation of the other. Evildoers exist in the world, and their existence immediately concerns me. This does not require taking the law into one's own hands; rather, it highlights, as I have tried to demonstrate, the ethical exigency of radical liberatory praxis. I do not read Levinas' approach to the ethical and the political, therefore, as an approach in which the relation between the two is kept in tension, each occasionally questioning the other, as some Levinas readers contend (such as Bernasconi).[31] My position is not to conflate Levinas' ethics with politics, but to insist on the immediate relevancy of his substituting praxis for the work of liberation.

Let us return to the question of the third as the persecutor: Does substituting praxis have something to say about the ways in which one approaches one's own or the other's persecutor in a liberatory struggle? On the surface, it seems that Levinas provides more ambiguity than answers to this question. After all, he is famous for saying that "in the trauma of persecution it is to pass from the outrage undergone to the responsibility for the persecutor" (OB 111) and for arguing that "the uniqueness of the self is the very fact of bearing the fault of another" (ibid., 112). Yet one can easily cite some of his comments to the opposite effect. One example is when he, in criticizing Simon Weil's advocacy of "platonic charity," distinguishes his position from the concepts of love and forgiveness in Christian morality by stating that "the extermination of evil by violence means that evil is taken seriously and that the possibility of infinite pardon tempts us to infinite evil" (DF 139).

I have highlighted these varying citations on persecution and violence in order to develop a context for my discussion of the role of violence in substituting praxis. Levinas' hyperbolic style prevents any clear, finalized interpretation; nonetheless, it is clear that he does not intend to blame the victim for her own persecution, nor does he mean to unconditionally reject political violence in the process of defending justice to the other. Having said that, his sayings cannot be confined to a phenomenological investigation that is without relevance to concrete political situations. Far from being irrelevant to political praxis, these sayings shed light on Levinas' approach to the third and on his conception of the spirit of liberatory praxis. I tend to agree with Bernasconi that in the face of injustice to the other, Levinas raises not so much the question of "Who should be blamed?," but rather, "What am I to do?"[32] This, as I read it, is a challenge to act. It is important to note, however, that it is almost impossible to raise the latter question if one reduces the work of justice to law and legal justice.

Yet one's approach to the third as the persecutor requires a more specific exposition, even if our attempt at this concretion risks betraying Levinas' saying. Insofar as the face of the other is inviolable, disregarding this inviolability is itself an unjust act. This means that in substituting praxis, effacing the face against whom one fights becomes an almost ethical impossibility. There are many places where Levinas alludes to this. In answering a question posed during an interview of whether an SS officer has a face, Levinas replied: "A very disturbing question which calls, to my opinion, for an affirmative answer. An affirmative answer which is painful each time!" (IRB 208). I read this quote to mean that the work of justice is expressed precisely in one's struggle against those who commit injustice, while at the same time keeping the dignity of their faces.

But again, this does not reduce our difficulty unless we can arrive at a more concrete understanding of what it means to keep the dignity of the other's face, including the face of the persecutor. If sincerity of substitution is the straightforwardness of the face-to-face relationship, can this relation be extended to my relationship with my political opponent? What does it mean to substitute myself for all others if some of these others are causing injustice? Does the work of substitution stop somewhere at the borders of political struggle? We cannot address these questions without addressing the ambiguity that exists in Levinas' own saying. Levinas is adamant that one's ethical relation with the other is expressed in rectitude and straightforwardness, but he is ambiguous about extreme situations of political hostility. Does ethics stop, or abandon some of its demands, when political struggle begins? Clearly, his ethical relation confronts us with an ambiguity when it comes to the role of violence in liberatory praxis. He expresses this ambiguity most succinctly when he writes:

> The modern world has forgotten the virtues of patience. The rapid and effective action to which everyone is committed for a single moment has furnished the dark gleam produced by the ability to wait and suffer. But the glorious deployment of energy is murderous. We must recall these virtues of patience not so as to preach a sense of resignation in the face of revolutionary spirit, but so that we can feel the essential link which connects the spirit of patience to true revolutions. This revolution comes from great pity. The hand that grasps the weapon must suffer in the very violence of that gesture. To anaesthetize this pain brings the revolutionary to the frontiers of fascism. (DF 155)

For Peter Atterton, this passage demonstrates Levinas' approval of political violence if and only when "it is used to defend the third party from the injury caused by others."[33] He further concludes that for Levinas it is not fear for one's life that should make one hesitate before resorting to violence, but fear for the other's death.[34] I agree with Atterton that in Levinas' ethical relation, violence is only justified to defend the other from injury. Yet to my mind, Levinas' qualification of violence goes much deeper than Atterton's reading. Levinas is more than simply acknowledging that political violence is justified in the face of atrocities committed against the other. Indeed, he rejects the sense of resignation we feel when faced with great evil where he tells us that "this resignation at the base of the most active charity" promotes infinite pardon but nonetheless tempts us to infinite evil (DF 140). Sometimes Levinas call this resignation "non-resistance to evil" (see OB 177; EN 105). Atterton conflates this with "non-violent resistance" and concludes that Levinas is rejecting non-violence as a way of confronting one's political enemy.[35] Levinas himself seems to adhere to this reading when, for example, he states that to take evil seriously means, in some context, to use violence against it (DF 138–41).

However, Levinas' restrictions on the use of violence are heavy; for him, contrary to Atterton's reading, violence is not automatically justified even in the name of defending the other. He condones the use of violence only when he uses diabolical terms such as "evil," which indicates the heavy qualification he places on the use of violence. Almost always, when he condones violence it is in a context where he addresses the notion of "evil." Even in his much debated and controversial comments about Palestinians, he articulates his position in terms of defending those who are close in the face of violence, rather than denying the face of Palestinians. In fact, Levinas expresses his dilemma in the form of a question, asking: "But if your neighbor attacks another neighbor or treats him unjustly, what can you do?" (LR 294). Whether Levinas is correct in his judgment about the historical facts of the Israeli–Palestinian conflict is not the point here. I am highlighting that he does not deny the Palestinian the status as the neighbour, nor does he deny the face of this neighbour; rather, he sees the Palestinian as a neighbour whose aggression against another neighbour calls for defending the one who is under attack.[36] It is significant that at almost all times, when talking about persecution and the persecutor, Levinas acknowledges that there exists a human face worthy of respect. Levinas' insistence on going to an extreme to emphasize that the persecutor has a face (even if that face belongs to an SS officer) and deserves respect and a defence, is meant to say something important about ethical justice. The acknowledgment of the face of the persecutor clearly indicates that Levinas does not condone violence except in extreme situations of evil.

The only time, to my knowledge, that Levinas denies the face of the other – the ultimate violence in his ethical relation – is when he is confronted with the question of "whether the executioner has a face." He replies that "the executioner is the one who threatens my neighbor and, in this sense, calls for violence and no longer has a Face" (EN 105). To me, it is important to point out the significance of the word "executioner." It seems that Levinas denies the face of the other only when the other approaches as the executioner; only the executioner's face can be forfeited. Here, violence is no longer a threat; the executioner is no longer a being who is trying to thematize the other – she is neither a tyrant nor a political enemy nor a persecutor. Clearly, the presence of an executioner conveys the imminent death of the other; her presence testifies that the death of the other is right here, in this very moment. Indeed, in historic sociopolitical situations the lines drawn between a political opponent, an enemy, a persecutor, and an executioner are not self-evident – not even for Levinas himself – and one's inescapable responsibility is to judge. Nonetheless, these figures show the extent to which one's obligation to the other's face demands the necessity to avoid, suspend, postpone, and withdraw from violence; Levinas calls this the act of revolutionary patience (DF 155).

Although Levinas is not specific as to how, in liberatory political praxis, his ethics can be expressed as both "revolutionary" and "patient," it is apparent that non-violence plays a major role in his ethicopolitical conception of rebellion against injustice. That is to say that substituting praxis demands nothing short of a revolutionary spirit, an ethical rebellion against injustice in substitution. The "ethical," here, underscores the non-violent spirit of the praxis. To demand justice for the other is to first be non-violent towards the one who inflicts the injury; it is to fear his death more than one's own. To this end, Levinas writes: "Justice without passion is not the only thing man must possess. He must also have justice without killing" (DF 147).

Conclusion

Substitution is an enabling moment in which radical passivity commences the subject to suffer for the suffering of the other. It demands a response to the plea of the other's face, which is a call for a form of praxis. Insofar as substitution is a call to act in the radical passivity of one's exposure, it can be read as an affirmative instant – or better, as an affirmative possibility of a praxis that does not fall back into the passive–active dichotomy. The radical passivity of substituting for the suffering of the other is the possibility of action by the subject; this raises the possibility of addressing a praxis that evades the intentional structure of the object–subject relation, in which the other is always falling prey to the subject's objectifying grasp, characteristic of the reciprocal economy of rational peace.

Levinas not only radically departs from the modern approach to praxis, which is based solely in terms of the agency of the will, but also opens up the possibility of reconceptualizing the contours of liberatory struggle. Substituting praxis is more than a demand that I be just to the other; it is also the demand that I rebel against injustice done to the other and all others (which I call ethicoliberatory praxis). But this demand is radically different from liberation and liberatory struggles as they have so far been formulated in the Western political tradition. This difference, first, is expressed in a different conception of freedom and responsibility: substitution reveals my freedom as the enabling moment of my response to the other's demand for justice. This structure reformulates the relations of freedom and responsibility vis-à-vis the subject engaged in liberatory praxis: freedom is no longer the first, nor the last; rather, freedom is seen as the realization of my responsibility for the other within my concrete sociopolitical determination. This conception radically departs from the Western tradition – including both liberalism and Marxism – which found social praxis in the will of an autonomous, virile agent. Instead it is sincerity and youth that can be accounted as two indispensable moments in substituting praxis; these two dimensions stand outside the economy of utility, opening the subject to another dimension of time that is not hers but the other's.

These two moments function as a reminder that substituting praxis does not permit a reduction of the other's plea to a mere demand on the subject to be just and charitable in her public and private affairs. This form of praxis also signifies that ethical relation is not only a sociopolitical act but also one that is accomplished through liberatory struggle – a rebellion against injustice to others. This rebellion situates the (im)possibility of (non-)violence as both ethical and political exigency. Thus the third, at one level, signifies the possibility of political violence, of injustice, as well as my ethical responsibility vis-à-vis two seemingly contradictory demands – to rebel against injustice while respecting the face of the persecutor. Going back to Levinas' notion of the third, the ethical leaves us with an acute dilemma – I am simultaneously obliged to rebel against injustice and to not violate the face of the third. Most literatures on this issue avoid this contradiction by discussing Levinas' notion of the third in ways that have no direct bearing on the concrete or collective political struggle. Levinas' notion of ethical justice does not abandon one in favour of the other; rather, the entry of the third as persecutor intensifies my responsibility, so much so that I must not only defend the other from a third who is an aggressor but also respect the dignity of the one who inflicts injury.

This is a dilemma, but it also represents a possibility to overcome violence. Levinas leaves us with two demands – to be revolutionary and at the same time to be patient – yet he does not tell us how this is possible in real liberatory struggle. His insistence on non-violence must be taken more seriously, and its implication for a liberatory political praxis must be further explored. In the next chapter, by drawing similarities between Levinas' spirit of patient revolution and Gandhi's non-violent praxis, I hope to find traces of Levinas' saying in a historical liberatory struggle.

4
Levinas and Gandhi: Liberatory Praxis as Fear for the Other

Peace is produced as this aptitude for speech. The eschatological vision breaks with the totality of wars and empires in which one does not speak.

Levinas, TI 23

One, who would sacrifice his life for others, has hardly time to reserve for himself a place in the sun.

Mahatma Gandhi[1]

(i) Levinas and Gandhi: Can There Be a Dialogue?

Levinas describes an ethical subject whose liberatory inspiration radically departs from that of the traditional Marxian or liberal agent of social change. His phenomenology of the face situates radical passivity at the heart of the sociopolitical subject and consequently posits substituting praxis as an ethical form of political action, one that cannot be reduced to characterizing the rebellious potential of the subject in terms of her virility. However, although he occasionally points to social movements such as Paris 1968, whose participants' goals transcended a mere transfer of power, he avoids explicitly articulating how this ethicopolitical subject acts politically or how it initiates radical political change. Despite his emphasis on responsibility for the suffering of the other as the basis of one's rebellion against injustice, he is not clear on how his ethics enters the political. Examples from Gandhian political praxis demonstrate, first, that Levinas' ethics leads us to a radical political praxis that is not founded in the violent agency of the subject, and second, that they reject the goal of attaining a negative freedom merely extended to another space called the political.

Mohandas Karamchand Gandhi[2] (1869–1948) was one of the few political leaders of the twentieth century who articulated political struggle and radical social praxis in terms of *Satyagraha* – non-violent rebellion against, and passive resistance to, injustice.[3] Throughout his life, Gandhi strove to articulate a *Satyagrahi*[4] (an agent of social change), whose core disposition was *ahimsa* (non-violence) and whose goal was infinite *anasakti* (selfless service to and responsibility for the other). Indeed, Gandhi described himself as someone whose political praxis was guided by the spirit of service to the other: "Action is my domain, and what I understand, according to my lights, to be my duty, and what comes my way, I do. All my action is actuated by the spirit of service."[5] Gandhi's writings cross the boundaries of religion, politics, economics, society, ethics, and gender. Although they are monumental (his collected works are almost one hundred volumes), well-known Gandhian scholar Raghavan Iyer states that Gandhi articulated neither a definitive political theory nor a political manifesto.[6] In a sense, Gandhi's writings, much like Levinas', are elusive and multi-layered. Furthermore, despite an impressive amount of literature on Gandhi, a systematic engagement of Gandhi's ethical and political thought with Western philosophy is still much needed.[7] But although Gandhi was not systematic in articulating his philosophy,[8] he was one of the only leaders of a social movement engaged in a political praxis based on non-violent struggle against injustice, with a genuine sense of responsibility for his political opponents. He inspired millions of political activists and leaders such as Nelson Mandela and Martin Luther King.

I view Gandhi as the closest political leader-activist to Levinas insofar as both argue for the insufficiency of the political when left to itself. Although Gandhi offers a more explicit and coherent approach to one's responsibility for the political opponent, both thinkers view ethics, seen as one's irreducible and irreplaceable responsibility for the other, as the foundation of the social and the political. Both present a radical critique of the autonomous, rational subject of modernity and deeply problematize the idea of human reason and progress as the sole means and end of human life. Yet in their attempts to explore the intersections of ethics and politics beyond the discourse of modernity, they do not assume an uncritical regression to traditionalism. Nor do they fall back on the conceptions of ethics and politics represented by institutional and historical religions. Instead they strive to tell a radically alternative ethicopolitical story. In light of the philosophical, ethical, and political affinities between Gandhi and Levinas, and their contemporaneity, it is surprising that there has never been a direct intellectual dialogue between the two, nor a serious and systematic exploration of the relationship between them.[9] This may be because Levinas' lifelong project was a dialogue with Western philosophy, particularly in terms of the question of "being" and the primacy of ethics in relation to ontology. For his part, Gandhi's main priority was to find the requirements of a radical political praxis that could liberate India from British colonialism[10] and to construct a liberatory discourse that did not repeat the same, or some other, pattern of domination, violence, and injustice. Although it may seem that Gandhi's and Levinas' lives and thoughts bear no relation to each other, I argue that the central purpose for both was to articulate an ethicopolitics whose foundation is not the rights and freedom of autonomous individuals, but one's responsibility for the other.[11]

(ii) Parallels between Levinas and Gandhi

Subject in Levinas and Gandhi

Gandhi's discussions on subjectivity are usually posited in terms of human "nature," and take the tone and categories of modern discourse, partly due to the time in which he wrote, but more so because he was not a trained philosopher.[12] When talking about subjectivity and the subject, Gandhi's language is different from that of Levinas. On the surface, Gandhi's language fits more easily into modernist discourse of the individual and its nature. He repeatedly uses words such as the individual, evolution, progress, nature, autonomy, truth, and virtue without much effort to problematize these concepts – at least not in the way of Levinas, who made the philosophical inquiry of these concepts his lifelong project. This style of writing has kept the interpretation and the implications of Gandhi's work, for the most part, within the bounds of a modernist discourse.[13] As a result, despite the general agreement that the Gandhian subject is different from the modern Western subject (with important implications for his political philosophy), this difference has not been fully illuminated.[14]

One fundamental misunderstanding about Gandhi arises from his frequent and unproblematic use of the word "individual." Gandhi employs the concept to simultaneously designate the subjectivity of the subject and uphold the subjection to the other (in the form of selfless service to the other) as the essence of what he deems human. This apparent contradiction raises the question of how his notion of the individual differs from the Western notion, and whether his approach to the subject is that of autonomy or heteronomy. One explanation for this apparent contradiction is that Gandhi was heavily influenced by Jainism. In Jainism there is no contradiction between *kaivalya* (a completely fulfilled self-hood) and heteronomy (defined as inter-subjection), which is a quite different concept than the liberal or Habermasian concept of intersubjectivity.[15] In *kaivalya*, the supreme Jaina religious goal, the self is neither attached to nor influenced by the world. However, the emphasis on the self in Jainism is founded on the theory of autotely rather than autonomy.

Ram-Prasad, writing on the self and heteronomy in Jainism, argues that autonomy is defined as the law of selfhood. In contradistinction, autotely is the goal of selfhood reached through both an insight into the multiplicity of reality and an ethical engagement with multiple otherness.[16] In this light, the goal of selfhood in Jainism is on par with heteronomy and indeed actually requires it. Therefore Gandhi's simultaneous emphasis on the self and on selfless service for the other is not contradictory but consistent. This framework, I argue, brings Levinas' and Gandhi's articulations of the self and the other much closer than those of Gandhian scholars who posit the Gandhian self in contradistinction to the Levinasian. For example, Ram-Prasad argues that Gandhi's Jaina-derived heterology is different from Levinas' insofar as it gives equal importance to oneself and the other. Ram-Prasad contends that Levinas' heterology, in contrast, gives significance to oneself only through being at the mercy of the other.[17] Here Ram-Prasad is ambiguous about the word "significant": does it mean importance, priority, or the possibility of signification? Ram-Prasad seems to offer a cursory reading of Levinas insofar as for Levinas, the self and the other are not contemporaneous. Therefore the issue of chronological priority of one over the other is irrelevant. For Levinas, the call of the other, and one's response to that call, is the possibility of signification, of signifyingness. This, however, cannot be translated, nor can it be reduced to the question of the priority of one over the other. Ram-Prasad quotes Levinas as saying that "the other must hold me hostage in order to deliver me"[18] to conclude that Levinas understands the subject only through "being at the mercy of the Other."[19] However, "being at the mercy of the Other" can also be translated as one's irreducible and irreplaceable responsibility for the other. In Levinasian terms, the subject is signified through her ability to respond to the call of the other; in Gandhian terminology, it is her selfless service that delivers her. In this sense she is hostage to the other for deliverance – "I" can only become "me" in the modality of subjection to the other's call (I discussed this as post-individual individuation in chapter 2). Therefore Gandhi's emphasis on individual autonomy comes much closer to Levinas' notion of separation, that is, absolute separation in proximity. Furthermore, both ground the responsibility for the other in the individual and as a result insist on the integrity of the individual. This affinity between Levinas and Gandhi, I argue, is of utmost importance insofar as their radical conception of the subjective lays the foundation for their ethical intervention into politics. One important implication of this parallel approach is that both Levinas and Gandhi firmly reject a liberal approach, one that defines the relation between the self and the other through the principle of pluralism. For both, pluralism simply acknowledges the alterity of the other, leaving the solipsism of the subject intact. For Levinas the "I" left to itself only intensifies the violence it wants to combat (BPW 30). Gandhi concludes his autobiography by stating, "I must reduce myself to zero. So long as a man does not of his own free will put himself last among his fellow creatures, there is no salvation for him. *Ahimsa* is the farthest limit of humility."[20]

Gandhi insists on preserving a notion of the individual partly so that the subject will be able to resist (a) assimilation into a totality or the modern state, and (b) the reduction of the state to an amalgamation of autonomous individuals. Anthony Parel, a well-known Gandhian scholar, correctly points out that for Gandhi there is a large difference between a nation formed as community (*praja*) and a nation of individuals held together by state power (*rashtra*). Those who interpret Gandhi's individual as autonomous cannot explain why, if Gandhi believes in a modern, autonomous individual, his conception of a nation-state is not an amalgamation of these same individuals?[21] Therefore, notwithstanding his insistence on the integrity, reality, and autonomy of the individual, Gandhi's approach to the individual cannot be reduced to a modernist one. Gandhi's distinction between *praja* and *rashtra* demonstrates that for him, the individual is born in his responsibility for the other. His notion of autonomy both insists and affirms that responsibility for the other is anchored in the individual subject before it is expressed in any institution or legal procedure. Thus, both Levinas and Gandhi use the concept of the individual, but they hold a radically different conception of the word, one that signifies heteronomy rather than autonomy as the constitutive moment of the subject. The individual, as a concept, is important insofar as the meaning of the individual arises out of its indispensability for justice before its indispensability to itself (LR 256).

For both Levinas and Gandhi, the individual acquires meaning only insofar as justice and the fight against injustice require a stable base, an interiority, a person to which it can be anchored. For both, the individual can only preserve its dignity – and, more important, can only become the subject proper – if it originates in its radical exposure and response to the suffering and death of the other. For both, the basis of both the social and the political is one's irreducible responsibility for the suffering and death of that singular face.

Further separating Gandhi and Levinas from the major trends in Western philosophy is their contention that the subject is primarily constituted not through its agency and freedom (and/or in opposition to the other's agency and freedom), but rather through its vulnerability and infinite responsibility for the other in proximity (who, in the case of Gandhi, can be human or non-human). For Levinas, the subject, before being a consciousness, is a conscience – it is oneself-for-the-other. For Gandhi, the other conditions consciousness – the subject can only free itself from its own conditioning through ethics, the responsibility for the other. As Gandhian scholar Jitendranath Mohanty[22] argues, Gandhi is much influenced by Vedantic tradition, which holds that consciousness is irreducible to awareness, knowledge, or purposiveness. Philosophers belonging to Samkara's school of Advaita Vedanta, for example, argue that there is a primordial order, prior to consciousness, in which there exists a non-intentional mode of relating to exteriority. For these philosophers, intentional consciousness must first make things its own object, and so cannot admit to any difference within it. Consciousness is therefore a unifying and homogenizing force. For Gandhi, the other (human or non-human), before revealing itself as the object of thought, exposes itself as that with which the subject has affinity or acquaintance. It is only after this event that the possibility of an intentional consciousness and the process of objectification occur; one cannot desire to know that with which you have no affinity or acquaintance.

Gandhian Selfless Service and Levinasian Irreplaceable Responsibility

Three aspects of Gandhian selfless service are very close to Levinas' articulation of responsibility, and together these aspects help both of them to view responsibility as a praxis above and beyond reciprocal rights and duties. This has important implications for the kinds of politics they endorse. First, for Gandhi (as for Levinas), responsibility for the other is infinite not because there is an infinite amount of suffering in the world, and not because there are infinite numbers of people for whom one is responsible, but because infinite responsibility is the core constitutive element of individuation. Insofar as being an individual means being able to respond, one can never stop being an individual. Gandhi contends that "the moment you adapt the attitude I suggest, the field of service becomes limitless. You limit your own capacity by thinking and saying that you must proselytize."[23] Second, for both Levinas and Gandhi, ethical responsibility is fundamentally non-reciprocal. For Gandhi, *anasaki* signifies selfless or non-reciprocal service.[24] Gandhian selfless service is founded in what Levinas would call a "dis-interested" modality rather than an interested investment. In this sense, Gandhi's and Levinas' approach to responsibility as infinite and non-reciprocal goes beyond the discourse of modernity, which primarily views responsibility as a contractual, reciprocal exchange of limited obligation and commitment to one another. Yet their distinction from modern notions of responsibility does not mean a return to selfless service as advocated by traditional discourses such as that of Christianity. For example, although very Christian in tone and deeply influenced by Christian values, Gandhi's notion of selfless service departs from traditional and mainstream Christian interpretations of selfless service. In the traditional interpretation of Christianity, Gandhi saw a coercive invitation to embrace a Truth. Therefore he strongly objected to those Christian missionaries in India who, under the guise of benevolence, attempted to convert segments of India's population to Christianity. Gandhi very explicitly says that the problem with Christianity is that it attempts to help the other by reducing her to the same.[25] Insofar as Gandhi's and Levinas' articulations of responsibility stand outside of reciprocity and utility, they differ from charity, benevolence, pity, and/or assimilating the other into the same. One is responsible not because one has a mission to spread the truth, and not because one is impelled to act by a sense of charity, but because someone is suffering. To be in selfless service to the other is to be responsible for the other's suffering and death irrespective of her being right or wrong, good or evil. In other words, the moment of responsibility cuts across these dualities. Gandhi's rejection of the solution offered by Christian missionaries to the problem of untouchables – the lowest social group in India's caste system at the time – exemplifies this approach. He repeatedly objected to missionaries who argued that the best solution for the problem of untouchability was to convert the untouchables to Christianity, and that untouchables would be better off if they became Christians. Gandhi, on many occasions, stated his distrust of any discourse based on the conversion of one person by another, even if this was done in the name of one's responsibility. He argued: "I disbelieve in the conversion of one person by another. My effort should never be to undermine another's faith but to make him a better follower of his own faith."[26]

Third, "proximity" plays a central role in both Gandhian political praxis and Levinasian ethical relation. For this reason, both Levinas and Gandhi repeatedly use the term "neighbour" to signify the structure of one's relationship to the other. For both, responsibility arises in the immediacy of the face-to-face relationship with the concrete other before its congealment in a universal idea or thought. For Gandhi, proximity is the ontic relation between self and other; people literally live and breathe in one another's proximity. Gandhi and Levinas both recognize the vulnerability and exposedness at the heart of the subject, who is born in proximity to the other. For Gandhi, non-violence, as the essence of the subject, points to the vulnerability of that which is sensible – the human. This conception is more radical than its reduction to a mere cognitive process. Along this line, Ram-Prasad argues that for Gandhi the other in the same is acknowledged both in thoughts and in deeds.[27] As such, the core similarity between Gandhi and Levinas is that for both, subjectivity arises from the intrigue of the other in the same based on passive exposure of one to the other in peace.

For Gandhi, one's return to self is the concrete experience of non-violence. In his phenomenology, non-violence is a corporeal event, an embodied experience that carries the human beyond her limits and exposes her to the infinite. In this sense he believes that one cannot get to the idea of non-violence through abstract reasoning alone. Non-violence must appeal to the heart, which for Gandhi is the locus of one's sensibility and receptivity. Contrasting soul force to brute force, he posits non-violence as the primordial orientation of the subject. This state, however, is not a given, nor is it a permanent order; its foundation is the fluid domain of the social, material, and political reality of the lives of the subjects, who are finite and fallible. Far from being an absolute law, the truth of non-violence has, for Gandhi, a contextual, experiential, and experimental form; therefore, one can only, at best, experiment with this truth. Levinas arrives at the same conclusion from a different trajectory. He challenges the Cartesian dualism of mind and body and radically disrupts their separation. For him the an-archic exposure of one to the other, and to the idea of infinity, is deeply rooted in the body and its sensibility: the body is referential from the beginning and as such is the locus through which one is exposed to the idea of infinity. Therefore the body, because of its bondage and its susceptibility, is open to the other's suffering and death. For both Gandhi and Levinas the ethical experience, beyond being a cognitive process, is deeply corporeal and material. However, Gandhi believes that since this experience is grounded in and conditioned by the social, political, and cultural context of the subject (a point with which Levinas would agree but which he does not elaborate), one's analysis should start from the construction of the human as it is (in its concrete material situation) and then peel off the layers of oppression and domination that chain the human. In a sense – and in contrast to Gandhi, who starts from the present – Levinas' phenomenological project compels him to start from the primordial, the pre-original, and the an-archic beginning. This difference means two different trajectories but not necessarily (as discussed above) two different outcomes.

Starting from the human as it is, the urgent task for Gandhi is to formulate a process of social and political change, as well as a subjectivity corresponding to this aim, in which the human can undergo the life-affirming ethical experience. One may argue that in Gandhi's mind, sociopolitical changes, however radical and transformative they may be, are not self-legitimizing. What legitimizes a social movement is neither the extent of its radicalism nor its success in overthrowing a political regime or existing social power structure. What is important is how the agent of change – individually and in a collective – acts, thinks, and feels in this process, and the approaches it adopts in achieving these sociopolitical changes. Gandhi names the ethicopolitical agent of social change *Satyagrahi*, which signifies non-violent disobedience to unjust laws and unfair social and political practices.[28] *Satyagrahi* is Gandhi's conception of an ethicopolitical subjectivity, and through it he introduces his most important ethical principle – non-violence – into politics; that is, *Satyagrahi* is to embrace the ethical imperative of "thou shalt not kill."[29] In this way, *Satyagrahi* embodies simultaneous non-violent resistance and responsibility for the welfare of others, the ethical principle held by Gandhi as the universal truth of social life. He posits two dimensions to *Satyagraha:* the first is non-violent resistance to injustice and exploitation; the second is the "truth force," which is the responsibility for the welfare of the other.[30]

(iii) Entry into Non-Violence through Eschatology

Although Levinas' eschatology does not specify non-violent forms of political struggle, I contend that it introduces the formal structure of non-violent revolutionary praxis into history. And far from being metaphysical, irrational, and subjective, his eschatology is the claim of an ethical peace that posits the principle of non-violent struggle for justice in the here and now – it is not a doctrine but a vision leading to engagement with the world in the form of a praxis. As Bernasconi rightly argues, Levinas' understanding of eschatology is not a "spiritual relationship; it leads to action. To see it is already to act."[31] This form of praxis, as I read it, is a saying that inspires the doing of peace; Levinas' eschatology is to begin to render violence as the ultimate injustice to the self and to the other(s). As such, his eschatology simultaneously criticizes rational peace and proposes an ethical peace, one that subordinates the rational peace of the state to its social promise, thereby creating the possibility for a human to see the face of the other (see LR 261). This social promise, for which eschatological vision holds the state responsible, is not the peace of empires imposed on the rest, a peace issued from war and resting on violence (TI 22); rather, it is a peace that comes with the work of justice for the other. In a sense, Levinas' understanding of eschatology cannot be but an ethical call to engage in a political struggle for justice in this world.

Levinas insists that war should not become "insaturation of a war in good conscience" (OB 160); eschatological vision has it that violence and war do not have the status of an origin. Within this vision, to demand justice is simultaneously revolutionary and peaceful. Levinas introduces an ethical vision of liberatory praxis, one that provides an ethical resistance to totalizing forces and the pressures of war: "if it causes war, it is not eschatology."[32] To claim that eschatology is not in opposition to war is to posit eschatology as an event that interrupts the constant alternation between war and rational peace; it is to radically reconceptualize the ethos of the political and of the rebellion against injustice. This is not to return the political realm to once again lay religion's traditional moral claim on politics. Rather, it is to expand on the work of liberation and to attain by peaceful means the demand for justice of the other as the inspiration for a non-totalizing liberatory struggle. As Asher Horowitz rightly asserts, this vision is one that "will attempt to describe 'a relation or an intentionality of a wholly different type' than the synoptic, objectifying and totalizing vision, the vision that is proper to representation."[33] The vision of ethical peace then stands beyond the tensions between peace and war. As such, the non-violence of ethical peace is not just a challenge to war, but an alternative vision and approach to the political, distinct from the vacillation between war and rational peace.

So I read Levinas' eschatology as a challenge to both dominatory forces and most liberatory movements, which view politics as an oscillation between war and ceasefire. The work of eschatology within history functions as a radical challenge to those politics that hold violence as necessary and unavoidable and that issue violence in the name of freedom, justice, truth, and/or responsibility. Levinas introduces eschatology as an event that "institutes a relation with being beyond the totality or beyond history, and not with being beyond the past and the present … It is a relationship with a surplus always exterior to the totality, as though the objective totality did not fill out the true measure of being" (TI 22). This surplus, in politics, is the non-violent struggle amidst the brute violence espoused by both the state and those forces that fight in the name of liberation. Political violence and its rational peace attempt to fill the political space with only one choice: war to eliminate war. In the face of this reality, Levinas proposes eschatology as that which is exterior to totality, as the vision of an ethical peace that needs to be brought into history through non-violent liberatory political praxis, as an alternative to the logic of war and violence. The concretion of eschatological vision in history is non-violent liberatory praxis in which peace is not merely an absence of war – the establishment of rational peace – but the realization of a "non-allergic" relation to the other.

Yet Levinas is aware that a philosophical discourse that posits a promise or a utopia in the form of a *telos* can easily be led to justify violence in the name of that same principle. He therefore has at least two problems to overcome in relation to eschatology: first, to avoid turning his eschatology into a metaphysical utopia that is always to come; and second, to resist making his notion of eschatology a totality. In this context he insists that his notion of eschatology is not a utopian goal to arrive at; rather, it is the event, the *doing* of peace that enters into time in every instant. Eschatology is within time and history without being reducible to totality: "It [eschatology] is reflected *within* the totality and history, *within* experience. The eschatological as the 'beyond' of history, draws beings out of the jurisdiction of history and the future; it arouses them in and calls them forth to their full responsibility" (TI 23). I agree, then, with Bernasconi, who concludes that Levinas' eschatology is not about the future, but rather about interrupting the present, about the making of peace in the here and now within history. Yet this interruption of the present is not in the hope of an immediate result for me; rather, it is inspired by a future that is not my own. Levinas repeatedly insists that his notion of eschatology does not act as a principle or a promise. In fact, he argues the opposite: "eschatology without hope for the self or without liberation in my time."[34] Rather than being the hope of redemption or salvation, eschatology is the expression of an inspiration that marks the ethical subject in her non-violent rebellion against injustice in history. Eschatology is to struggle for peace with peaceful means. As Bernasconi rightly states, this lack of hope for oneself cannot be equated with hopelessness.[35] Rather, it is a hope that breaks the boundaries of self-same and that as such cannot be reduced to a totality. For Levinas, the praxis that emanates from eschatological inspiration expresses the total gratuity of action and differs both from a labour and from a struggle whose target is one's own liberation in one's own time. In other words, eschatological vision frees praxis from the hold of presence. For Levinas, this praxis defines our present history, while its hope is for the world to come. Levinas offers few if any concrete examples in his discussion of the work of liberation that engenders an eschatological inspiration instead of emerging from a foundational totality. One of these rare examples is given to us in "Meaning and Sense," where Levinas pays tribute to Leon Blum.[36] He explains Blum's vision as

> 1941! – a hole in history – a year in which all the visible gods had abandoned us, in which god was really dead or gone back into his non-revealedness. A man in prison continues to believe in a nonrevealed future and invites men to work in the present for the most remote things, for which the present is an irrecusable negation. There is a vulgarity and a baseness in an action that is conceived *only* for the immediate. To act for far-off things at the moment in which Hitlerism triumphed, in the deaf hours of this night without hours – independently of every evaluation of the "forces in presence" – is, no doubt, the summit of nobility. (CPP 93)

(iv) Gandhi: Non-Violent Revolt and Eschatological Peace

The spirit of this non-violent eschatological praxis was expressed in Gandhi's political struggle against British domination in India. How did Gandhi's eschatological framework shape a different approach to building a community of resisters? For Gandhi, the "people" as a category was not constituted as oppositional to another "people"; rather, this category was to be born in the responsibility of each for the other. He did not see the Indian "people" as separate from the British, who held the political power. For Gandhi, the secret of dismantling the unjust dominant political power was not to confront it with greater power, but to confront it with a power that was different and beyond the economy that governed the dominant political authority. Therefore Gandhi's first principle was that the political must not be approached, or challenged and resisted, by another greater or violent power. The claim for justice should emanate from a place totally other than the traditional political articulation of justice. Ethicopolitical struggle must refuse to be co-opted into what Gandhi called "power politics or politics of power."[37] Power politics, Gandhi insisted, was the reduction of ethicopolitics to negative freedom of the individual, with the state as merely the regulator or defender of individuals' rights or freedoms. For Gandhi, this arrangement needed to be radically, yet peacefully, be replaced by a new vision of political power and political peace.

Gandhi insists that in liberatory struggle, peace entails much more than the absence of war. Peace, for both Gandhi and Levinas, is not the opposite of war, and non-violence is not just the absence of violence. Peace is not a utopian objective for which one wages war. Rather, peace has to find its concretion here and now. Gandhi's approach to liberatory struggle expresses a Levinasian saying that peace must emanate from non-violent rebellion against injustice, in such a way that it cuts across the vacillation between war and its absence and provides a radical and affirmative alternative to both. Indeed, Gandhian non-violent rebellion aims to disrupt the workings of power, not merely replace one power with another. For Gandhi, political power, more than a political problem, is a *social* problem emanating from the ways in which the subject is being signified and thus from how the inter-human relationship is conditioned in the political. For Gandhi, the view that power relations constitute all aspects of life and inter-human relationships is the logic of empire.

Gandhi would have agreed with Levinas that a philosophy that starts with being as the self-same is infused with power. In liberating India from colonial power, he did not draw liberatory inspiration, or its claims, from ontological or political categories; rather, he resorted to ethical ones. He realized there was a need for a separate category that did not express the political aspirations of Indian people in terms of a common substance or yet another totality, be it religion, ethnicity, geography, or the fact of India's victimhood. For Gandhi that separate category was ethical justice: responsibility for each and everyone, including the political opponent. In this sense, Levinas and Gandhi share the same approach to politics and political praxis. What makes both approaches to the political liberatory praxis unique is their belief that the only realm that can effectively halt the workings of "power for its own sake" is the ethical realm, signified through one's responsibility for the other – or as Gandhi calls it, selfless service. Levinas' and Gandhi's ethics transcend ontology and as such do not construct power relations as autonomous and constitutive of all that we call reality. Power is a by-product of the social rather than its founding element. In this sense a power relation is not the principal element that organizes the inter-human relation. Beyond and above the persuasiveness of power, the self is born into signification in responsibility for the other. In this way, Gandhi and Levinas not only reformulate the approach to the concept of political power but also propose a modality beyond imperialistic power.

One effect of such an approach to the political is encountered in Gandhi's insistence that the legitimacy of a liberatory struggle is not derived from the extent to which it succeeds in overthrowing the dominant power, nor is it derived from the extent to which it fulfils and provides for the rights and freedom of its own members. Although these matters are important, the legitimacy of a liberatory struggle is based on each person's substitution for the other's suffering and death regardless of identity, membership, and belonging. In liberatory discourse, this entails a constant questioning of how the community of resisters is constructed, who is left out and who is included, who is given a face and who is deprived of it, how the political enemy is constructed and encountered, the nature of the movement's opposition to dominant political power, and the place of violence in the struggle. In this sense, Gandhi believes deeply that the demands of justice must not only be posited and fought for through political power, but also (and equally) be practised within the social realm. An ethical political struggle must therefore adopt a different approach to the political, the state, and the social. In contradistinction to liberal ethics, Gandhi upholds that the goal of radical political praxis is to question the workings of the power itself, to overcome and dismantle the mechanisms of injustice through each and everyone's responsibility for the other.

To offer a radical alternative to this order, Gandhi insists on his politics of non-violence in contradistinction to the politics of "opposing or vanquishing anyone."[38] This distinction is important since it posits the goal of liberatory praxis as winning not through annihilating the enemy, but rather through changing the heart of the political opponent. For Gandhi there is a difference between "self-assertion" and non-violent resistance: in the former, political struggle is a cycle of reaction and counter-attack, of trying to defeat the enemy with greater power or more intense violence. Gandhi insists that a liberatory discourse that sustains itself on the construction of a common enemy does not necessarily serve justice. Both Gandhi and Levinas are attuned to the totalizing danger of this construction. The concern they raise is the possibility of being caught in negation instead of initiating an affirmative radical praxis. The existence of a political enemy may well be a reality of political struggle; however, Gandhi and Levinas force us to ponder the process of this construction and the ethical questions that arise in the face-to-face struggle with this enemy. Their warnings compel us to think about the reasons for our political alliances and friendships and the ways in which common enemies are constructed. Throughout his life Gandhi insisted that India's liberatory struggle should encounter its political enemies face-to-face, respecting their life and dignity; this, for Gandhi, meant a non-violent struggle against the British colonial forces in India. According to Gandhi, the goal of a liberatory movement is not only political victory but also the transformation of the heart of the enemy.[39] As such, embracing non-violence is not a tactic but a principle: peace is justice itself. Gandhi insists that it is *Satyagrahi*'s responsibility to see the enemy as a human being and to refuse to obliterate her face; only by refusing to return violence with greater violence can *Satyagrahi* have any hope of changing the enemy's heart and of calling her to reflect on her unjust deeds. There are many examples in Gandhian liberatory praxis that represent this approach. Concretely, his approach to liberation means that *Satyagrahi* is not a militaristic subjectivity, even if this militarism is employed in the name of justice. For Gandhi, militaristic subjectivity is another form of submission to the logic of empire; *Satyagrahi* cannot fight against empire by its own mechanisms:

> A nation becoming free after a violent struggle is bound to capture power in few hands and the suffering of India's large masses would not have changed if we became free by violent means. I wanted people of India to partner with the English people after independence, so a peaceful transfer of power was necessary.[40]

Where the empire applied violence and tyranny, *Satyagrahi* adopted the work of love and non-violence, reinscribing and redefining the political beyond the colonial approach to power and politics. This approach brought General Smuts in South Africa to his knees, forcing him to recognize the rights of "coolies," as all Indians were then called in South Africa. If you had hurt an Englishman, said Smuts, "I would have shot you, even deported your people. As it is, I have put you in prison and tried to subdue you and your people in every way. *But how long can I go on like this when you do not retaliate*?"[41]

There are many examples such as the above, illustrating that while many accused Gandhi of political pacifism, his *ahimsa*/non-violence was not a refusal to revolt; rather, it was a new concept of revolution; his *ahimsa* opened the possibility of the politics of ethical peace instead of the politics of suspended violence (i.e., rational peace). For Gandhi, this meant that *Satyagrahi* had to initiate a radical attempt to withdraw from the political cycle as it had hitherto been constructed, thus creating a liberatory alternative to an unjust system. Therefore, besides urging a non-violent struggle against enemies, Gandhi insisted that the liberatory movement approach other aspects of social and cultural life in the same spirit. If the colonizers maintained their dominatory power through economic exploitation, *Satyagrahi* would have reduced the effectiveness of that exploitation by creating alternative economic arrangements that sapped the colonizers' economic power. This is what motivated Gandhi to declare his spinning wheel revolution. He waged "war against the machine," going back to spinning with spinning wheels and weaving with looms, encouraging Indians to become self-sufficient and to burn British-made clothes. In 1921 he gave up wearing a shirt and cap and started wearing only a loin-cloth in devotion to homespun (*khadi*) cotton. To support local economies, he encouraged Indians to open shops that sold homespun cottons, and he presided over bonfires of foreign cloth, for which he was arrested repeatedly. Yet during his trip to England in 1931 he did not forget to apologize to English working men and women for all the economic harm that India's spinning wheel revolution had caused them. The reason for Gandhi's advocacy of small-scale, local economies – what he called village republicanism – was not merely economic, nor did it grow out of an irrational hatred of modernization; rather, it was to generate spaces in which people could create alternative social relations from those offered by the empire and its government. An equally important reason was the intimate link he perceived between centralization and violence: centralization, in order to sustain itself, had to resort to force and violence. For him, centralization and large-scale economic institutions were not conducive to non-violent structures – centralization was the manifestation of the universalizing tendency of Western philosophy by which individuals become particular instances of a totality. For him it was the self-sufficient and self-managed village republics that could produce, sustain, and perpetuate the grassroots, radical democracy and preserve the uniqueness of the individual.[42] Gandhi's non-violent approach to political struggle did not end after Indians assumed political power and became independent. Even after India's liberation, Gandhi continued to advocate unilateral disarmament as well as a non-violent national policy; he adopted this policy at a historical juncture when every state was racing towards escalating its military power.[43]

(v) Levinas: The Event of Speech and Eschatological Peace

It is important to note that Gandhi made the above decisions in the 1930s and 1940s, in a global political atmosphere of war, violence, and fear of international aggression. If Levinas could have given his views on Gandhi's insistence on the unilateral demilitarization of India or his other non-violent policies, he would have argued that these steps were traces of what he called "ethical peace within history," where embracing non-violence was not a tactical move but a principle.

Levinas himself sees in the praxis of speech the traces of ethical peace within history. Indeed, he reminds us that although philosophers profit from the "truth" of eschatological peace so as to announce their rational peace, they either relegate eschatological peace to the subjective realm or proclaim it as a revelation with no foundation. Returning eschatological peace to history, Levinas argues, cannot be done based on claims to philosophical evidence or theology. The real importance of eschatological peace lies elsewhere, in the pre-originary praxis of speech, which itself presupposes a renunciation of violence. In entering speech, one acknowledges the face of the other, and hence one disavows murder. Levinas writes: "The banal fact of conversation, in one sense, quits the order of violence … To speak, at the same time as knowing the other, is making oneself known to him. The other is not only known, he is *greeted [salute]*. He is not only name, but also invoked" (DF 7).

For Levinas, then, ethical justice transpires in the event of speech – or, restated, in a praxis that takes as its structure the logic and modality of speech where the subject is already positioned in a face-to-face relation to the other as an interlocutor. The event of speech and the structure it reveals is a modality of human praxis in which one is already accountable and answerable to another, already accused and responsible, and already substituted. Asher Horowitz elaborates on Levinas' approach to the event of speech, arguing that "the relation with an interlocutor is not only a knowing, or a participation in a common universality ... The relation with an interlocutor is also proximity: whatever the message is, whatever its possible validity, speaking is contact."[44] For Horowitz, insofar as language is the response to the call of the other and not a response to the call of a truth, the event of speech is the concretion of peace in human history.[45] Proximity, contact, and responsibility for the other are what make the event of speech possible. Levinas affirms the same point when he asks: "Can thought and truth force the other to enter my discourse, to become an interlocutor?" (CPP 125). In *Totality and Infinity,* Levinas expands on this reading, arguing that "the Desire for exteriority has appeared to us to move not in objective cognition but in Discourse, which in turn has presented itself as justice, in the uprightness of the welcome made to the face" (TI 82). As such, the event of speech can be reduced neither to what is communicated nor to an agreement between the parties – although the pre-originary event of speech sets the conditions for all these moments. To understand speech as reduced to negotiation, communication, and the exchange of truths, as Horowitz emphasizes, is to understand speech as anaesthetized and reified.[46] In a sense, Levinas divorces the origin of language from reason, truth, and the said and finds its pre-originary inspiration in peace. For him, the ethical significance of speech lies in the affirmative expression of one's substituting praxis for the other in speech. In the event of speech, before that which is communicated, one is substituted for the other in proximity. Horowitz stresses the same point: "A proximity concretized in speech, is a manifestation of the other to the same, but one where the other manifests by undoing and escaping his manifestation."[47] Thus to enter into speech with the other is to acknowledge the existence of the other as "other" and to be held responsible for her alterity. The event of speech expresses peace and concretizes the non-allergic relationship to the other. Gandhi, as I will argue later, expands this structure to liberatory political praxis and to his conception of liberation as peace with the "other" – justice.

Ethical Love as the Principle of the Social and the Political

Some Levinas scholars argue that the origin of language must take into account both violence and non-violence. Peter Atterton, in "Levinas and the Language of Peace: A Response to Derrida,"[48] addresses Levinas' approach to violence and non-violence in relation to language. In contradistinction to Derrida's claim that the non-violence of speech is the escape from the worst violence, Atterton argues that the non-violence of speech is a consequence of "escaping ethical violence,"[49] which he describes as the peace that is between me and the other but that nonetheless ignores and possibly excludes the third party. Therefore for Atterton there is both "the originary non-violence and originary violence, to which the violence of speech is to respond."[50] Both violence and peace are at the beginning, since "non-violence in relation to the Other would in turn be violence (negligence at least) against the third party and vice versa."[51] He admits that Levinas is one of the few thinkers who insists on the originality of peace;[52] nonetheless, he sees in the event of speech both violence and non-violence as co-present and "equiprimordial,"[53] meaning that "neither condition, neither peace nor violence could call itself primordial."[54] Atterton insists that positing both violence and non-violence as originary is important, because if the ethical relation were to be seen as a relation from which every violence was excluded, then we could not offer a satisfactory origin for language. Therefore the primordial peace, suggested by Levinas' eschatological peace, is insufficient insofar as it does not take into account the original violence – a reading that he admits would be not be accepted by Levinas.[55]

There are many reasons why Levinas would object to such a reading. For one, ethical violence, as Atterton describes it, is close to the violence of the state-of-nature theorists, for whom the non-violence of speech is the answer. In Atterton's reading the non-violence of speech is merely a commerce through which peace is maintained, a rational peace in which violence is still committed against an excluded third party. I think this framework is exactly what Levinas opposes when he posits speech as the concretion of the ethical peace. For Levinas it is crucial to leave a modality of peace, a vision of peace, that stands out of the economy of violence to which humanity can appeal and upon which it can act. There are many problems with Atterton's reasoning, but in the context of my argument one stands out in particular: he takes the third party as coming onto the scene only after the subject's relation with the other is established. He insists that the third exists from the beginning, yet he reads the relation between the subject and the other as "erotic," as disturbed only after the third comes to the scene.[56] Atterton's reading contains the same fallacy present in other liberal readings of Levinas' ethics, in which the private relation between the two is constructed in opposition to social relation, with the latter forever infested with violence.

This is not my reading of Levinas; as discussed before, the third is on the scene from the beginning, marking the ethical as sociality. Levinas, especially in his later works, acknowledges and separates the erotic, private relation from the work of ethical love in sociality; that is, love as peace and responsibility for the other. I think it is important to ask why Atterton views the privileging of one person over another as a violence on par with the violence of exploitation, oppression, murder, and so on. Levinas clearly makes a distinction between *logos* and speech (speech being the structure of the social), signifying the social as a structure in which one lives as if one always already has interlocutor(s) for whom one is infinitely responsible. That is to say, Levinas' event of speech should be read as profoundly social, signifying the principle of non-exclusion and peace. This reading is on par with Levinas' claim that the aim of ethical peace is to reduce violence so that it is no more than the marks left on the other by the thematization that is necessary to the ontological human condition (OB 7). The problem with Atterton is that he tries to address the question of violence by attempting to figure out whether, at the beginning, there was peace or war. Levinas' answer to this question would have been neither; before war and peace "there were alters" (CPP 124) – a proximity to, and peace with, the other. It is through this exposition that Levinas not only establishes peace as the originary event but also radically reconceptualizes its meaning – no longer does that meaning reference the peace–war duality with its chronological structure. Levinas argues that "as a manifestation of reason, language awakens in me and in the other what is common to us. But in its expressive intention, it presupposes our alterity and our duality" (CPP 36). This quote is important since it affirms that at some crucial level Levinas posits love as a structure that is not a private one – ethical speech cannot be reduced to a rational or erotic dialogue and/or an exchange between two individuals. It is intended to signify love and peace as the structure of sociality.

In contrast to Atterton, Horowitz understands Levinas' approach to speech structured as love. Horowitz reads the Levinasian event of speech, before its congealment in the said, as the "a surplus of sociality and love, where love is conceived first of all as fear for the other."[57] It is true that in his early writing, Levinas describes love as "the ego satisfied by the you" – and hence the erotic space carved between the two is not the beginning of society but its negation (CPP 31) – and he warns of the danger of positing this private inter-subjective love as the origin of sociality: "love makes blind the respect which is impossible without blindness toward the third person and is only a pious intention oblivious of the real evil" (CPP 31). Levinas rightly contends that for love to emerge from its containment in a couple, for it to go beyond a closed society of the two and include all those who remain outside the amorous dialogue, it has to become judgment and justice (CPP 32–5). However, as Levinas later argues, although love can always be reduced to the fundamental immanence, it also opens the possibility of transcendence. As Levinas so beautifully asserts, love contains the possibility of a desire and a "movement ceaselessly cast forth, an interminable movement toward a future never future enough" (TI 254). In his later writings he pays more attention to the ambiguity of the concept, exploring it as an event situated at the limit of immanence and transcendence (TI 254). Love, although reducible to need, still bears witness to and presupposes "the total, transcendent exteriority of the other, of the beloved," and more so, testifies to what is not yet, to a possibility more remote than the possible (TI 254). Although infinite responsibility for the other is not reducible to this event, this form of love – Eros – presupposes the face of the other (CPP 147n8). In other words, love is the possibility of feeling the frailty of the other (TI 256), of being affected and frightened by the nakedness and destitution of the other. As such, love situates the self in an asymmetrical relationship to the other in which the subject becomes the fear for the other's suffering and frailty and is prompted to assist the other. This urge does not occur in abstraction but in a dimension whose locus is the sensible subject. In Levinas' later writing, love is not an occurrence reducible to a private feeling, nor is it that which forgets the real evil. More important, its transformation into judgment and justice does not arise out of a disembodied, abstract reason or equality. Rather, the justice of love proceeds from the wounded body of the "sense-able," marked by the frailty of the other. It is this sense-able love that Levinas posits as the origin, as peace, and as an alternative to the categorical imperative originated in the universal reason of consciousness. This pre-originary sensibility can resist, and has been resisting, the reduction of ethics to abstract, universal laws that are acknowledged but hardly felt.

It is *this* love – the fear for the other's death and suffering – that makes the event of speech not a reconciliation of egos, but an event, one that in Horowitz's words makes possible "these egos ...'capable' of transcending egoism upon the approach of the other."[58] Horowitz correctly maintains that Levinas achieves this vision by radically separating his approach from that which he labels philosophy of Neuter.[59] In the latter approach, the subject, rather than having an absolute separation from the other, is perceived to have a distance from the "situation." For Levinas, as already discussed in chapter 2, the "I" is not at a relative distance from the other but is absolutely separate from the other and all others. This means, Horowitz insists, that for Levinas the primordial drive for the subject's entry into speech is not the fulfilment of a need, nor is it a desire for the desire of the other. Rather, the entry into speech emanates from a primordial order of desire that is one-for-the-other.[60] In Levinasian desire "the relationship between strangers who are not wanting to one another – desire in its positivity – is affirmed across the idea of creation *ex nihilo*" (TI 104). In her absolute separation, the subject's entry into speech with the other breaks away from totality as domination. Levinas argues that in entering into a conversation with another person, "I do not only *know* something, I am also part of society. This *commerce* which the word implies is precisely action without violence: the agent, at the very moment of its action, has renounced all claims to domination or sovereignty" (DF 9). For Levinas this event is an instance of a peace that can transcend rational peace; he calls this the peace of proximity, the ethical peace that is "peace as love of the neighbor, where it is not a matter of peace as pure rest that confirms one's identity but of always placing in question this very identity, its limitless freedom and its power" (BPW 167).

Political Opponent as Interlocutor

But can the praxis of speech, as Levinas approaches it, survive political conflict and hostility? Is rational peace not the ultimate goal one can hope to achieve in the political? How does the praxis of speech relate to the work of liberation and the struggle against injustice? Can Levinas' conception of speech, as a surplus of sociality and love, or love as sociality, reconceptualize the approach to liberatory political praxis and the justice it seeks? To what extent is liberatory praxis caught within the articulation of peace as merely rational, contributing to the perpetuation of violence? We have already discussed that for Levinas, eschatological or ethical peace is the principle of justice in history; but does he make a connection between peace as justice and the ethical demand to fight against injustice? If so, how? It should be obvious that for Levinas, love as fear for the other, although primordial and embodied, is overdetermined by social, political, and economic factors. As such, its awakening is a social endeavour rather than an essential property or a rational reflex. In this context, then, social speech is the medium through which the ethical fear for the other can be promulgated in inter-human relationships and within the social. That is to say, the social praxis of speech, addressing the other as one's interlocutor, can bring about what Gandhi calls a "change of heart" in the other. Although Levinas does not address the effect of ethical speech in liberatory praxis, that effect can be inferred from his thought that substitution for the other means an insistence on being in speech community, even with one's opponent, so as not only to convey a message but also – which is more important – to remain in a face-to-face relationship with her.

One rare case in Levinas' writings of a concrete example was his reference to Egyptian president Anwar Sadat's trip to Israel in 1977. Levinas hailed Sadat's visit as a gesture, and an instant of peace, one that was taken through a path that "lay beyond politics, whatever the actual role of the political route may have been in the itinerary of this peace" (LR 279). For all that had been said about Sadat's visit and the price he had to pay – his assassination by a Muslim extremist – what seemed to be central for Levinas was that this historic visit spoke to a surplus beyond the "mocking gaze of the political man" (TI 22). For Levinas it was precisely this gesture of welcome and peace that could not be exhausted in and by the logic and political necessities of war. Sadat's visit, during which he addressed the people of Israel from the Knesset, was seen by Levinas, irrespective of its outcome, as a break with totalization as presented in the logic of war or in the rational peace of the political, and as opening another path to the political.

Levinas is not very clear on how his conception of ethical love can be expressed in the political. In contrast, Gandhi's concept of *ahimsa* is love expressed in the political form. Furthermore, by extending the meaning of *ahimsa* to the realm of political conflict, Gandhi opened an alternative path for facing the political opponent. If the basis of sociality is love, Gandhi did not see any reason why it could not be the foundation of political struggle, one whose goal, before conquering power, was changing hearts. He insisted on the doctrine of unconditional love in politics; he did so even when most of his own comrades stood against him, arguing that to love the "enemy" or wrongdoer was to ignore the question of justice. Gandhi insisted that his notion of *ahimsa* was not pacifism in the face of injustice; rather, the "law of love," as he called it, was the search for the lost affinity with the other and for the human's infinite capacity to suffer for the other. In this way, he made a distinction between the non-violence of the "weak" and that of the "strong." *Ahimsa* of the strong has the infinite capacity to suffer for the other's suffering and does not bow to injustice. Gandhi describes this form of non-violence in the following terms: "Non-violence is not a cover for cowardice, but it is the supreme virtue of the brave ... Cowardice is wholly inconsistent with non-violence ... Non-violence presupposes ability to strike."[61]

However, *ahimsa* devoid of love and forgiveness, and backed by resentment, is the non-violence of the weak. It is important to note that while Gandhi views the *ahimsa* of the weak as ineffective in breaking the cycle of domination and oppression, he does not evaluate it as an inherent quality in some individuals or social groups. He understands it, rather, as the by-product of certain socioeconomic conditions, not as an intrinsic moral degradation. For Gandhi, there are circumstances in which a group of helpless people cannot defend themselves and must be saved by external forces, even if by violence. Yet even in these situations he never ceases to hope that *ahimsa* of the heart is possible, even if the political situation seems to declare otherwise. Thus Gandhi – unlike, say, Nietzsche, who viewed the powerless as eternally caught within the cycle of resentment – sees the powerless, the disenfranchised, and the marginalized as capable of elevating their political struggle to a non-violent movement based on love and goodwill.

(vi) Gandhi: Political Enemy as Interlocutor: Peaceful Struggle as Speech

Gandhi saw it as imperative to bring political hostility to the order of speech. For him, this was not so much a tactical move, or an opening for negotiation, but a way to provide the anti-colonial movement with a proper ethicopolitical dimension. He believed firmly that only a change of heart could end the rule of empire in India and bring about a lasting peace. For him, one measure of success at this project was the extent to which the political enemy could be turned into an interlocutor. The whole point of *ahimsa* is to enter into political struggle against one's enemy as if he is an interlocutor – as if, at some level, one is accountable to one's political opponent. This is to say that Gandhi's *ahimsa* urged the *Satyagrahi* to change her opponent's mind and heart and not merely to overpower the opponent. Gandhi, much like Levinas, approached justice from its narrow (formal) *and* broader (ethical) dimensions. For both, ethical justice went beyond the concern for one's rights and freedom and included one's responsibility for the life and dignity of the other – including one's political opponent. As such, Gandhi did not compromise in protecting the life and dignity of those deemed political enemies or outsiders, be they the English, the untouchables, the Muslims (for Hindus), or the Hindus (for Muslims). True, it is difficult if not impossible to feel responsibility towards the one who is directly participating in social–political–economic domination and in the killing of a nation or a people. It is also true that in light of today's political violence, Gandhi's approach seems like an impossibility. But Gandhi's political praxis aimed at this impossibility – at a face-to-face relation with his political enemies as if they were his interlocutors, for whom he was fearful, and to whom he was responsible. In a letter to Lord Irwin, Governor General and Viceroy of India at the time, Gandhi informed Irwin of his plan for a mass civil disobedience against the unjust Salt Law:

> My ambition is no less than to convert the British people through non-violence, and thus make them see the wrong they have done to India. I do not seek to harm your people. I want to serve them even as I want to serve my own people. I respectfully invite you to pave the way for the immediate removal of those evils, and thus open a way for a real conference between equals. But if you cannot see your way to deal with these evils and if my letter makes no appeal to your heart, on the eleventh day of this month I shall proceed … to disregard the provisions of the Salt Laws … I have no desire to cause you unnecessary embarrassment, or any at all, so far as I can help.[62]

Care for the well-being of his political opponent did not mean that Gandhi was not firm in his rebellion against British rule. He understood that political conflict is not merely between two opposing arguments, but between the interests of the rulers and those of the ruled. He knew that to achieve justice and to eliminate oppression, much more than reasoning with the political enemy is required. Yet he believed he could create a framework for liberatory struggle structured on the logic of love, embodying the peaceful spirit of human dialogue, transforming the "fear from the other" to a "fear for the other."

Ahimsa, for Gandhi, signified the heterological, heteronomical, and tendentious nature of desire – the core constitutive of the Gandhian subject. Based on this conception, Gandhi attempted to indicate a radically different sense of personhood, one whose impetus for political change came not from desire for power or from an abstract ideal of justice, freedom, or equality, but from love felt in one's heart. In a sense, to approach justice, freedom, or equality in a heteronomical order – meaning that they signify something beyond one's own private life and interest – these concepts must lead the subject to *ahimsa* and not away from it. Legal justice, although necessary, is not enough; there must be a non-violent awakening to the evil of injustice. One such example was the civil disobedience campaign begun in 1942, which lasted for three years and came to be known as the Quit India campaign. Against all of Gandhi's attempts to open a dialogue, the British government, within hours of the passage by the Indian National Congress of the Quit India Resolution, crushed the movement with all its might and arrested the leaders of the Congress, including Gandhi himself. The government's brutality provoked violent struggle throughout the country.[63] After his release from prison in 1944, Gandhi announced that he was deeply disappointed in his followers for ignoring the fundamental principle of non-violence: "The destruction of bridges and roads could not change the hearts of men."[64] Many saw Gandhi's objection to the Indian people's resort to violence as unreasonable, arguing that it was legitimate to resort to violence in the name of self-defence. They further insisted that violence might be necessary for the anti-colonial movement in its struggle to seize political power. Gandhi vehemently rejected these propositions: "Therein lies the Fallacy … A non-violent rebellion is not a programme of seizure of power. It is a programme of transformation of relationships ending in a peaceful transfer of power."[65] Throughout his years of struggle against the British authorities, Gandhi's belief in *ahimsa* as the supreme ethical principle obligated him to acknowledge the face of his political opponents. Throughout his struggle, Gandhi appealed repeatedly to the British colonizers for a more sympathetic approach to Indians and for equal treatment of Indians; he urged them to live in India not as colonizers but as part of the people.[66] For Gandhi, the doctrine of *Satyagraha* required one to make the opponent see and realize the injustice in which he was engaged. He insisted that without a complete change of heart, there could be no reconciliation between Indians and the English:

> I have said on many platforms that the British race is with us … I do believe that it is possible for India if she would but live up to the tradition of

> the sages of whom you have heard from our worthy President, to transmit a message through this great race, a message not of physical might, but a message of love. And then, it will be your privilege to conquer the conquerors not by shedding blood but by sheer force of spiritual predominance.[67]

Gandhi's stance echoed Levinas' insistence that the relationship with the other, be it friend or enemy, is not a togetherness but a facing. For Gandhi, facing the other at times of political conflict meant hanging on to whatever humanity was left in the oppressor and insisting on one's responsibility for him – a responsibility that mere opposition to an enemy would have denied. At a number of crucial junctures, Gandhi stopped the march of revolution in India, halted the *Satyagraha* campaign, and began a hunger strike to protest people's violence against the colonial forces. In 1919, for example, he suspended *Satyagraha* campaign, called it a "Himalayan miscalculation," and fasted for three days because people had resorted to widespread violence. In 1922 he suspended mass disobedience because of people's attacks on the police and fasted until people stopped their violence. Gandhi fasted on seventeen different occasions: three of these were for self-purification, but the rest were in protest against violence aimed at British authorities or against violence arising from ethnic and religious divides.[68]

Gandhi's profound commitment to face-to-face relationships with his political opponents was exemplified by his insistence on dialogue with them. Indeed, he maintained that dialogue was more than the medium of negotiation – it was the event of peace. His commitment to talking to his enemies in situations of political hostility has long since been copied around the world and has spawned impressive scholarly work.[69] Although to a large extent his approach has been reduced to conflict resolution programs and manuals, these literatures merit some attention in terms of his philosophy of non-violence. For example, Thomas Weber, a well-known Gandhian scholar in the field of international relations,[70] in discussing Gandhi's contributions to conflict resolution strategies, lists the following as established maxims in the field: that violence is invited from opponents if they are humiliated or provoked; that personal contact with opponents should be sought; that opponents should not be judged harder than the self; that opponents should be trusted; and that a weakness in an opponent should not be exploited.[71] Gandhi's approach to the British personnel who worked for the empire in India exemplified these maxims. He tried diligently to implement these principles to reach his liberatory end, in face-to-face encounters with his opponents, in his foreign policy after India became independent, and in his reluctant and painful acceptance of the partition of Pakistan from India when he finally realized that millions of lives would be lost if he insisted on the unity of Muslims and Hindus.

Yet Gandhi maintained that caring for opponents, insisting on face-to-face relations with them, and even being responsible for their welfare did not contradict firmness and resolve in political struggle. One of the best examples of this approach was his famous Salt *Satyagraha* of 12 March 1930, which he called "right against might." To protest the colonizers' monopoly over salt production (a vital source of income for millions of Indians), Gandhi, at age sixty-two, marched 241 miles in twenty-four days to the sea at Dandi, where he and thousands of others who had joined him on the way defiantly broke the law by picking up salt at the seashore as the whole world watched. Before the march began, Gandhi had communicated his plan to the Viceroy, Lord Irwin, telling him that his ambition was "no less than to convert the British through non-violence."[72] Gandhi received no response from British authorities and so started the march. At first the British authorities, along with many of Gandhi's intellectual colleagues in the Congress who saw his plan as irrelevant, ridiculed Gandhi's breach of the salt laws as "Mr. Gandhi's somewhat fantastic project."[73] They could not fathom how an empire could be overthrown by "boiling sea water in a kettle." Instead of responding to Gandhi's initial communication, Lord Irwin crushed the movement, and in May arrested Gandhi along with 60,000 other civil resisters. Yet Gandhi's march exhilarated the whole of India – on shore, Indians started making salt out of seawater. This round of civil disobedience lasted about twelve months and led to Gandhi's release. Gandhi's Salt March forced the British authorities to open a dialogue with Gandhi, which led to the Gandhi–Irwin Pact in March 1931.[74] Bal Ram Nanda, a Gandhian scholar, argues that among all the mass civil disobediences, the Salt March came closest to Gandhi's conception of *Satyagraha*. Gandhi had called off two previous civil disobediences, in 1919 and 1920, after they turned to violence. But the Salt March had all the elements of what Gandhi viewed as non-violent struggle. Nanda lists them as follows:

> the careful preparation, the articulation of the moral issue, the intuitive choice of symbols and instruments, the cautious beginning, the slow acceleration and, finally, the successful mobilization of the people without hatred and violence, simultaneously with the willingness to build bridges with the enemy for an eventual meeting of minds.[75]

Although Gandhi was a nationalist and as such adamant that the British Empire release its grip on India, his approach to liberation differed sharply from that of other nationalists. He made a clear distinction between harming the interests of a colonizing force and committing violence against the individuals participating in that domination. He argued that nationalists must win over the British by their genuine love and responsibility for the life and death of these subjects. He believed that the power of empire was concentrated in its economic and social structures rather than in individuals. Those who served the colonizing system, even the highest-ranking officers, were foremost human beings whose actions and ideas had to be firmly opposed but whose lives and dignity had to be safeguarded. It was *Satyagrahi*'s responsibility to reduce the possibility of violence when two groups of people came face-to-face and when one group had guns to the others' heads. Not even in an unequal situation – in the name of self-defence – was *Satyagrahi* relieved from her responsibility towards her enemy. Nothing could change Gandhi's view on this fundamental ethical responsibility.

(vii) Liberation as Substitution: Fearing for the Other Instead of Fearing from the Other

Gandhi does not insist on non-violence in liberatory struggle because he gives a divine or sacred status to blood or to human life. In fact, he resists fetishizing non-killing.[76] He states on many occasions that although non-violence is better than violence, violence better than cowardice or indifference. The more important question, for him, is not whether blood will be shed or not, but rather "*whose blood* is going to be shed" (as Arvind Sahrma puts it).[77] Gandhi, much like Levinas, dreads the murder of the other more than one's own death (see TI 244–6). He insists that in liberatory struggle, self-suffering is preferred over the infliction of pain on others:

> When I consider what is going on today in India, I think it is necessary for us to say what our opinion is in connection with the political assassinations ... You the student would have to beware, lest mentally or morally you give one thought of approval to this kind of terrorism. I, as a passive resister, will give you another thing very substantial for it. *Terrorise yourself*; search within[,] by all means resist tyranny wherever you find it; by all means resist encroachment upon your liberty, but not by shedding the blood of the tyrant.[78]

In contrast to the politics of violence-rational peace, Gandhi contends that power and violence are not the foundations of realistic politics. He repeatedly contends that violence – even in most cases of proclaimed self-defence – emanates from the fear of the other. Indeed, for both Gandhi and Levinas, modern politics is based on the fear of the other – the stranger, always constructed as a "potential threat" – whose menace must be controlled by a higher power. A politics based on such a foundation necessitates a state whose primary ethos is to prevent a war of all against all and to protect individuals from one another's aggression. Therefore both Gandhi and Levinas attempt to provide an ethicopolitics that transforms this fear *of* the other into a fear *for* the other. For example, Levinas on a few occasions indicates his objection to the Hobbesian state by criticizing its foundations and their implications for human political liberation.[79] What is fundamentally problematic with a politics and a state based on this allergic relationship is that its workability can only be guaranteed by the spectre of violence; peace in the Hobbesian state is an armed peace, and its justice arises in order to preserve commerce among competing members of that society.

Levinas' criticism of viewing the political as an allergic relationship with the other needs to be accompanied by more grounded studies, ones that analyse the historical mechanisms through which this allergic relation is intensified and transformed into an inevitable ontological human condition, so that the structures of domination, exploitation, and inequality persist and serve the interests of a few. In his struggle for liberation, Gandhi looks more closely at the political implications of this allergic relation and refuses to succumb to fearing the other, whether this fear is real or illusory. That is why he insists that in a liberatory struggle, *ahimsa* – love and non-violence, even for one's opponent – needs to substitute for violence and power struggle:

> If we are not possessed by the desire to power and a feeling of jealousy, why has so much bitterness spread around us? Why do these people come to Malikanda and shout violent slogans? ... Why don't you try to win them over with love? Why don't the leading workers among you go to them and talk to them lovingly?[80]

Both Gandhi and Levinas, in their own terms, offer conceptual categories for imagining such a non-allergic, fearless relation to the other. As discussed in the previous chapter, Levinas' substitution paves the way for a substituting praxis in which political praxis is imagined as the work of an ethicopolitical subject who is for-the-other's suffering and death. Both Gandhi's *Satyagrahi* and Levinas' ethicopolitical subject embrace genuine openness that involves the risk of dying for the other and share the anxiety for the other's death. Suffering is an event that occurs both within and without and that disrupts boundaries separating the inside and the outside. This substitution for the other's suffering emanates simultaneously from laying oneself open and offering oneself to the other and from a responsibility to alleviate the injustice done to the other.

For both Gandhi and Levinas, suffering occupies a significant space: "suffering for" concretizes transcendence in immanence; it opens the horizon of human sociality and politics to service for the other and offers substituting praxis as a viable alternative to the politics of violence-rational peace. For Gandhi, self-suffering is the embodied form of taking responsibility for the other and all others. *Satyagrahi* must take the burden of suffering on his or her own shoulders: "I urge you to speak sedition – but at your peril. You must be prepared to suffer the consequences."[81] Yet this substituting praxis can be concretized only when *Satyagrahi* has reduced herself to zero: "LOVE can only be expressed fully when man reduced himself to a cipher. This process of reduction to cipher is the highest effort man or woman is capable of making."[82] For Gandhi, reducing oneself to a cipher means that a *Satyagrahi* goes beyond her own solipsism and her own self-interest, revealing the primordial exposure of one to the other. For Gandhi, this going beyond is not necessarily opposition to one's being, nor is it an abstract transcendence. In the latter the transcendental move is an intentional progression to a faceless universal, or a general idea or form. Gandhian transcendence is much closer to Levinas: it is a going beyond to reach, to touch, and to feel another human's suffering in the modality of radical passivity and exposure; it is the process of "never enough emptying myself of myself" (CPP 169); it is to substitute one for the other. In Gandhi, this concrete transcendental move is the founding moment of an ethical politics and the constitutive event of *Satyagrahi*. Although Levinas' substitution, as discussed in the previous chapter, opens the possibility of a praxis that is provoked by one's sensibility rather than by the strength of one's will, he is not definite about the implications of his own concept – it is not clear what role, if any, his notion of substitution plays in the political. What does it mean to substitute one-for-the-other in the political sense? His concept, therefore, remains suggestive in the political. For Gandhi, to be non-indifferent to the other's suffering and death prior to knowledge and will means literally to die for the other and to be responsible even for one's political opponents: "when we put ourselves in our opponents' shoes we will do them justice."[83]

Gandhi suggests that when reasoning fails and dialogue is impossible, voluntary suffering at the hands of the political opponents may bring about a change of heart and remove obstacles to their understanding of their injustice. For example, after Gandhi's Salt March millions of Indians across the country began mass civil disobedience and broke the unjust salt laws everywhere. Webb Miller, a journalist for United Press in the United States and an eyewitness to the non-violent march at the Dharasana salt depot, wrote a famous description of the events of that march. His moving report offers a detailed account of the police atrocities conducted against stubbornly peaceful marchers:

> Suddenly, at a word of command, scores of native policemen rushed upon the advancing marchers and rained blows on their heads with their steel-shod *lathis.* Not one of the marchers even raised an arm to fend off the blows. They went down like ten-pins. From where I stood I heard the sickening whack of the clubs on unprotected skulls. The waiting crowd of marchers groaned and sucked in their breath in sympathetic pain at every blow. Those struck down fell sprawling, unconscious or writhing with fractured skulls or broken shoulders ... Group after group walked forward, sat down, and submitted to being beaten into insensibility without raising an arm to fend off the blows. Finally the policemen became enraged by the non-resistance.[84]

What inspired these non-violent foot soldiers (as they came to be known to the world) was the Gandhian belief that *Satyagrahi* must abstain from using violence for his or her just cause. Moreover, there is a "truth" in not returning violence with higher violence – the "truth" in self-suffering is that it reveals the workings of injustice to others who witness such brutality, even to individuals who participate in such violence. Gandhi insists that by suffering for the other, *Satyagrahi* exposes injustice around him[85] and throws into question who is powerful and who is not. For Gandhi and for millions of others who followed him, *ahimsa* – non-violence in its social, economic, political, and physical forms – was the justice they sought. This relationship to justice forbade them to adopt a political praxis that hurt anyone except themselves. Although Gandhi's non-violence has been criticized as pacifist and ineffective in bringing change in the realm of realpolitik, the non-violent struggle of these foot soldiers was an instance that broke the passive–active dichotomy and that transcended the mere negation of power. This event came very close to what Levinas calls a positive affirmation of the ethical dimension, from which justice is demanded and the responsibility of one for the other is issued. Between 1906 (in South Africa) and 1942 (the final nationwide *Satyagraha* campaign in India), Gandhi led many individual and mass civil disobediences in a variety of forms. Although many Indians' blood was shed by soldiers of the British Empire during these non-violent struggles, Gandhi, in the name of the same justice he sought for his own people, allowed no violence towards the British colonizers.

Gandhi was the first political leader-activist to make an intimate connection between the ethical demand of non-violence to others and liberation. Liberation is only sustainable in a non-violent mode appropriate to the ethics of proximity, and *ahimsa* is not a private virtue, reserved for one's intimate community. Rather, *ahimsa* is the ethical command "thou shalt not kill" brought into sociality and political strife. Levinas regrets that this command has yet to govern the social and political reality of social life. While appreciating the existing universal rights of man, he reminds us that the two ethical commands "thou shalt not kill" and "thou shalt love the stranger" have been, for thousands of years, waiting to enter into and govern the inter-human relationship (EN 155).[86] Although Levinas' reminder can be reduced to, for example, a ban on capital punishment, Gandhi expanded this demand to situations of political strife. By positing *ahimsa* as the guiding principle of one's interaction with the other, Gandhi situated the subject's radical vulnerability and fear for the other's death as the origin of sociality and political engagement. Levinas talks about this fear:

> The alterity of the other is the extreme point of the "thou shalt not kill" and, in me, the fear of all the violence and usurpation that my existing, despite the innocence of its intentions, risks committing. The risk of occupying – from the moment of the *Da* of my *Dassein* – the place of an other and thus, on the concrete level, of exiling him, of condemning him to a miserable condition in some "third" or "fourth" world, of bringing him death. Thus an unlimited responsibility emerges in this fear for the other. (EN 169)[87]

To fear for the other in substitution means to be responsible even for the faults of others. In reading Job's encounter with God, Levinas tells us that after Job complains to God about his misfortune, God poses a question to Job: "Where were you when I founded the earth?" (CPP 184).[88] Levinas reads this exchange as one's responsibility for everything and everyone. He rhetorically asks whether this irreducible responsibility for, and solidarity with, creation is not the humanity of the human: "that is, [man] is responsible for what was neither one's self nor one's work, and if this solidarity and this responsibility for everything and for all, which cannot occur without pain, is the spirit itself?" (CPP 184). This irreducible responsibility signifies itself in politics in terms of *ahimsa* towards one's political enemy. Gandhi's political praxis and his ethical demands from *Satyagrahi* are relevant examples of what Levinas would want to signify here. For Gandhi, the fear of doing violence to the other occupies a crucial place in his ethicopolitics. In one sense, it is analogous to one's irreducible responsibility for the other's suffering. As such, for Gandhi it is imperative to transform these prohibitive commands into an affirmative engagement with alterity. For example, in the midst of India's struggle for independence from the British Empire, there were at least three incidents in which people, against Gandhi's appeal, became violent in their response to police brutality. The first occurred at Malegaon in April 1921 when a policeman and four constables were killed during a protest. Gandhi compared this violence to a "black particle floating in milk," took responsibility for his followers' violence, and did not hesitate to publicly announce his shame. In the second incident, in Bombay on 17 November 1921, many Parsi and Indian Christians were viciously attacked and killed as they took part in the welcoming of the arrival of the Prince of Wales to India. Gandhi immediately renounced the violence and confessed his responsibility: "I am more instrumental than any other in bringing into being the spirit of revolt."[89] He never hesitated in implicating himself in a deed that was not his own, to the point of blaming himself both in the public and in his subsequent court trials. In a public show of apology for the violence of his followers, Gandhi said:

> I cannot face again the appealing eyes of Parsi men and women that I saw as I passed through them. Nor can I face Andrews[90] when he returns from East Africa if we have done no reparation to the Indian Christians whom we are bound to protect as our own brothers and sisters ... I must do the utmost reparation to this handful of men and women who have been the victims of forces that have come into being largely through my instrumentality.[91]

The third incident of violence occurred in the Chauri Chaura riot of 4 February 1922, when Gandhi's followers killed twenty-one policemen. Instead of viewing these as necessary moments in the revolutionary struggle of his people, Gandhi saw himself as personally responsible, and called these violent events an "index finger pointing accusingly at him"[92] and at the non-cooperation movement in general. Gandhi, who at that time used the term "satanic" for the British Empire, immediately announced that those who fought with "Satanic means have no right to regard or describe the opponent as Satan."[93] Gandhi took responsibility for the fault of his followers not only in words but also in deeds, by fasting for days every time one of these violent events occurred. Although this shamed others for their violence, his fast was the result of a deeper belief: fasting, for Gandhi, was a protest as well as warning to his followers about the inhumanity and injustice in violence. But more than that, fasting was a concrete expression of the debt he felt for the victims and a concrete expression of expiation for the violence within the movement.

Levinas' comments about responsibility for one's persecutor, and Gandhi's approach to the political enemy, have been criticized for ignoring the question of justice. Gandhi was one of the few political leaders of a social movement who insisted explicitly on an ethical approach to one's political opponent – that *Satyagrahi* was responsible for the life and dignity of her enemy. This responsibility, he emphasized, did not start after the political victory over the enemy; rather, it began with *Satyagrahi*'s entry into the political struggle; substitution for the other must occur from relations almost unimaginable. He directly linked one's treatment of the political enemy to the outcome of that movement, and he insisted that the spirit of revolt not contradict the spirit of non-violence – that is, a liberatory movement does not become revolutionary through a greater degree of violence. He repeatedly emphasized that in liberatory struggles, if *Satyagrahi* shirked responsibility towards the enemy, if she adopted violence to annihilate the oppressor, then she was merely reproducing that against which she was fighting. If a revolution started and continued with violence, the violence would not stop after the political victory. It would continue, producing other enemies whose annihilation through violent means would become necessary to the movement's survival. Both Gandhi and Levinas saw the non-violent face-to-face encounter and the responsibility for an enemy as intrinsic parts of the work of justice: "Our religion is based on *ahimsa*, which in its active form is nothing but love, love not only to your neighbors, not only to your friends but love even to those who may be your enemies."[94] Justice can have no other meaning than non-violence towards the person(s) whom *Satyagrahi* fights. Gandhi would have absolutely agreed with Levinas' extreme saying that "to a certain extent (my God keep me from being reduced to it as a rule of daily usage) I am responsible for the other even when he bothers me, even when he persecutes me" (EN 106).

Gandhi's two strategies of passive, non-violent resistance to, and non-cooperation with, British colonial rule in India were concrete expressions of this ethical orientation in liberatory politics. For Gandhi, non-violent rebellion (civil disobedience) and passive resistance (non-cooperation) were two of the concrete liberatory praxes best suited to ethical peace; they allowed *Satyagrahi* to fight against injustice without reproducing the same cycle of violence.[95] Gandhi saw a continuation of the same imperial political order if India's liberatory movement resorted to the empire's own tactics. This, for Gandhi, would mean that India must arm itself against Britain, and for that India needed to become Europeanized. It had to accumulate capital, industrialize, and become a technological society – that is, become that against which it would fight.[96] Therefore, for both Gandhi and Levinas it was imperative to find an ethical path to peace and justice that transcended the purely political thinking of realpolitik.[97] Gandhi's non-violent resistance, translated into political praxis, meant non-cooperation (*swadeshi*) with the ruling power. This meant a refusal to cooperate with "evil" when one did not have the capacity to undo it through non-violent means.[98] Once in the political and social realm, if one cannot practise *Satyagraha*, one can always refuse the workings of power and violence.

Gandhi also advocated non-violent resistance and non-cooperation when face-to-face dialogue with the colonizers was not possible; this was aimed at pressing the British to resume their dialogue with the movement. Gandhi started his first great non-cooperation campaign against the British Empire on 1 August 1920. He travelled across the country urging people not to cooperate with the empire and its state. He even encouraged students not to go to the colleges and universities built and run by the British Empire. Gandhi hoped that through non-cooperation, Indians would dissipate the fear the British Empire provoked in them, that they would stop being fearful of the other even when this other possessed military power. He hoped that without shedding blood, Indians would come to realize that the empire and its system were no longer omnipotent. Through non-cooperation, and without violence, India's decolonization movement succeeded in paralysing the government and challenging its role and legitimacy.[99]

Conclusion

Through the concepts of *ahimsa* and *Satyagraha,* Gandhian political praxis addresses the central concern that Levinas raises repeatedly – to recall a more an-archic modality of peace and justice that is based on something beyond and more fundamental than individual rights and freedom, beyond the definitions articulated in the modern conception of the political. Levinas echoes Gandhi's ethical concern when he voices his own:

> But the European conscience is not at peace ... Thousands of years of political – and bloody – fratricidal wars, of imperialism in the guise of universality, of contempt for human beings and exploitation, including in this century, two world wars, oppression, genocides, the Holocaust, terrorism, unemployment, the never-ending poverty of the Third World, the ruthless doctrines of Fascism and National Socialism, and the supreme paradox in which the defense of the person is inverted into Stalinism ... A challenging by Europe itself of its philosophical privilege which was to guarantee its peace! (EN 191)

For both Gandhi and Levinas, a permanent peace cannot arise out of rational peace signed under the shadow of war. Such a peace assumes nothing beyond a totality under which individuals conduct commerce and political systems function in fear of one another. Ethical peace requires an eschatological vision that resists subsumption into the totality of war. Levinas' approach to the event of speech is one example of eschatological peace breaking the work of totality and its violence.

For both Levinas and Gandhi, it is imperative that sociality and politics be irreducible to people associating with one another based on their similarities or their differences. Sociality is initiated prior to all verbal expression, and in turn it conditions the possibility of speech; it starts from one's fear for the other's death. Responsibility, and only responsibility, contains the secret of sociality as "love of one's neighbor" (EN 169). For both, the principle of liberal pluralism, presented as an ethical solution to the problem of totality and inter-human relation, still holds the self-same as the point of comparison and relatedness. In pluralism, reason establishes points of comparison between humans so as to establish peace and justice (EN 190–1). As such, the irreducible alterity of the face of the other is reduced to a theme, a fixed, knowable identity merely different from the self, an abstraction that is recognizable and comprehensible by thought. For Levinas and Gandhi, however, difference, before its abstraction, signifies a singularity – the uniqueness and irreducible alterity of every human face. It is in the relation of facing this irreducibly singular other, and in one's ability to respond to her demand, that the individual and the social are signified. Thus, for Gandhi, non-violence is not private: "For me non-violence is something to be shunned if it is a private virtue. My concept of non-violence is universal ... We were born to prove that truth and non-violence are not just rules for personal conduct. They can become the policy of a group, a community, a nation."[100] So it is fair to say that for both Gandhi and Levinas the entry into the political is not through the laws of the political; their intervention into the political comes not from the ontology of war but from the laws of sociality – proximity, love, and substitution for the other's suffering.

Indeed, for Levinas, after the birth of consciousness, legal justice, and the state, it is still the saying, the infinite responsibility of one for the other, that haunts this totality and remains a surplus to it; it is this surplus that can transform this totality into an open-ended process. For Levinas, after the betrayal of the saying in the said, after the reduction of ethical justice to law and legality, one's non-allergic relation to the other still precedes all the abstractions involved in the institutionalization of justice. Although both Gandhi and Levinas use concepts such as justice, freedom, law, and equality, they insist that what has been lost in thematization is the locus where these concepts originate. Far from being the product of a consciousness, of a thought, or of a categorical imperative produced by universal reason, these concepts are signified in the order of the face-to-face relationship with another human being. Their origin is neither in the togetherness of equals nor in the peaceful, regulated coexistence of differences. Rather, these concepts come forth in the an-archical relation of a facing in which oneself is substituted for the other. Therefore the primordial plane of sociality is not the identity of one with the other, nor is it the similarities or commonalties we share, nor is it a unity towards a set goal. This means, as Levinas insists, that the institution of justice must create a possibility in which humanity can face the other and through which the other is enabled to actualize herself as unique and singular (LR 261). Gandhi attempts to bring the structure of this surplus into the political struggle, opening a different approach to, and a new vision of politics, justice, and liberation.

For Levinas and Gandhi, what makes the "I" a subject in the social is its substitution for the other's suffering and death, in proximity and affinity, a closeness that is never close enough to be fixed in a theme or a political regime. Substitution is the event in which the subject finds itself responding to, and responsible for, the suffering and the death of the other, without the prior cognitive or conscious requirement of finding a meaning for that suffering and death. What comes before the representation of suffering and its meaning making is the event of substitution – the other's suffering concerns me and, as such, I am uniquely and irreducibly responsible. For both Levinas and Gandhi, no other events in the experience of humanity can establish a just politics. In this sense, substitution is the event that transgresses the separation between ethics and politics. Without assimilating or reducing one into the other, substitution underscores that the individual is already born into a sensibility and non-indifference towards the injustice committed to the other.

Substitution presents a radical alternative to a notion of politics that demands justice only for those with whom the subject forms a community of the same. Without denying the significance of these identities – be it a nation, a community, a religion, a flag, or a concept such as liberty – substitution reveals the insufficiency of these categories for a just politics and for a lasting peace. Gandhi's political fasts to protect the most vulnerable, the marginalized, those who were deemed irrelevant in India's liberation, or even to protest against violence done to his oppressors, are just one example of this orientation. Another example is his lifelong struggle against India's caste system. Gandhi believed that inclusion in the structures of domination and oppression was a matter of degree and that no one stood outside of those structures. All Indians were implicated in this cycle, even those who were victims of the system. Amidst India's fight for independence against a more important enemy (the British Empire), Gandhi never ignored the dominatory practices and injustices in his own culture. He simultaneously opposed the British government, the Indian government, imperialism, and India's caste system.[101] He did not fight against the British Empire by insisting on a false sense of unity among Indians, ignoring the internal workings of domination and oppression. He did not allow the fight against a powerful enemy to distract *Satyagrahi* from unjust practices within his own community, nation, or culture. For him, there was no ethicopolitical prioritizing: the struggles against colonialism and Indian princes (and the caste system) had to go hand in hand. He knew that if the aim was political victory over British rule, India could have gained its independence years earlier. But he believed that a target of India's liberatory movement was also the annihilation of the internal workings of domination such as untouchability. While fighting against the British Empire, he repeatedly argued that *Swaraj* – home rule – was unattainable without complete compensation for all the oppression against untouchables, women, and religious minorities such as Muslims.[102] He insisted on the Hindus' one-way responsibility for non-violent engagement with the Muslim community. For example, he put his life seriously in danger when in September 1924 he went to the home of Mohammed Ali, an Indian Muslim, and conducted a twenty-one-day "great fast" as penance for communal rioting between Hindus and Muslims.

Despite decades of colonialism and British support of the caste system, Gandhi did not view the problem of untouchables as merely a by-product of external exploitation, nor did he see its maintenance as the result of systematic support of India's caste system by the British. Rather, he viewed the problem as intimately related to Hinduism and its internal hierarchy, and maintained that other faiths could render little help in this regard: "The removal of untouchability is purely a question of the purification of Hinduism. This can only be effected from within."[103] For Gandhi, the fight against untouchability was not just an abstract political and cultural problem, but an immediate ethicopolitical exigency for all Hindus – this responsibility had to be taken in a face-to-face situation, while being fought in the political realm. In 1915, against all the objections, Gandhi admitted an untouchable family to one of his *Satyagraha* ashrams, which were places of communal living that Gandhi had begun establishing after his return from South Africa. In fact, most of Gandhi's hunger strikes were not against British rule but against untouchability. Between 1932 and 1934, Gandhi observed five hunger strikes (some of them while in British jail) ranging from two to thirty days, to protest India's caste system. In 1933, while India's liberatory struggle was in full bloom, he began a ten-month tour of every province in India to help end untouchability – a journey that was viewed as a distraction by many of his comrades. He did not hesitate to give his life for the rights and freedom of the most marginalized and oppressed group among his own people.

Gandhi's substitution for the other has a close affinity with Levinas': both offer a decisive break with Western liberatory discourse insofar as they remind us that neither the struggle against injustice, nor the absence of unjust structures, is enough to form a just community.

Although unjust social, political, and economic structures always exist where justice is excluded, justice is not simply the absence of these unjust orders. Equally important are the order in which the ethicopolitical subjectivity is constituted and the means by which a liberatory struggle rises to eradicate the structures of domination and subjugation. As applied to liberatory movements, the event of substitution is Levinas' intervention into the praxis of social and political struggles. The agent of social change is not the one who, by shedding the false consciousness of her existence, finally realizes her own unfreedom and bondage. Neither is this agent the one who, through benevolence, identifies with the other's suffering and tries to alleviate that pain through charity. The agent of social change is an ethicopolitical subject who finds herself in substitution and who suffers for another with whom she may have nothing in common. Substitution, therefore, is the ethical condition of the possibility of a just radical praxis: "not to see the suffering of the world is not to bring this suffering to an end" (NTR 188). Gandhi also believed that in revolt, the ethicopolitical subject should take the burden of suffering on her own shoulders alone. For him, justice that is reduced to a fight for one's own rights and freedoms can after its realization maintain itself only through closure, exclusion, and violence against those who are left outside. Gandhi knew that a liberatory movement that is exclusively built on the demand for the freedom of its members first has to decide who can be defined as a member and who cannot, who is inside and who is outside, who is included and who is not. Throughout the long years of India's liberatory struggle, Gandhi's ethicopolitics obligated him to make decisions never taken by any other political leader-activist, decisions that defied dominant political thinking, especially that of the West – from the liberal to the most radical. For Gandhi, what was absent from all these theories of change was an ethical orientation, a claim on justice based on the rights and freedom of the other. In this, Gandhi was the political leader-activist who most closely adhered to Levinas' ethics.

For Gandhi, substituting for the other also entails not taking away humanity from oneself or from the other, even if that other is one's enemy. This ethical concern obligated him to articulate different strategies for a liberatory praxis, starting from negotiation, followed by self-suffering, and ultimately by non-violent direct action. Underlying all these strategies was an effort to encounter his enemy in a face–to-face situation where speech supersedes violent political action.[104] As difficult as it may have been, Gandhi tried to take every political step, such as civil disobedience, non-violent rebellion, and non-cooperation as though he had an interlocutor, and tried to change his enemy's heart rather than seize power. For Gandhi, a non-violent struggle was the only way that a social movement could stand up to its own radical potentials, breaking the power of empire without itself being caught in its power dynamics, and creating an alternative to the empire's power structure without being merely a reaction to it. Therefore he waged a non-violent war against the colonizing power. He adopted a political praxis corresponding to this aim – namely, ongoing nationwide *Satyagraha* campaigns of mass civil disobedience. Thus in both strategies of non-violent rebellion (civil disobedience) and passive resistance (non-cooperation), Gandhi felt deeply responsible for the lives and dignity of those against whom he waged war. This responsibility expressed itself in his refusal to use violence against his political enemy. Although winning India's independence was Gandhi's lifelong commitment, he was always adamant that this independence could not be sustained by humiliating, harming, or annihilating his opponents. So he took every occasion to remind the Indian people that "it is often forgotten that it is never the intention of a *Satyagrahi* to embarrass the wrongdoer."[105] Gandhi believed that the one who finds himself in proximity adapts a non-violent rebellion against injustice, and Levinas argues that the state and its institutions must be inaugurated out of proximity. Levinas would have agreed with Gandhi, who insisted that non-violence be the overriding principle of liberation. Levinas would add that "justice is not a legality regulating human masses, from which a technique of social equilibrium is drawn, harmonizing antagonistic forces. That would be a justification of the State delivered over to its own necessities. Justice is impossible without the one that renders it finding himself in proximity" (OB 159). Gandhi would have added that only non-violence can fulfil this promise.

Conclusion

Politics left to itself bears a tyranny within itself.

Levinas, TI 300

Emmanuel Levinas, writing during and after the cruelest and bloodiest war of the twentieth century, developed a vision of ethical relation that places sensibility at the heart of an ethical subject. I suggest that an important aspect of this sensibility is the radical immediacy it establishes in the political, and its conception of justice.

Levinas, in the span of almost fifty years of writing, may have occasionally lent his support to the liberal state, yet he quite clearly understood that a political approach to liberation, freedom, peace, and justice needs to be informed by a vision beyond the one offered by Western liberalism. This vision takes the radical openness to the suffering other as the ground for one's irreducible responsibility, which must be concretized in a sociality informed by a curvature of social space – that is, the asymmetrical relationship between the subject and the other.

Suffering for the other – substitution – presupposes a radical passivity at the heart of the subject. In chapter 2, I discussed Levinas' phenomenological approach, which signifies the subject as the incarnation of two uneasy moments – on the one hand, primordial sensibility to the suffering of the other, and on the other, responsibility for the other's (in) justice. Radical passivity presupposes an interiority that is much more fundamental and primordial than the one imagined in the concepts of autonomy and individualism. This interiority does not point at that which can later be called the essence of being; more important, it does not foreclose the subject to the outside. Rather, it exposes the other at the heart of the subject and reveals the intrigue of the other in me. This interiority is the unique inscription that the other's suffering leaves in me. Levinas puts it as follows: "this suffering *in me* is so radically mine that it cannot become the subject of my preaching. It is as suffering *in me* and not as suffering in general that welcomes suffering [of the other]" (EN 241n5). Although this inscription signifies the subject as a trauma and a hostage, it does not paralyse nor does it lock the subject into an eternal existential crisis. Levinas sees this inscription as a positivity, as an affirmation, and as the event of sociality.

This conception of subjectivity holds the social not as the amalgamation of autonomous and equal individuals who form a collectivity in order to conduct reciprocal commerce, nor as a plurality fighting to establish its freedom against another freedom. Nor is it the association of equal friends in pursuit of a higher truth. The social engenders itself in the approach of the face whose suffering has already conditioned the corporeal interiority of the subject. As such, the social is already an unequal space; sociality is my radical exposure and vulnerability to the other whose approach I cannot escape and whose demand I cannot ignore. The social is a curved space marked by the asymmetrical relationship between me and the other. Even the arrival of the third and her demand for equality does not disrupt the asymmetry; even in a society of equals, the social bond is marked by asymmetry. Hence Levinas reminds us that "we" is not "the plural of I" (CPP 43). As such, justice as equalization points at only one dimension of justice – formal justice. As important as this justice is, Levinas insists that formal justice cannot sustain or affirm the uniqueness and singularity of the other. In contrast to most readers of Levinas, who see the third as an abandonment of ethical relation in the political, I suggest that the third embodies the demand for an equality that does not negate the asymmetry of the social; formal equality is already enveloped in a relation of height. As Robert Gibbs reminds us in *Correlations*, "the equalization of the other with me occurs by reference to the third, for whose sake we must both serve" (234).

The third is a significant moment in Levinas' ethical relation, and in its relevance to a radical conception of the political. Is not the entry of the third the ultimate saying in the said – one that simultaneously demands equality and asymmetry? And is not her demand for justice accompanied by a prohibition of violence? The third does not imply the abandonment of my irreducible responsibility for the other and all others. Rather, the third raises the question of one's responsibility to defend the other in the face of injustice; and in this way, she brings up the possibility of both violence and its prohibition at the same time. This is to say, both commands – to defend the other and to not commit violence – are carried into the sociopolitical order as the ethical demand of the face. In short, the political order of justice cannot be reduced to the work of formal, universal justice. Sometimes it seems that Levinas reduces his notion of justice to that of formal justice – to the universal equality of human freedoms and rights in liberal democracy. Other times, he seems to be suggesting it is a deepening, or radicalization, of the liberal regime. Yet this is a reductionist reading of Levinas. Ethical justice from the beginning proclaims the irreducibility of the human to a genre or a species, and its aspiration is to free humans from all categories (EN 6–9). Within ethical justice lie two intrinsically linked dimensions – the first, non-indifference to the suffering and death of others, and the second, the demand to "repair the world" (HO xxxvii). As such, even when the uniqueness of the face must in some context be covered and reduced to a notion of "universal equality of all men," it must simultaneously unmask the violence that underpins this reduction. Therefore at some level, the former notion of justice denounces the latter's violence without abolishing its work totally.

Moreover, justice as equalization exists so that "we" serve a third who commands "us" from height. That is to say, I and you may become equal, but "we" are not equal to the third: asymmetry never leaves sociality. Levinas, until the end, kept his reservation about the ability of liberal society to accommodate, despite its formal and legal equality, the ethics of the asymmetrical relationship.[1] He alludes succinctly to what I have been discussing so far:

> Modern antihumanism, which denies the primacy that the human person, free and for itself, would have for the signification of being, is true over and beyond the reason it gives itself. It clears the place for subjectivity positing itself in abnegation, in sacrifice, in a substitution which precedes the will. Its inspired intuition is to have abandoned the idea of person, goal and origin of itself, in which the ego is still a thing because it is still a being. Strictly speaking, the other is the end; I am a hostage, a responsibility and a substitution supporting the world in the passivity of assignation, even in an accusing persecution, which is undeclinable. Humanism has to be denounced only because it is not sufficiently human. (OB 127–8)

When the state enters into the political through the primordial "law" of ethicosociality, it becomes subordinated to its social promise: the state exists to create the possibility for a human to see the face of the other. We can only begin to think about the legitimacy of the state in terms of the relation to the face before me. So Levinas contrasts two visions of the state as follows: "whereas, in Hobbes's vision – in which the state emerges not from the limitation of charity, but from the limitation of violence – one cannot set a limit on the state" (EN 105). Since Machiavelli and Hobbes, political power has become the glue that unifies us amidst violent freedoms; the spectre of violence becomes that which organizes and manages the social and the political. Every effort thereafter is merely an attempt to distribute political power and its violence equally among different spheres in order to reach a state of equilibrium. As such, the difference between the liberal regime and the original conception of Leviathan is found in the extent to which this political beast, which originally came to limit the violence of each against all, can itself be restrained from below. Levinas' suggestion that the political must arise out of the substitution of one-for-the-other is therefore not just a deepening of liberal politics, but a proposition that the political is the human endeavour that attempts to fulfil the demand of justice for the other in a way that embodies the exceptional place of the face and that establishes a non-allergic relation between the self and the other – ethical justice.

Substitution not only is the ground of the political but also informs political praxis in its quest for ethical justice. This vision of justice is realized in substituting praxis, which cannot be taken as some form of an internal dialogue that is supposed to make a radical transformation in the subject's constitution. Substituting praxis is expressed in one's non-indifference and rebellion against injustice – to repair the world – for a time that may not be the time of my ego. Here lie the fundamental limits of social struggle in Western progressive discourse – even in its most radical forms in which anti-racist, anti-sexist, and anti-imperialist agendas are added to its platform. These movements may deliver more freedom and rights to their constituencies, and they may announce an end to economic exploitation and violence as their ethos, yet they still fall short of accomplishing liberation as it is imagined in the notion of ethical justice. Despite its success in guaranteeing and advancing the freedom and rights of individuals, the ethos of this form of social struggle is still invested in the virility of an autonomous agent who is unable to take a critical distance from the imperialism of his virility, for it owes its very achievements to this imperialism. This imperialism forecloses the non-reciprocal responsibility of one for the other because to embody such an orientation it must renounce that same imperialism. This form of social struggle can only explain its responsibility to the other insofar as obligation relates back to one of the constitutive elements of its own ego – be it to the ego's time, to its alter-ego, to class solidarity, or to its hope of salvation. The appeal of ethical justice cannot be addressed to one's consciousness, but only to something much older and more primordial than the ego of the individual. This task involves an undoing of one's relation to time and its colonizing economy, so as to fight for the other without making her into a totality. Moreover, speaking concretely, this imperialism is complicit with the imperialistic spirit that steers the work of global exploitation, of political violence, and of fixing economic poverty as the permanent face of the alterity of the other. Ethical praxis demands a substituting praxis, which begins its defence of the other human by struggling against the injustices of global economic exploitation and to end political violence. Both Levinas and Gandhi share this vision.

Levinas and Gandhi share and imagine the ethicopolitical subject as one who is substituted for the other in the radical passivity of her exposure to the suffering of the other. Imagining the radical subject of social change on this ground does not merely take away the imperialistic edge of the subject, whose pathos of social change is rooted in extending its own same-self to the rest of the world; it also means that this subject approaches the political from the law of sociality – ethical love – and adopts non-violent rebellion against injustice. Gandhi's ethical approach to liberatory politics forces him, literally against all odds, to find alternative political strategies such as civil disobedience and non-cooperation, which correspond to the ethical order from which his politics is issued. As such, his liberatory praxis aims at finding an interlocutor in his political opponent.

The traces of Levinas' ethicopolitics can be seen in Gandhi's political rebellion and in his simultaneously non-violent and revolutionary, patient and demanding, praxis. This notion of liberation has been made possible by holding on to an eschatological vision of peace whose laws of love and substitution resist disappearing into power politics. Gandhi's political praxis can help us understand the relevancy of Levinas' ethics of one-for-the-other for the radical politics of liberation – it is a praxis that keeps Levinas' ethics from being reduced to an individual virtue or collective charity and that enables us to see his ethicopolitics as the ground for a radical collective mobilization.

Notes

Introduction

1 Levinas, *Difficult Freedom*. Hereafter cited as DF.
2 Throughout, I will use "agent of social change," "radical-political subject(ivity)," "the subject of political struggle," "the subjectivity of revolt," and "the subject in revolt" interchangeably.
3 For studies on Levinas' ethics and politics, see, among others, Caygill, *Levinas and the Political*; Simmons, *An-Archy and Justice*; Cohen, "'Political Monotheism'"; Alford, "Levinas and Political Theory"; Dussel, *Philosophy of Liberation*; Gibbs, *Correlations in Rosenzweig and Levinas*; Horowitz and Horowitz, *Difficult Justice*; Bergo, *Levinas between Ethics and Politics*; Critchley, "Five Problems."
4 See Horkheimer and Adorno, *Dialectic of Enlightenment*, 118–19. Hereafter cited as DE.
5 I will elaborate on this theme in chapters 2 and 3.
6 I am using the concept of humanity with an awareness of its exclusionary history. I continue using the concept as a rhetorical strategy, but also in a modified sense – one that is open-ended and fluid and that is not reducible to notions of rights and freedoms. This modified version of the concept also acknowledges that the natural world is not there to sustain humans; rather, it is an essential constitutive modality of humanity itself.
7 Levinas uses the male pronoun in his writings. To avoid the constant use of he/she, I have chosen to use "she" wherever I discuss the subject, the other, and the third.
8 Dignity is meant to convey the human ability to free itself from what has been, from everything that links it or engages it with something. See Levinas, "Reflections." Hereafter cited as RPH. See, in particular, page 66.

9 To simplify access to Levinas' work, I will be citing him in the text. All other citations are written as endnotes.

10 Here, I have borrowed Asher Horowitz's elaboration of this theme in "Beyond Rational Peace." For Levinas' discussion of this theme (the logic of betrayal), see, in particular, OB, 37–51; 153–62.

11 *Ahimsa*, literally, means non-violence, and *Satyagraha* represents the force that is born of truth and love or non-violence. In chapter 4, I will elaborate on these two concepts.

1. Levinas' Ethicopolitics

1 For religious, philosophical readings of Levinas, see Cohen, *Elevations*; and Handelman, *Fragments of Redemption*. For excellent phenomenological works on Levinas, see Libertson, *Proximity*; Peperzak, *Beyond*; and Manning, *Interpreting Otherwise Than Heidegger*. For the question of the status of ethics in relation to deconstruction, see Derrida's articles on Levinas, "Violence and Metaphysics" in *Writing and Difference*; and "At This Moment in This Work Here I Am," in *Re-Reading Levinas*. Derrida later revises some of his positions in "Violence and Metaphysics" in his extensive engagement with Levinas in *Adieu to Emmanuel Levinas*. For feminist engagements with Levinas, see Chanter, *Feminist Interpretations of Emmanuel Levinas*; and Sandford, *The Metaphysics of Love*.

2 See Caygill, *Levinas and the Political*; and Simmons, *An-Archy and Justice*.

3 Authors who read Levinas along the line of liberal politics include Cohen, "'Political Monotheism'"; Alford, "Levinas and Political Theory"; Simmons, *An-Archy and Justice* and "The Third"; and Susan A. Handelman, *Fragments of Redemption*.

4 Caygill reads Levinas from the left tradition and does offer new insights where Levinas' politics is at its most difficult juncture, such as his response to the Israeli–Palestinian situation. However, Caygill founds his interpretation of Levinas' thought almost entirely on his reading of Levinas' stance towards Zionism, interpreting Zionism as the hidden politics of Levinas' ethics (see chapters 3 and 5 in particular). According to Caygill, Levinas' political responses to the Israeli–Palestinian situation both contravene his ethical philosophy and follow from it; the distinction between the "other" and the "third" as well as Levinas' commitment to Judeo-Christian monotheism give rise to racist tendencies. I believe that by adopting this orientation, Caygill misses the chance to engage productively with the difficult relationship between ethics and politics, and the promises it holds, in Levinas' thought. But more problematically, this has resulted in a serious

misreading of Levinas' central concepts such as his critique of identity as essence (see ch. 2), peace of eschatology (see ch. 3), and the other and the third in Levinas (see ch. 4). I will treat these issues – in particular, Caygill's treatment of the other and the third – later in the book.

5 See, for example, Rorty, *Achieving Our Country;* Bernstein, "Evil and the Temptation of Theodicy"; and Putnam, *Ethics beyond Ontology.*

6 For notable exceptions, see Dussel, *Philosophy of Liberation;* and Gibbs, *Correlations in Rosenzweig and Levinas.* In chapter 10, "Marx and Levinas: Liberation in Society," Gibbs explores the intersection of Levinas' ethics and Marx's political economy to underscore the place of economic justice in Levinas' ethical relation. See also excellent essays in Horowitz and Horowitz, *Difficult Justice.*

7 Levinas, "Philosophy, Justice and Love," in *Entre Nous: Thinking-of-the-Other.* Hereafter cited as EN.

8 Badiou, *Ethics.*

9 Ibid., 10–34.

10 Spivak, "French Feminism Revisited," 77. Recently, however, Spivak has become more open to Levinas' ethical relation and has implicitly acknowledged, although cautiously, his relevance to pressing political issues. See, for example, her article, "Righting Wrongs."

11 Hereafter cited as TI.

12 Bernasconi, "Different Styles of Eschatology," 7.

13 Ibid., 7.

14 Ibid., 6.

15 Levinas, *Time and the Other.* Hereafter cited as TO.

16 For an insightful discussion of these categories, see Bernasconi, "Strangers and Slaves." For an application of this reading see, for example, Shannon Bell, "Levinas and Alterity Politics." Using Levinas' category of the "stranger," Bell treats this category as the principle of fluidity and openness. She discusses the ethical responsibility for the sexual outcast who is a stranger in an Oedipalized regime.

17 Levinas, "Freedom and Command," in *Collected Philosophical Papers.* Hereafter CPP.

18 A cursory reading of Derrida's text may interpret "undecidability" as inability to decide. However, as Derrida explains in several of his interviews, "undecidability" connotes fear and trembling at the time of decision making. For example, see "Hospitality, Justice, and Responsibility."

19 Levinas, "Peace and Proximity," in *Basic Philosophical Writings.* Hereafter BPW.

20 Levinas, "No Identity."

21 Levinas, *Otherwise Than Being or Beyond Essence.* Hereafter OB.
22 I will elaborate on this theme in chapter 2.
23 Levinas, "Useless Suffering."
24 Levinas signifies the ethical implication of this inward journey by the term "oneself," which is one-for-the-other in radical passivity. I will elaborate on this in chapter 2.
25 Horowitz, "Beyond Rational Peace."
26 Ibid., 33–4.
27 For such an argument see Cohen, "'Political Monotheism.'" Cohen's liberal reading of Levinas will be discussed below. An exception to this line of argument is Miguel Abensour's insightful approach in "An-archy," wherein he reads Levinasian ethics as an-archy that provokes the disturbance of politics. For Abensour, the political, far from proceeding from the limitation of violence, is born of the limitation of an-archy (proximity, substitution, radical passivity, one-for-the-other).
28 Horowitz, "Beyond Rational Peace," 30.
29 Ibid., 31.
30 Ibid., 31–4.
31 Ibid., 36; cited from OB, section 4, subsection b.
32 Ibid., 35.
33 Ibid., 39.
34 Ibid., 39–41.
35 It is here that I see the limits of works by Levinasian scholars who read the role of ethics as "anarchical disturbance" of the political (see Abensour's "An-archy" and Critchley's "Five Problems"). Reading Levinasian ethics as a disturbance of the political misses a deeper pre-originary tension between ethics and politics, which Levinas' work reveals. That is, the tension is marked by the debt of politics to ethics for its betrayal of ethical relation, a tension that calls for the political to be responsive, and responsible to the call of the ethical.
36 For such a reading of the "third," see, for example, Paul W. Simmons, "The Third"; Robert J.S. Manning, *Beyond Ethics;* Adriaan Peperzak, *To the Other,* 181; Jacques Derrida, *Adieu,* 63. Even Annabel Herzog, despite her radical reading of Levinas' ethicopolitics, stays within this dominant reading of the "third": see Herzog, "Is Liberalism 'All We Need'?," 209.
37 Levinas, *Is It Righteous to Be?,* 205. Hereafter IRB.
38 Caygill's *Levinas and the Political* (ch. 4) is one example of this approach. Caygill argues that because the other is singular, the third cannot be an other (p. 131). The "I" can ally itself with the other but not the third. The "I"'s responsibility to the third is delegated through the other's

responsibility to the third as an other. This, according to Caygill, rules out the possibility of an alliance between the "I" and the "third" against the "other" (p. 133). This misreading stems from Caygill's understanding of Levinas' proximity as a relation of identity so that the other who is closer to me in identity cannot be passed by in the name of the "third." Consequently, according to Caygill, Levinas potentially justifies the worst form of the state (read Israel) in the name of the other.

39 See Kant, *The Metaphysics of Morals*, 58.

40 Abensour offers the same reading in his article "An-archy."

41 Levinas, "Difficult Freedom," in *The Levinas Reader*. Hereafter LR. This essay is one of few places where Levinas is most explicit in his approach to the political.

42 Robert Gibbs, *Correlations in Rosenzweig and Levinas*. Hereafter CRL.

43 CRL, 229.

44 Horowitz, "Beyond Rational Peace," 31.

45 Unfortunately, not many Levinasian scholars have paid enough attention to the two significations of justice in Levinas. For example, Abensour in "An-archy" envisions an an-archic disturbance of politics by proximity, substitution, speech, and the responsibility of one-for-the-other. Yet he still offers a unified notion of justice in Levinas and hence interprets it as that which is ensued with the appearance of the "third" (see 15–16).

46 Levinas, *Beyond the Verse*. Hereafter BV.

47 Levinas, *Humanism of the Other*. Hereafter HO.

48 Levinas, "The Ego and the Totality."

49 See Critchley, *Ethics, Politics, Subjectivity;* and Manning, *Beyond Ethics*.

50 Ibid., 117–18.

51 For exceptions to this dominant reading, see Gibbs, *Correlations in Rosenzweig and Levinas*. In chapter 10, "Marx and Levinas: Liberation in Society," Gibbs provide a different approach to Levinas' third and explores its significance for a conception of liberation as a non-private affair (see 229–34). See also Dussel, *Philosophy of Liberation*; and Herzog, "Is Liberalism 'All We Need'?"; and Horowitz and Horowitz, "Is Liberalism All We Need? Prelude via Fascism."

52 For an extremely insightful reading of this essay, see Horowitz and Horowitz, "Is Liberalism All We Need?"

53 The history of worker's unions in Western democracies, their gradual transformation from organized sources of liberatory struggles to bureaucratic machines concerned mainly with negotiating their members' rights and privileges, is but one example of Levinas' insightful criticism of Marxism. Here, the point is not to deny the importance of labour unions

in protecting workers against inhuman capitalist labour laws, but to draw attention to this regressing process in the history of workers' unions. Recently in North America, especially in Canada, unions are aligning themselves with broader struggles on a variety of social justice issues. On the other hand, throughout Europe and North America, unions are still hostile and exclusionary when it comes to "guest workers," or "foreign workers," such as Turkish workers in Germany.

54 See Cohen, *Ethics*, 10; Cohen, "'Political Monotheism.'"
55 Cohen, *Ethics*, 10; Cohen, "'Political Monotheism,'" 3–4.
56 Ibid., 1.
57 Levinas, "Transcendence and Height."
58 Cohen, "'Political Monotheism,'" 7.
59 See Cohen, *Ethics*, 10–24, 271–82.
60 Cohen, "'Political Monotheism,'" 11.
61 No authors have so far made use of Levinas' radical passivity as a central investigative theme in discussing the relation between his ethics and politics. All discussions on Levinas' radical passivity and its relation to politics are cursory. For example, see Ciaramelli, "Levinas' Ethical Discourse." Comprehensive works that engage with the concept of radical passivity in Levinas are mostly in the fields of phenomenology, communication, and literature: see Libertson's *Proximity*. For an appreciation of Levinas' radical passivity in literary theory, see Wall's *Radical Passivity*.
62 Cohen, "'Political Monotheism,'" 35.
63 Ibid., 43.
64 Here I am using Walter Benjamin's notions of law-making, law preserving, and divine violence discussed in "Critique of Violence."
65 Ibid., 284–300.
66 Ibid., 288.
67 Levinas, "Judaism and Revolution," in *Nine Talmudic Readings*. Hereafter NTR.
68 See, for example, Atterton, "In Defense of Violence."
69 Two points have to be made briefly: First, for Levinas the issue of violence is a matter of degree. There is an ethical difference between thematizing the other in language, for example, and being indifferent to the other's suffering. And both are very different from killing the other. I will elaborate on this issue later in my thesis. Second, Levinas does not equate ontology with violence, but rather sees the entrapment in ontology, without an opening to transcendence, as potential ground for violence.
70 This "other," according to Peter Atterton, has been omitted in Lingis's translation. This omission holds an important signification, since, as I will

be arguing on Levinas and non-violent political struggle, it refers to the "other" of the West and the importance of radical but peaceful means to overcome violence. See Atterton, "In Defense of Violence."

71 See my discussion of this concept in the fourth section of this chapter. Briefly, created and fundamental freedom signifies the absolute separation between the self and the other, which makes possible both disengagement and non-reciprocal relation with the other.

72 Levinas states: "The soul's detachment is not an abstract state; it is the concrete and positive power to become detached and abstract" (RPH, 66).

73 Levinas, "Damages Due to Fire."

74 Cohen, *Ethics*, 14.

75 Ibid.

76 Gibbs, *Correlations in Rosenzweig and Levinas*, 229–30.

77 See, for example, Cohen, *Ethics*, 10–11, and Cohen, "'Political Monotheism,'" 11–12.

78 Herzog, "Is Liberalism 'All We Need'?" See, in particular, 219–23.

79 Marx, "Critique of the Gotha Program," 531.

80 Horowitz, "Beyond Rational Peace," 31–4.

81 Ibid., 37–9.

2. Radical Passivity, the Face, and the Social Demand for Justice

1 For example, see Ciaramelli, "Levinas' Ethical Discourse."

2 See Drabinski, *Sensibility and Singularity*.

3 For an insightful phenomenological investigation of Levinas' radical passivity and communication, see Libertson, *Proximity*; in literature, see Wall, *Radical Passivity*. See also MacAvoy, "The Other Side of Intentionality."

4 Bernasconi, "What Is the Question," esp. 238–9.

5 Levinas, "Philosophy and the Idea of Infinity."

6 Levinas develops this idea most lucidly in OB, especially in ch. 4, section II, "Recurrence," 102–9.

7 Here, by totalization I mean a dimension that constructs subjectivity as closure.

8 By distinguishing between the other and its alterity, I want to point to the inevitable process of thematization and appropriation of the other – the other can be thematized, but her alterity is always a saying, beyond the said: an inspiration.

9 Critchley, *Ethics*, 65.

10 Bernasconi, "What Is the Question," 238–9.

11 These themes will be elaborated in ch. 3.

12 In ch. 3, I elaborate on the significance of diachrony for a radical political praxis.

13 But from the outset one must be aware of the irreducibility of this moment to identity and ontology. This instant is not reducible to womanhood, to motherhood, or to the female sexed body; rather, it signifies a structure of an openness and a vulnerability at the heart of creation, which is Goodness itself.

14 Levinas, "Damage Due to Fire," esp. 181–3.

15 Irigaray, *Je, Tu, Nous*, 38.

16 Ibid., 40–1.

17 There are many problems with Irigaray's approach to Levinas' ethics that cannot be addressed here. For an insightful elaboration of Irigaray's relationship to Levinas, see Chanter, *Ethics of Eros* and *Feminist Interpretations of Emmanuel Levinas*.

18 I will return to the issue of violence and political praxis in chs. 3 and 4.

19 Waldenfels, "Levinas and the Face of the Other," esp. 71–2.

20 Here I use "poverty" in a phenomenological sense, beyond its cultural-economic meaning, as fragility and nakedness.

21 Hereafter PM.

22 Although a diversion, it is important to note that Levinas' saying that "expression invites one to speak to someone" cannot be reduced to the act of communication. Expression of the face, and its non-assumability, cannot be reduced to either the source of communication or to the incessant flight of the signified from its signifier. Although both these moments refer to something beyond their own horizons, they still fall short of signifying the expression of the face beyond the power of intentionality and totalization. In dialogue, the power inscribed in the reciprocity among interlocutors who, in agreement or disagreement, are present to one another, still attests to the workings of the structure of intentionality. Here I am referring to Libertson's *Proximity*. Although Libertson's insightful exposition of Levinas' notions of proximity, power, and alterity has influenced my own work, I differ with the implications of his inquiry in few important places, one of which is the centrality of communication, parole, in the engagement of the self with alterity, which, according to Libertson, gives rise to subjectivity. I am suggesting that what underlies communication and parole is the saying of the demand for justice giving rise to the subject in communication with and for the other. Therefore, prior to two interlocutors in communication with each other, prior to my verbal response to the other's invitation, there is the involuntary sensibility and vulnerability of contact

in proximity: "the act of speaking is the passivity in passivity" (OB, 92). Moreover, in the infinite withdrawal of the signified from that which stands as signification of it, one still deals with a structure of purposive movement – albeit a displaced one. This structure does not break from the constitutive correlation and the grip of power; instead, it is the signified that is invested with the higher power enabling it to escape/evade/elude the signifier's attempt to thematize it into a fixed meaning (OB, 48–9). In other words, the withdrawal of the signified from appropriation by a signifier is attributed to its higher power, and not to the weight of its proximity in separation (and here, I am referring to one of Levinas' central criticisms of Derrida. See OB, 5). Rather than attributing this withdrawal to the passivity intrinsic to the expression of the face, this structure is still caught within the play of power in signification – between the signifier and the signified. Having said that, it is important to note that both moments bear the mark of a subjectivity who, prior to signification and communication, had been inspired by the invitation that comes from the expression of the face. The reason I made this diversion is to insist that the expression, beyond being merely an invitation to respond in communication, is about one's passive exposure to, and responsibility for, the suffering and death of the other. This is an important moment for the idea of an ethicopolitical subjectivity that enters into communication with someone who is already constructed as its opponents. Levinas' approach helps us see that communication, beyond reaching a consensus with the other, is already about the impossibility of ignoring the expression of the other's face; it is about that which reminds us of the pre-originary peace between me and the other.

23 Critchley, "Introduction," 16.

24 Derrida, "Hospitality, Justice, and Responsibility," 71.

25 Benjamin, "Analogy and Relationship."

26 Ibid., 207.

27 See, for example, TI, section III, "Exteriority and the Face."

28 Howard Caygill in *Levinas and the Political*, ch. 4, rightly points out that Levinas' aim to derive human rights from alterity means to look at rights not appositionally, as traditional political theory does, but from freedom as responsibility,

3. Substituting Praxis and Political Liberation

1 Maloney, "Levinas, Substitution, and Transcendental Subjectivity."

2 Ibid., 52.

3 Ibid., 58.

4 Ibid., 53.
5 Bernasconi, "What Is the Question."
6 Ibid., 235.
7 Ibid.
8 Ibid., 245.
9 Ibid., 250.
10 Ibid.
11 Ibid., 241.
12 Ibid., 248.
13 Ibid.
14 Ibid.
15 Ibid.
16 Ibid., 250.
17 Bernasconi, "The Ethics of Suspicion."
18 Ibid., 17n8; italics added.
19 Bernasconi, "What Is the Question," 249.
20 Critchley, Introduction, in *The Cambridge Companion to Levinas,* 18. It must be noted, however, that Critchley limits this application to Derridian deconstruction.
21 Bernasconi, "What Is the Question," 238–9.
22 Levinas, "Ideology and Idealism."
23 Levinas, "The Temptation of Temptation."
24 For Levinas' allusion to these two concepts, see, for example, "No Identity" and "Meaning and Sense," in CPP; OB, 31–4; TI, 220–47.
25 Levinas, "No Identity."
26 Levinas, "Meaning and Sense."
27 See, for example, TO, 39–42.
28 Horkheimer and Adorno, *Dialectic of Enlightenment*, 44–5.
29 Levinas, "Philosophy, Justice, and Love."
30 For examples of this take on Levinas' notion of the "third," see note 34 in chapter 1 of this book.
31 See, for example, Bernasconi, "The Third Party," 77.
32 Bernasconi, "What Is the Question," 240. Yet Bernasconi limits his insight to a question of individual responsibility rather than expanding it to a social–political scene.
33 Atterton, "In Defense of Violence," 3.
34 Ibid., 16.
35 Ibid.
36 I do not intend to go into the details of this interview. Suffice it to say that, contrary to some readings, Levinas not only does not deny the face

of Palestinians but also closes his comments by indirectly condemning killing in the name of homeland, saying that "a person is more holy than a land, even a holy land" (LR, 297). Yet Levinas has been criticized for his disturbing one-sided defence of the State of Israel and for his inability to extend the implications of his own ethics to the Israel–Palestine conflict. In this context, Bernasconi, for example, criticizes Levinas for his "simplistic image of messianism" and for privileging Zionism. For more discussion on this issue, see Bernasconi, "Different Styles of Eschatology: Derrida's Take on Levinas' Political Messianism" and "Who Is My Neighbor?" Other scholars, such as Caygill, read Levinas' work almost entirely in light of a perceived relationship to Zionism and his comment on Israel–Palestine (see Caygill, *Levinas and Political*). Simon Critchley, although offering a more generous reading of Levinas' comment on Palestine–Israel, still, like Caygill, views his comment as seriously compromising his ethics (see "Five Problems").

4. Levinas and Gandhi

1 Gandhi, *Selected Writings of Mahatma Gandhi*, 52. Hereafter SWMG.

2 Gandhi emerged as the leading voice of the National Congress Party in 1920 because he proposed a non-violent protest against the British Raj. From 1920 to 1948, the time of his assassination by a Hindu extremist, he was the voice of India's non-violent struggle against colonialism. The people of India gave the title Mahatma (Great Soul/Self) to Gandhi. He very much disliked the title because he was reluctant to be deified. Against all his protest, Indians continue to call him Mahatma, and recently the Library of Congress has listed him under "Gandhi, Mahatma."

3 Gandhi first started using "passive resistance" during his early campaign in South Africa, but later replaced that term with "non-violent resistance" in order to avoid equating the concept with weakness, and to break away from the passive–active dichotomy. Over time he also realized the need to underscore the significance of the non-violent aspect of the resistance (see Gandhi, *Moral and Political Writings of Mahatma Gandhi*, hereafter MPWG). It clearly demonstrates that the Gandhian notion of passivity is interchangeable with non-violent struggle. In a letter to Madame Edmond Privat, he wrote: "I see that you have grasped the fundamental difference between passive resistance and non-violent resistance. Resistance both forms are, but you have to pay a very heavy price when your resistance is passive, in the sense of the weakness of the resister. Europe mistook the bold and brave resistance full of wisdom by Jesus of Nazareth for passive

resistance, as if it was of the weak ... I detected no passivity, no weakness about Jesus as depicted in the four gospels" (MPWG, 25–6).

4 *Satyagrahi* is the subject-agent who spends his or her life in *Satyagraha,* which is a firm responsibility to non-violent resistance and/or rebellion against injustice.

5 MPWG, 2.

6 Ibid.

7 One important reason for such a lack, according to Douglas Allen, is that Gandhi's religious and philosophical assumptions are viewed in the West as contradictory, pre-modern, and sometimes even reactionary for the modern realities of life, and therefore as irrelevant to contemporary political thinking. But Allen, among others, argues that the Gandhian critique of the modern subject, of the self–other relation, and of Western-style politics is still highly relevant and holds radical potential for the present and the future. See Allen, "Gandhi, Contemporary Political Thinking."

8 Douglas Allen argues that there is no single true and authentic political thought that can be attributed to Gandhi. In fact, he argues that there are diverse and contradictory Gandhian positions on many political issues. This is because Gandhi focused on political practice and paid little attention to formulating a coherent, systematic political theory. Ibid.

9 Two such works are Ram-Prasad, "Non-Violence and the Other," and Giri, *Conversations and Transformations.*

10 Another reason may be Gandhi's position on the Holocaust in Nazi Germany and on the conflict between Israel and Palestine. In a well-known letter, Gandhi encouraged German Jews to adopt a non-violent resistance against Hitler. Later, in his widely circulated editorial in *Harijan,* Gandhi supported the Arabs' claim to the land in Palestine. While he sympathized with the Jewish cause, stating that "I do believe that the Jews have been cruelly wronged by the world," nevertheless he urged them to seek the goodwill of the Arabs by discarding "the help of the British bayonet" (*Harijan,* 11 November 1938). Gandhi's position generated many reactions, notably one from Martin Buber – one of Levinas' intellectual interlocutors. In February 1939, Buber sent a letter to Gandhi strongly criticizing his position. Gandhi ignored the letter. This historical background may have contributed to the lack of any intellectual encounter between Levinas and Gandhi. For historical details of Buber and Gandhi's dialogue, see Buber, *Pointing the Way.*

11 Note that this is not a comparative study of the two thinkers, although this would constitute a worthwhile endeavour in its own right. Gandhian example in this chapter is mainly to demonstrate the applicability of Levinas' ethics to a concrete historical event.

12 The problem of Gandhi's approach to the subject is a complex one, since, as Douglas Allen argues, there is no single Gandhi; there are as many Gandhis as there are Gandhian scholars. See Allen, "Gandhi, Contemporary Political Thinking."
13 See, for example, the writings of two important Gandhian scholars, Raghavan Iyer and Bhikhu Parekh.
14 As discussed previously, part of the reason may be that this was not a primary project for Gandhi himself; consequently, his criticism of the modern subject remains scattered and unsystematic. Therefore, due to the lack of systematicness in Gandhi's discussion of his break from the modern conception of the subject, my discussion of it in this section remains symptomatic and suggestive.
15 More specifically, what this means is that Gandhi's notion of inter-subjection is much closer to Levinas' subjection to the other than to Habermas's communicative intersubjectivity. Gandhi never formulates, as Levinas does, the relation between the self and the other as asymmetrical, and subjectivity as subjection to the other. Yet his notion of selfless service as the ground of one's individuation brings his approach to self–other relation much closer to Levinas' asymmetry than to Habermas's intersubjectivity, which assumes reciprocity among communicative subjects as its foundation.
16 Ram-Prasad, "Non-Violence and the Other."
17 Ibid., 13.
18 Ibid., n47.
19 Ibid., 13.
20 Gandhi, *An Autobiography*, 420. Hereafter cited as ASMET.
21 Parel, *Gandhi, Freedom, and Self-Rule.*
22 Mohanty, *Essays on Indian Philosophy.*
23 MPWG, I:462.
24 Ibid., 4.
25 Ibid., 461.
26 Ibid., 457.
27 Ram-Prasad, "Non-Violence and the Other," 11.
28 For an in-depth discussion of *Satyagrahi*, see Herman, *Community, Violence, and Peace*, 76.
29 This issue is discussed at some length in De Bary, *Sources of Indian Tradition*, 259–62. Hereafter SIT.
30 See Baum, *Nationalism, Religion, and Ethics*, 46. Hereafter NRE.
31 Bernasconi, "Different Styles of Eschatology," 4.
32 Ibid., 5.
33 Asher Horowitz, *Ethics at a Standstill*, 19.

34 A quote by Levinas cited in Bernasconi, "Different Styles of Eschatology," 8.

35 Ibid., 9.

36 Leon Blum (1872–1950), was the first Socialist (and the first Jewish) Prime Minister of France, presiding over the Popular Front coalition government in 1936–7. When the Germans occupied France in June 1940, Blum was arrested by the Vichy authorities and held as a prisoner in various locations in France and Germany till May 1945. While in prison he wrote his best-known work, *For All Mankind*, trans. W. Pickles.

37 MPWG, I:413–18.

38 Ibid., I:422.

39 Ibid., I:418.

40 A quote from Gandhi cited in Kamat's "Potpourri; Mahatma Gandhi Album," http://www.kamat.com/mmgandhi/whyahimsa.htm.

41 MPWG, I:396. Italics are mine.

42 See, for example, Gandhi's editorial in *Harijan*, 1942, 13.1.

43 For an in-depth discussion of Gandhi's insistence on unilateral disarmament, see Saraswati, *Culture of Peace*, section III.

44 Horowitz, "How Can Anyone Be Called Guilty?," 301.

45 Ibid., 295.

46 Ibid., 307–8.

47 Ibid., 302.

48 Atterton, "Levinas and the Language of Peace."

49 Ibid., 67.

50 Ibid., 68.

51 Ibid.

52 Ibid., 59.

53 Ibid., 68.

54 Ibid.

55 Ibid.

56 Ibid., 67.

57 Horowitz, "How Can Anyone Be Called Guilty?," 295.

58 Ibid., 299.

59 Ibid., 308.

60 Ibid.

61 Gandhi, *Non-Violence in Peace and War*, I:59. Hereafter NVPW.

62 Cited in Chandra, *Rediscovering Gandhi*, 289–91.

63 Nanda, *In Search of Gandhi*, 82–4.

64 Ibid., 85.

65 Ibid.

66 For a discussion of Gandhi's role during the non-cooperation movement, see Emilsen, "Wrestling the Serpent," 150; and Gandhi, *The Collected Works of Mahatma Gandhi*, XIX:173 and XX:367. Hereafter CWMG.
67 WPMG, I:372.
68 Parekh, *Gandhi's Political Philosophy*, 159–60.
69 See, for example, Joan Bondurant, *Conquest of Violence*; Johan Galtung, *The Way Is the Goal*; Gene Sharp, *The Politics of Nonviolent Action;* and Thomas Weber, *Conflict Resolution and Gandhian Ethics.*
70 See Weber, "Gandhian Philosophy."
71 Ibid., 496.
72 Cited in Nanda, *In Search of Gandhi*, 79.
73 Ibid.
74 Ibid., 80.
75 Ibid., 81.
76 Parekh, *Colonialism, Tradition, and Reform*, 135.
77 Sharma, "Does Hinduism Teach Peace or War?," 17.
78 MPWG, I:373 (italics added).
79 For example, see BPW, 168–9; EN, 105; NTR, 188.
80 MPWG, I:432.
81 MPWG, I:373.
82 CWMG, XXIII:452.
83 Cited in Weber, "Gandhian Philosophy," 506.
84 Cited in Chandra, *Rediscovering Gandhi*, 296.
85 MPWG, III:2.
86 Levinas, "The Rights of Man and Good Will."
87 Levinas, "Diachrony and Representation."
88 Levinas, "Transcendence and Evil."
89 Cited in Emilsen, "Wrestling the Serpent," 149.
90 Charlie Freer Andrews (1871–1940) was an English Anglican priest and one of the closest friends and colleagues of Gandhi. He fought alongside Gandhi both in South Africa during the civil rights struggle and in India during the Indian independence movement. He was the only person who called Gandhi by his nickname "Mohan."
91 Ibid.
92 Ibid., 150.
93 Ibid., 145.
94 MPWG, I:373.
95 MPWG, III:5–7.
96 Ibid., I:373.
97 See LR, 283.

98 MPWG, I:415–21.
99 CWMG, XIX:124.
100 MPWG, I:430.
101 See Emilsen, "Wrestling the Serpent."
102 CWMG, XIX:521.
103 MPWG, I:456.
104 For a thorough discussion of these steps, see Weber, "Gandhian Philosophy," 496.
105 *Harijan*, 25 March 1939.

Conclusion

1 As indicated in one of Levinas' last works, "Peace and Proximity."

Bibliography

Abensour, Miguel. "An-archy between Meta-Politics and Politics." *Parallax* 24 (July–September 2002): 5–18.

Alford, C. Fred. "Levinas and Political Theory." *Political Theory* 32, no. 2 (2004): 146–171. http://dx.doi.org/10.1177/0090591703254977.

Allen, Douglas. "Gandhi, Contemporary Political Thinking, and Self-Other Relations." In *Contemporary Political Thinking*. Edited by B.N. Ray. 129–70. New Delhi: Kanishka Publishers, 2000.

Atterton, Peter. "In Defense of Violence: Levinas and the Problem of Justice." http://ghansel.free.fr/atterton.html.

Atterton, Peter. "Levinas and the Language of Peace: A Response to Derrida." *Philosophy Today* 36 (1992): 59–70.

Badiou, Alain. *Ethics: An Essay on the Understanding of Evil*. Translated by Peter Hallward. New York: Verso Books, 2001.

Baum, Gregory. *Nationalism, Religion, and Ethics*. Montreal and Kingston: McGill–Queen's University Press, 2001.

Bell, Shannon. "Levinas and Alterity Politics." In *Difficult Justice: Commentaries on Levinas and Politics*. Edited by Asher Horowitz and Gad Horowitz. 111–26. Toronto: University of Toronto Press, 2006.

Benjamin, Walter. "Analogy and Relationship." In *Walter Benjamin: Selected Writings*, vol. 1. Edited by Marcus Bullock and Michael W. Jennings. 1913–26. Cambridge, MA: Belknap Press, 1996.

Benjamin, Walter. "Critique of Violence." In *Reflections*. Edited by Peter Demetz. 277–300. New York: Schocken Books, 1978.

Bergo, Bettina. *Levinas between Ethics and Politics*. Boston: Dordrecht, and London: Kluwer Academic Publishers, 1999.

Bernasconi, Robert. "Different Styles of Eschatology: Derrida's Take on Levinas' Political Messianism." *Research in Phenomenology* 28, no. 1 (1998): 3–198. http://dx.doi.org/10.1163/156916498X00010.

Bernasconi, Robert. "The Ethics of Suspicion." *Research in Phenomenology* 20, no. 1 (1990): 3–18. http://dx.doi.org/10.1163/156916490X00018.

Bernasconi, Robert. "Strangers and Slaves in the Land of Egypt: Levinas and the Politics of Otherness." In *Difficult Justice: Commentaries on Levinas and Politics*. Edited by Asher Horowitz and Gad Horowitz. 246–61. Toronto: University of Toronto Press, 2006.

Bernasconi, Robert. "The Third Party: Levinas on the Intersection of the Ethical and the Political." *Journal for the British Society for Phenomenology* 30 (1999): 76–88.

Bernasconi, Robert. "What Is the Question to Which 'Substitution' Is the Answer?" In *The Cambridge Companion to Levinas*. Edited by Robert Bernasconi and Simon Critchley. 234–51. Cambridge: Cambridge University Press, 2002. http://dx.doi.org/10.1017/CCOL0521662060.011.

Bernasconi, Robert. "Who Is My Neighbor? Who Is the Other?" In *Ethics and Responsibility in the Phenomenological Tradition*. Ninth Annual Symposium of the Simon Silverman Phenomenology Center. 1–31. Pittsburgh: Simon Silverman Phenomenology Center, Duquesne University, 1991.

Bernstein, Richard J. "Evil and the Temptation of Theodicy." In *The Cambridge Companion to Levinas*. Edited by Simon Critchley and Robert Bernasconi. 252–67. Cambridge: Cambridge University Press, 2002. http://dx.doi.org/10.1017/CCOL0521662060.012

Blum, Leon. *For All Mankind*. Translated by W. Pickles. New York: Viking Press, 1946.

Bondurant, Joan. *Conquest of Violence: The Gandhian Philosophy of Conflict*. Berkeley: University of California Press, 1965.

Buber, Martin. *Pointing the Way: Collected Essays*. Translated and edited by Maurice S. Friedman and K. Paul. London: Routledge, 1957.

Caygill, Howard. *Levinas and the Political: Thinking the Political*. London: Routledge, 2002.

Chandra, Yogesh. *Rediscovering Gandhi*. London: Century Books, 1997.

Chanter, Tina. *Ethics of Eros: Irigaray's Re-writing of the Philosophers*. London: Routledge, 1995.

Chanter, Tina. *Feminist Interpretations of Emmanuel Levinas*. University Park: Pennsylvania State University Press, 2001.

Ciaramelli, Fabio. "Levinas' Ethical Discourse between Individuation and Universality." In *Reading Levinas*. Edited by Robert Bernasconi and Simon Critchley. 83–105. Indianapolis: Indiana University Press, 1991.

Cohen, Richard A. *Elevations: The Height of the Good in Rosenzweig and Levinas*. Chicago: University of Chicago Press, 1994.

Cohen, Richard A. *Ethics, Exegesis, and Philosophy: Interpretation after Levinas*. New York: Cambridge University Press, 2001. http://dx.doi.org/10.1017/CBO9780511488238.

Cohen, Richard A. "'Political Monotheism': Levinas on Politics, Ethics, and Religion." In *Essays in Celebration of the Founding of the Organization of Phenomenological Organizations*. Edited by Chan-Fai Cheung, Ivan Chvatik, Ion Copoeru, Lester Embree, Julia Irbarne, and Hans Rainer Sepp. Organization of Phenomenological Organizations. http://www.o-p-o.net.

Critchley, Simon. *Ethics, Politics, Subjectivity: Essays on Derrida, Levinas, and Contemporary French Thought*. New York: Verso Books, 1999.

Critchley, Simon. "Introduction." In *The Cambridge Companion to Levinas*. Edited by Robert Bernasconi and Simon Critchley. Cambridge: Cambridge University Press, 2002. http://dx.doi.org/10.1017/CCOL0521662060.

Critchley, Simon. "Five Problems in Levinas's View of Politics and the Sketch of a Solution to Them." *Political Theory* 32, no. 2 (April 2004): 172–85. http://dx.doi.org/10.1177/0090591703261771.

De Bary, W.M. Theodore, ed. *Sources of Indian Tradition*. New York: Columbia University Press, 1968.

Derrida, Jacques. *Adieu to Emmanuel Levinas*. Stanford: Stanford University Press, 1997.

Derrida, Jacques. "At This Moment in This Work Here I Am." In *Re-Reading Levinas*. Edited by Robert Bernasconi and Simon Critchley. 11–48. Bloomington: Indiana University Press, 1991.

Derrida, Jacques. "Hospitality, Justice, and Responsibility: A Dialogue with Jacques Derrida." In *Questioning Ethics: Contemporary Debates in Philosophy*. Edited by Richard Kearny and Mark Dooley. 65–83. London: Routledge, 1999.

Derrida, Jacques. "Violence and Metaphysics: An Essay on the Thought of Emmanuel Levinas." In *Writing and Difference*. 79–153. Chicago: University of Chicago Press, 1978.

Drabinski, John E. *Sensibility and Singularity: The Problem of Phenomenology in Levinas*. Albany: SUNY Press, 2001.

Dussel, Enrique. *Philosophy of Liberation*. Maryknoll: Orbis Books, 1985.

Emilsen, William W. "Wrestling the Serpent: Gandhi, Amritsar, and the British Empire." *Religion* 24, no. 2 (1994): 143–53. http://dx.doi.org/10.1006/reli.1994.1011.

Galtung, Johan. *The Way Is the Goal: Gandhi Today*. Ahmedabad: Gujarat Vidyapith Peace Research Centre, 1992.

Gandhi, Mahatma. *An Autobiography or The Story of My Experiments with Truth*. 2 vols. Translated by Mahadev Desai. Ahmedabad: Navajivan Publishing, 1927–9.

Gandhi, Mahatma. *The Collected Works of Mahatma Gandhi*, vols. 19, 29, and 33. New Delhi: Publications Division, Ministry of Information and Broadcasting, Government of India, 1988.

Gandhi, Mahatma. *The Moral and Political Writings of Mahatma Gandhi*, vols. 1 and 3. Edited by Raghavan Iyer. Oxford: Oxford University Press, 1986–7.

Gandhi, Mahatma. *Non-Violence in Peace and War*, vol. 1. Ahmedabad: Navajivan Publishing, 1948.

Gandhi, Mahatma. *Selected Writings of Mahatma Gandhi*. Boston: Beacon Press, 1951.

Gibbs, Robert. *Correlations in Rosenzweig and Levinas*. Princeton: Princeton University Press, 1992.

Giri, Kumar Ananta. *Conversations and Transformations: Towards a New Ethics of Self and Society*. Lanham: Lexington Books, 2002.

Handelman, Susan. *Fragments of Redemption: Jewish Thought and Literary Theory in Benjamin, Scholem, and Levinas*. Bloomington: Indiana University Press, 1991.

Herman, A.L. *Community, Violence, and Peace: Aldo Leopold, Mohandas K. Gandhi, Martin Luther King, Jr, and Gautama the Buddha in the Twenty-First Century*. Albany: SUNY Press, 1999.

Herzog, Annabel. "Is Liberalism 'All We Need'? Levinas' Politics of Surplus." *Political Theory* 30, no. 2 (2002): 204–27. http://dx.doi.org/10.1177/0090591702030002002.

Horkheimer, Max, and Theodor Adorno. *Dialectic of Enlightenment*. Translated by John Cumming. New York: Continuum Publishing, 1995.

Horowitz, Asher. "Beyond Rational Peace: On the Possibility/Necessity of a Levinasian Hyperpolitics." In *Difficult Justice: Commentaries on Levinas and Politics*. Edited by Asher Horowitz and Gad Horowitz. 27–47. Toronto: University of Toronto Press, 2006.

Horowitz, Asher. "How Can Anyone Be Called Guilty? Speech, Responsibility, and the Social Relation in Habermas and Levinas." *Philosophy Today* 44 (2000): 295–317.

Horowitz, Asher. *Ethics at a Standstill*. Pittsburgh: Duquesne University Press, 2008.

Horowitz, Asher, and Gad Horowitz, eds. *Difficult Justice: Commentaries on Levinas and Politics*. Toronto: University of Toronto Press, 2006.

Horowitz, Asher, and Gad Horowitz. "Is Liberalism All We Need? Prelude via Fascism." In *Difficult Justice: Commentaries on Levinas and Politics*. Edited by A. Horowitz and G. Horowitz. 12–23. Toronto: University of Toronto Press, 2006.

Irigaray, Luce. *Je, Tu, Nous, Towards a Culture of Difference*. London: Routledge, 1993.

Kant, Immanuel. *The Metaphysics of Morals*. Translated by Mary Gregor. Cambridge: Cambridge University Press, 1991.

Levinas, Emmanuel. *Basic Philosophical Writings*. Edited by Adriaan T. Peperzak, Simon Critchley, and Robert Bernasconi. Bloomington: Indiana University Press, 1996.

Levinas, Emmanuel. *Beyond the Verse: Talmudic Readings and Lectures*. Translated by Gary D. Mole. Bloomington: Indiana University Press, 1994.

Levinas, Emmanuel. *Collected Philosophical Papers*. Translated by Alphonso Lingis. Pittsburgh: Duquesne University Press, 1998.

Levinas, Emmanuel. "Damages Due to Fire." In *Nine Talmudic Readings*. Translated by Annette Aronowicz. 178–97. Bloomington: Indiana University Press, 1990.

Levinas, Emmanuel. "Diachrony and Representation." In *Entre Nous: Thinking-of-the-Other*. Translated by Michael B. Smith and Barbara Harshav. 159–77. New York: Columbia University Press, 1998.

Levinas, Emmanuel. *Difficult Freedom: Essays on Judaism*. Translated by Sean Hand. London: Athlone Press, 1990.

Levinas, Emmanuel. "Difficult Freedom." In *The Levinas Reader*. Edited by Sean Hand. 249–66. Oxford: Blackwell Publishers, 1989.

Levinas, Emmanuel. "The Ego and the Totality." In *Collected Philosophical Papers*. Translated by Alphonso Lingis. 25–45. Pittsburgh: Duquesne University Press, 1998.

Levinas, Emmanuel. *Entre Nous: Thinking-of-the-Other*. Translated by Michael B. Smith and Barbara Harshav. New York: Columbia University Press, 1998.

Levinas, Emmanuel. "Freedom and Command." In *Collected Philosophical Papers*. Translated by Alphonso Lingis. 15–23. Pittsburgh: Duquesne University Press, 1998.

Levinas, Emmanuel. *Humanism of the Other*. Translated by Nidra Poller. Urbana: University of Illinois Press, 2003.

Levinas, Emmanuel. "Ideology and Idealism." In *The Levinas Reader*. Edited by Sean Hand. 235–48. Oxford: Blackwell Publishers, 1989.

Levinas, Emmanuel. In *Is It Righteous to Be? Interviews with Emmanuel Levinas*. Edited by Jill Robbins. Stanford: Stanford University Press, 2001.

Levinas, Emmanuel. "Judaism and Revolution." In *Nine Talmudic Readings*. Translated by Annette Aronowicz. 94–119. Bloomington: Indiana University Press, 1990.

Levinas, Emmanuel. *The Levinas Reader*. Edited by Sean Hand. Oxford: Blackwell Publishers, 1989.

Levinas, Emmanuel. "Meaning and Sense." In *Collected Philosophical Papers*. Translated by Alphonso Lingis. 75–107. Pittsburgh: Duquesne University Press, 1998.

Levinas, Emmanuel. *Nine Talmudic Readings*. Translated by Annette Aronowicz. Bloomington: Indiana University Press, 1990.

Levinas, Emmanuel. "No Identity." In *Collected Philosophical Papers*. Translated by Alphonso Lingis, Alphonso. 141–51. Pittsburgh: Duquesne University Press, 1998.

Levinas, Emmanuel. *Otherwise Than Being or Beyond Essence*. Translated by Alphonso Lingis. Pittsburgh: Duquesne University Press, 1998.

Levinas, Emmanuel. "The Paradox of Morality: An Interview with Emmanuel Levinas." In *The Provocation of Levinas: Rethinking the Other*. Edited by Robert Bernasconi and David Wood. Translated by Tamara Wright, Peter Hughes, and Alison Ainley. 168–80. London: Routledge, 1988.

Levinas, Emmanuel. "Peace and Proximity." In *Basic Philosophical Writings*. Edited by Adriaan Peperzak, Simon Critchley, and Robert Bernasconi. 161–69. Bloomington: Indiana University Press, 1996.

Levinas, Emmanuel. "Philosophy and the Idea of Infinity." In *Collected Philosophical Papers*. Translated by Alphonso Lingis. 47–59. Pittsburgh: Duquesne University Press, 1998.

Levinas, Emmanuel. "Philosophy, Justice, and Love." In *Entre Nous: Thinking-of-the-Other*. Translated by Michael B. Smith and Barbara Harshav. 77–90. New York: Columbia University Press, 1998.

Levinas, Emmanuel. "Reflections on the Philosophy of Hitlerism." Translated by Sean Hand. *Critical Inquiry* 17, no. 1 (1990): 63–71. http://dx.doi.org/10.1086/448574.

Levinas, Emmanuel. "The Rights of Man and Good Will." In *Entre Nous: Thinking-of-the-Other*. Translated by Michael B. Smith and Barbara Harshav. 155–58. New York: Columbia University Press, 1998.

Levinas, Emmanuel. "The Temptation of Temptation." In *Nine Talmudic Readings*. Translated by Annette Aronowicz. 30–50. Bloomington: Indiana University Press, 1990.

Levinas, Emmanuel. *Time and the Other*. Translated by Richard A. Cohen. Pittsburgh: Duquesne University Press, 1987.

Levinas, Emmanuel. *Totality and Infinity: An Essay on Exteriority*. Translated by Alphonso Lingis. Pittsburgh: Duquesne University Press, 1961.

Levinas, Emmanuel. "Transcendence and Evil." In *Collected Philosophical Papers*. Translated by Alphonso Lingis. 175–86. Pittsburgh: Duquesne University Press, 1998.

Levinas, Emmanuel. "Transcendence and Height." In *Basic Philosophical Writings*. Edited by Adriaan Peperzak, Simon Critchley, and Robert Bernasconi. 11–31. Bloomington: Indiana University Press, 1996.

Levinas, Emmanuel. "Useless Suffering." In *Entre Nous: Thinking-of-the-Other*. Translated by Michael B. Smith and Barbara Harshav. 91–101. New York: Columbia University Press, 1998.

Libertson, Joseph. *Proximity, Levinas, Blanchot, Bataille, and Communication*. The Hague: M. Nijhoff, 1982.

MacAvoy, Leslie. "The Other Side of Intentionality." In *Addressing Levinas*. Edited by Eric Sean Nelson, Antje Kapust, and Kent Still. 109–18. Evanston: Northwestern University Press, 2005.

Maloney, Philip J. "Levinas, Substitution, and Transcendental Subjectivity." *Man and World* 30, no. 1 (1997): 49–64. http://dx.doi.org/10.1023/A:1004228124719.

Manning, Robert J.S. *Beyond Ethics to Justice through Levinas and Derrida: The Legacy of Levinas*. Quincy: Franciscan Press of Quincy University, 2001.

Manning, Robert J.S. *Interpreting Otherwise Than Heidegger: Emmanuel Levinas' Ethics as First Philosophy*. Pittsburgh: Duquesne University Press, 1993.

Marx, Karl. "Critique of the Gotha Program." In *The Marx-Engels Reader*, 2nd ed. Edited by Robert C. Tucker. 525–41. New York: Norton, 1978.

Mohanty, Jitendranath. *Essays on Indian Philosophy*. Delhi: Oxford University Press, 1993.

Nanda, Bal Ram. *In Search of Gandhi: Essays and Reflections*. New Delhi: Oxford University Press, 2002.

Parekh, Bhikhu. *Colonialism, Tradition, and Reform: An Analysis of Gandhi's Political Discourse*. New Delhi: Sage Publications, 1999.

Parekh, Bhikhu. *Gandhi's Political Philosophy: A Critical Examination*. Notre Dame: University of Notre Dame Press, 1989.

Parel, Anthony. *Gandhi, Freedom, and Self-Rule*. Lanham: Lexington Books, 2000.

Peperzak, Adriaan. *Beyond: The Philosophy of Emmanuel Levinas*. Evanston: Northwestern University Press, 1997.

Peperzak, Adriaan. *To the Other: An Introduction to the Philosophy of Emmanuel Levinas*. West Lafayette: Purdue University Press, 1993.

Putnam, Hilary. *Ethics beyond Ontology*. Cambridge, MA: Harvard University Press, 2004.

Ram-Prasad, Chakravarthi. "Non-Violence and the Other: A Composite Theory of Multiplism, Heterology, and Heteronomy Drawn from Jainism and Gandhi." *Angelaki: Journal of the Theoretical Humanities* 8, no. 3 (2003): 3–22. http://dx.doi.org/10.1080/0969725032000154359.

Rorty, Richard. *Achieving Our Country*. Cambridge, MA: Harvard University Press, 1998.

Sandford, Stella. *The Metaphysics of Love: Gender and Transcendence in Levinas.* London: Athlone Press, 2000.

Saraswati, Baidyanath, ed. *Culture of Peace: Experience and Experiment.* New Delhi: Indira Gandhi National Centre for the Arts / D.K. Printworld, 1999.

Sharma, Arvind. "Does Hinduism Teach Peace Or War? The Story of Gandhi and his Assassin." *Voices across Boundaries: A Multifaith Magazine* 1 (2003): 17–20.

Sharp, Gene. *The Politics of Nonviolent Action.* Boston: Porter Sargent, 1973.

Simmons, Paul W. *An-Archy and Justice: An Introduction to Emmanuel Levinas' Political Thought.* Lanham: Lexington Books, 2003.

Simmons, Paul W. "The Third: Levinas' Theoretical Move from An-archical Ethics to the Realm of Justice and Politics." *Philosophy and Social Criticism* 25 (1999): 83–104.

Spivak, Gayatri C. "French Feminism Revisited: Ethics and Politics." In *Feminists Theorize the Political.* Edited by Judith Butler and Joan W. Scott. 54–85. London: Routledge, 1992.

Spivak, Gayatri C. "Righting Wrongs." *South Atlantic Quarterly* 103, nos. 2–3 (2004): 523–81. http://dx.doi.org/10.1215/00382876-103-2-3-523.

Tahmasebi, Victoria. "Levinas, Nietzsche, and Benjamin's 'Divine Violence.'" In *Difficult Justice: Commentaries on Levinas and Politics.* Edited by Asher Horowitz and Gad Horowitz. 172–90. Toronto: University of Toronto Press, 2006.

Waldenfels, Bernhard. "Levinas and the Face of the Other." In *The Cambridge Companion to Levinas.* Edited by Robert Bernasconi and Simon Critchley. 63–81. Cambridge: Cambridge University Press, 2002. http://dx.doi.org/10.1017/CCOL0521662060.003.

Wall, Thomas Carl. *Radical Passivity: Levinas, Blanchot, and Agamben.* New York: SUNY Press, 1999.

Weber, Thomas. "Gandhian Philosophy, Conflict Resolution Theory, and Practical Approaches to Negotiation." *Journal of Peace Research* 38, no. 4 (2001): 493–513. http://dx.doi.org/10.1177/0022343301038004006.

Weber, Thomas. *Conflict Resolution and Gandhian Ethics.* New Delhi: Gandhi Peace Foundation, 1991.

Index

www.ingramcontent.com/pod-product-compliance
Lightning Source LLC
LaVergne TN
LVHW090159080826
844660LV00013B/867/J

* 9 7 8 1 4 4 2 6 4 2 8 4 3 *